MOSES WROTE ABOUT ME

"47 But if ye [all of you] believe not his writings,
how shall ye believe My words?" John 5:47

By: Philip Mitanidis

Dedicated to my son: *Kevin*

www.beehivepublishinghouse.com
e-mail: thehive@beehivepublishinghouse.com

Moses Wrote About Me
First Edition 2011. Printed in Canada.
ISBN 978-0-9866246-0-5
Revised Edition 2013. Printed in USA
ISBN 978-0-9866246-3-6

Published work by Philip Mitanidis:

The Creator of Genesis 1:1—Who is He?

The Covenant—A Contract Rejected

No God and Saviour Beside Me

According to a Promise

Christians Headed Into the Time of Trouble

Ghosts Demons UFO'S and Dead Men

Moses Wrote About Me

Blaspheming the Holy Ghost

What is the Sign of Christ's Second Coming and the End of the World

IV__ACKNOWLEDGEMENTS & ABBREVIATIONS

In my references from the (OKJV) Bible, I have changed the first letter of the pronouns into capital letters, which refer to God the Creator; and I have translated the Hebrew word "יהוה" and the Greek word "Κυριος" to read "LORD," whenever the Scriptures refer to God the Creator of Genesis 1:1.

Please refer to the Hebrew and to the Greek inspired Scriptures in order to verify my opinions.

All Bible references are given from the Old King James Version (OKJV) unless otherwise indicated.

Greek Scripture references are quoted from Η Αγια Γραφη, Βιβλικη Εταιρεια, Αθηναι 1961.

Front cover produced by Philip Mitanidis
The artwork in this book is produced by the Author Philip Mitanidis.

When you speak to theologians, church ministers, and laymen regarding the God of the Old Testament (OT), they will quickly tell you that the God of the Old Testament is the God of Abraham. And, if you ask them to identify the God of Abraham, they will tell you that the God of Abraham is God the Father, as we know him now in the New Testament (NT); and more than likely, they will refer you to the following verses to support their claim: "15 And God said moreover unto Moses, Thus thou [you] shalt say unto the children of Israel, The LORD God of your fathers, the God of Abraham, the God of Isaac, and the God of Jacob, hath sent me unto you: this is My name for ever, and this is my memorial unto all generations." "4 Hear, O Israel: The LORD our God is one LORD" (Exodus 3:15; Deuteronomy 6:4).

But, by you reading the above verses, do they really reveal to you who is the God of Abraham and of Israel?

Obviously not, since one of the major disturbing problems theologians, church leaders, and laymen have with the (OT) is the fact that they cannot decide how to answer the above verses because the prophets of the LORD of hosts reveal sometimes two Individuals by the name of "LORD God" and sometimes they reveal three Individuals by the name of "LORD God" in the Torah (5 books of Moses); in fact, the same revelation is found throughout the Old Testament. Therefore when they come across verses as the above and as in Psalms 82:1, they are unable to distinguish who is who and why two or three Individuals are identified by the name of "God"?

As an example, the Hebrew text in Psalms 82:1 reads as follows: "1 God stands in the midst of God, He judges in the midst of the judges." Psalms 82:1 (Translation is mine.)

Thus in order to avoid any controversy to their one God (God the Father) belief, the translators and theologians either remove the second word "God" from the above verse, as they have done in many Bibles; or they replace it with other names, such as "divine"—check your Bible.

Ironically, in most Bibles, which I have read, the theologians and translators have removed to their detriment the wrong word (God) from the above verse (Psalms 82:1). The reason I say they have removed the wrong word (God) is due to the fact that they think that the second word (God), which they have removed, does not refer to God the Father. Unfortunately for them, the second word (God), which they have removed from the verse, does refer to God the Father; and, the first word (God), which they left in the verse, refers to Christ the LORD of hosts, and that does not sit too well with them, when it is brought to their attention.

Although theologians, translators, and church leaders, have removed One Individual from Psalms 82:1 verbally and from paper, they cannot escape the fact that the Old Testament like the New Testament reveals three Individuals by the name of "LORD God." And therefore when they run into similar verses as in Psalms 110:1, which says, "1 The LORD said unto My LORD, Sit Thou [you] at my right hand, until I make Thine [Your] enemies Thy footstool," they cannot remove the first or second word "LORD" from the verse because it ties into too many references throughout the Bible, which reveal more than one Lord.

So! Who is King David's LORD? And who is talking to King David's LORD? And what God is standing in the midst of another God?

Good questions don't you think?

But even more devastating and trying for the theologians, translators, church leaders, and laymen, are references that state that there is "no God beside Me."

Here is one reference of many: "8 Fear ye [all of you] not, neither be afraid: have not I told thee [you] from that time, and have declared it? ye [all of you] are even My witnesses [the children of Israel]. Is there a God beside Me? yea, there is no God; I know not any." Isaiah 44:8

The personal pronoun "Me" and "I" of the LORD God of Israel, in the above verse, pose a question, "Is there a God beside Me?" Then, He answers; "yea, there is no God; I know not any." As a result, how can the above statement be uttered, when two more Individuals, in the (OT), claim to be God?

And on top of that emphatic declaration, there is even more confusing and frustrating comment, for many, and that is the fact that Christ the LORD of hosts claims that the Torah (5 books of Moses) is all about Him and not about God the Father as we know him in the (NT)! (See John 5:46, 47.)

So! Now what?

How are the theologians, translators, and church leaders going to explain the above verses and Christ's claim when the Old Testament and the New Testament reveal three separate Individuals by the name of "LORD God"?

Unfortunately, they cannot give you the answers; all they can do is to explain away the Scriptures, and that makes it their opinions. They cannot identify who is who in the above verses, and why Christ claims Moses and the rest of the prophets wrote about Him (John 5:39) and not about God the Father? If they were able to, they would have done it by now; but, then again, probably not!

But, not to despair, this book that you are reading right now (Moses Wrote About Me *by: Philip Mitanidis*), removes what appears to be the discrepant maze of uncertainty from the Old Testament by identifying each Individual, who claims to be "God," by their character names; in doing so, it illuminates the Old Testament pages as you have never seen them before. Therefore when you read the Old Testament, this book will help you to understand who is the God of Abraham, the LORD of hosts, the King of Israel, Shiloh, Rock, the Most High God, the Highest God, the God of Israel, and who led the children of Israel out of Egypt and into the Promised Land? Who dwelt in His Sanctuary in "Shiloh" and in "Jerusalem"? Why the Sanctuaries in "Shiloh" and in "Jerusalem" were destroyed? And, as a prerequisite, to identify the LORD God of Abraham, this book reveals Abraham's interaction with God and where Abraham's journey took him after he left his hometown "Ur," and much, much more.

At the end, this book is going to send a surge of excitement for the clarity it brings to the Old Testament, for identifying who is who in the Old Testament, and for confirming Christ's claim that Moses and the rest of the prophets of old primarily wrote about Him and not about God the Father

The author

CONTENTS

Abraham Leaves His
Hometown Ur of the Chaldees

Before I present Abram (Abraham) to you, I want to give you a real time frame from the time Adam sinned, to Noah, the flood, and all the way down to the birth of Abraham, by providing you with dates, which are in Anno Mundi (A.M.). It should be noted; the starting date begins from the time Adam sinned and not from the time Adam was created sinless.

Therefore, from the year Adam sinned, to the time the flood came, the Hebrew text places Noah and the flood in 1656 A.M. At this point, Noah was 600 years old. And from the flood to the birth of Abraham, which was in 2008 A.M., the time span was 352 years. And 75 years later, in 2083 A.M., Abraham was told by the LORD of hosts to leave Haran and go to Canaan.

Having given you the above time frame, I hope it will help you to relate more realistically to the following presentation, which starts 120 years before the flood came upon planet earth.

Noah lived six hundred years before the flood came; but before the flood came,

* "For one hundred and twenty years the message of grace and mercy went forward to the giant descendents of Adam and Eve. In spite of their high intellect and stature, many of these individuals were incapable of making a moral judgment and save themselves from the flood that was to come upon them. With the help of the evil angels, they were steeped in sin so deep that it clouded their judgment. They had become like the evil angels who emulate Satan their leader. The antediluvians had put on the evil character of

Abraham Leaves His Hometown Ur

Satan. In doing so, they hated God the Creator for not letting them live in sin and therefore they loved death.

Therefore, God the Creator was left with no choice, if He was going to save the repentant sinners, He had to stop sin and the unrepentant sinners from overtaking the whole earth. "13 And God said unto Noah, The end of all flesh is come before Me; for the earth is filled with violence through them; and, behold, I will destroy them with the earth." "18 But with thee will I establish My covenant; and thou shalt come into the ark, thou, and thy sons, and thy wife, and thy sons' wives with thee" (Genesis 6:13, 18).

The Creator's patience was running out. The sinners on earth went beyond the Creator's forbearance. They were gone to the point of no return. God the Holy Spirit could not reason with them any more. They abandoned Him and the Creator. (See 1 Peter 3:18-20.)

God the Creator gave the antediluvians plenty of time to repent, but they chose not to. He also gave them plenty of evidence of the things Noah was preaching about. That evidence was true because the Creator foretold what was going to take place before the flood came. But, the antediluvians laughed at Noah when he said to them that the rain would precede the catastrophic events of the world. In response, they said, "It does not rain Noah! We do not have rain—remember? Why are you making this up?" And when Noah said that he was going to build a ship, they said, "There is no water here Noah; can't you see? You are standing on dry ground?" When Noah said to them that the animals were going to come into the ark (ship) two by two, and the clean animals will come in the ark by sevens, they said, "It is impossible to accomplish that task Noah." "The animals and the dragons will tear you apart Noah, if you try to capture them!" "Besides Noah, how are you going to collect all of these animals and birds in your lifetime? Are

Abraham Leaves His Hometown Ur

you going to sprout wings?" "Noah, you are going to be too old to walk by the time you gather all of the species in the ark!"

The antediluvians scorned Noah and his sons, but seven days before the flood came, the animals and the birds started to come into the ark as Noah had said. People began to wonder how this was done? How were all of the animals and birds coming into the ark so orderly by themselves without killing each other—they wondered?

Instead of wondering how Noah managed to get the animals into the ship, so orderly, they should have thought of the signs, which Noah gave them, and of the events that were going to take place before the flood came upon them. And they should have taken heed to these signs, which Noah revealed to them. They should have repented and entered into the ship and be saved. Instead they continued to mock and ridicule Noah and his family.

While the antediluvians were wondering about the animal procession, Lucifer (Satan) and his evil angels were not wondering at the scene. Although man could not see God's angels bringing the animals into the ark, Lucifer and his angels saw the holy angels directing the animals and the birds into the ark. And that brought chills upon Lucifer's spine. He began to worry because he did not take the Creator's words seriously enough, when Noah said that a flood was coming. A flood could not harm Lucifer and his angels. But now, he realizes that this is more than a flood, and he wondered how catastrophic it was going to be? But, he was not worried because he thought he could always hitch a ride in the ark (ship).

Meanwhile, Noah, after one hundred and twenty years of warning the people, his sons, and their wives went into the ark as God the Creator told them to. When everybody had settled in, and no one else wanted to go in, an unseen hand

Abraham Leaves His Hometown Ur

lifted the huge door of the ark, and closed it shut. The Creator, personally, closed the door and no one could open it. Not even the mighty evil angels. Noah's ark was protected by the Creator's hand; and no one could enter in it, and that included the millions of evil spirit beings, who dwell on earth, called evil angels (Revelation 12:9).

At this point Lucifer began to really worry because he saw with his own eyes how the Creator closed the huge door of the ark (ship). Satan remembered the words of the Creator that were spoken by Noah. He also knew that God the Creator does not lie. In his anxiety, Lucifer began to plan for his safety because now, he knew that he could not hitch a ride in the ark. He started to think how the water, which enveloped the earth, was going to come down upon the earth, and what role and effect the water that was upon the earth and beneath the crust of the earth would have upon him; and what would he do to escape a crushing death? At this point, Lucifer was not worried about anybody else; he was worried mainly about his own safety.

When his commanding angels saw Lucifer acting strange, they inquired of their outcome during the deluge. He told them that the water would not be detrimental upon them; but they were not that stupid, they were concerned because, if the deluge were going to be prolonged, they would not be able to stay in the water too long. Nonetheless, Satan managed to assure them that if they could hover and stay sandwiched between the water that was above the ark and below the ark, they would be OK. Although they were still skeptical, they thought that the plan was logical enough to follow.

But what Satan and his evil angels did not anticipate was the awesome lightnings that were going to take place during and before the release of the water, which enveloped planet earth? You see, the millions of kilowatt lightning and

Abraham Leaves His Hometown Ur

thunder that was going to drape the sky, at will, worried Satan. He wondered if that wattage was large enough to kill him or any of his evil angels. He knew that any one of his angels who fell in the path of these awesome deadly lightning bolts would have a severe time to survive its destructive strike.

Although the evil angels spent a lot of time planning their escape, there was nothing they could do at that point but to wait for the deluge to come. They were left on their own. It was a solemn time for the evil angels because they were not allowed to leave planet earth and take refuge somewhere else. As far as the human race was concerned, it was going to have a rude awakening. All of those individuals who chose not to enter in the safety of the ark were headed on the road of dismay, pain, anxiety, terror, and destruction.

As I stated before, after the birds, reptiles, animals, Noah, and his family went into the ark, the Creator closed the ark's door. For seven days, the antediluvians laughed and scorned Noah and his zoo; but then, raindrops were felt! Could it be that Noah was right—some reasoned? The rain came lightly at first, and then, it became progressively stronger. When the people saw what was happening, they rushed towards the ark; but the ark's door was closed! They could not get in. As the rain got stronger, and streams of water began to flow violently towards the low lands, those mighty giants began to rush to the ark screaming for the door to be lowered. But, the call of mercy that fell upon their deaf ears for one hundred and twenty years was over. The antediluvians made their choice to stay out of the ark, and when the door of the ark was closed, probation was over. The door was sealed, and no un-repented sinner could go in.

The crowd that was pushing, shoving, and trampling each other on the way to the ark was in frenzy because they

Abraham Leaves His Hometown Ur

could not get to the ark fast enough. Children, wives, husbands, and old people were abandoned. It was survival time for every one. Many that were able to reach the ark clung to the wooden hull to only find themselves overtaken by someone stronger than himself or herself—to no avail. The torrential rains came; and the powerful streams, which turned into huge rivers, came crashing upon the crowds, sweeping them away like refuse. The water currents were so violent and swift, men, women, and children could not hold on to the slippery ark and to the trees, which they thought they had refuge in. Noah's ark, which was as big as a football field, was lifted securely with its cargo to ride the mauling and battering rising water.

The hand of the Creator sustained the ark during the devastating turbulent deluge.

Meanwhile, the deluge, which covered the earth with its mauling and brutal currents of water, churned, and coiled across the globe; and by their shear brute force turned the world upside down, tore the single continent into pieces, and created new landscapes.

We are told, "17 the flood was forty days upon the earth; and the waters increased, and bare up the ark, and it was lift up above the earth. 18 And the waters prevailed, and were increased greatly upon the earth; and the ark went upon the face of the waters. 19 And the waters prevailed exceedingly upon the earth; and all the high hills, that were under the whole heaven, were covered. 20 Fifteen cubits upward did the waters prevail; and the mountains were covered. 21 And all flesh died that moved upon the earth, both of fowl, and of cattle, and of beasts, and of every creeping thing that creepeth upon the earth, and every man: 22 All in whose nostrils was the breath of life, of all that was in the dry land, died. 23 And every living substance was destroyed which was upon the face of the ground, both man, and cattle, and the

Abraham Leaves His Hometown Ur

creeping things, and the fowl of the heaven; and they were destroyed from the earth: and Noah only remained alive, and they that were with him in the ark. 24 And the waters prevailed upon the earth an hundred and fifty days" (Genesis 7:17-24)." 1*

For five months, in 1656 A.M., the megalithic storm created mayhem on the planet and in the planet. The water, which surrounded the atmosphere, kept pouring upon the face of the earth; and the underground turbulent water kept rising above the land until it reached fifteen cubits above the highest newly formed mountain peak. Those rolling hills, before the flood came, looked like dwarfs in comparison to the tallest mountains of today. For over a year new mountains were continuously forming upon the fragmented continents. At the end of the fifth month, the devastating storm and the mauling ocean currents, which created new landscapes, stopped breaking the continent into pieces. The surface of the water began to settle as the internal mauling currents continued to configure their watery highway, by snaking around the fragmented continents, and establishing their under water imprint. And so did the fragmented continents secure their real estate upon the hotbed of newly formed Tec-Plates. The huge clawing waves, mega watt lighting, and the blowing relentless winds subsided, and the vast ocean began to calm down on the twelfth month.

Now the ark (boat), which was as big as a football field, stopped its turbulent moves. And in the calm ocean water, the God of Abraham directed the ark to drift towards the newly created mountain range of Ararat (north of Iraq). There as the vast ocean began to recede, the hand of the

---

1*   Mitanidis, Philip. *The Creator of Genesis 1:1—Who is He?* Pgs. 48-49. BeeHive Publishing House Inc. 2003.

Abraham Leaves His Hometown Ur

LORD of hosts kept the ark over the mountain range until the seventh month, and caused the ark to drift within its clasp.

But it was not until the tenth month that the tops of Mount Ararat could be seen. Although the mountaintops were visible the land was still covered with water. Therefore Noah waited for forty days before he felt that he was safe on solid ground, or if the ark would sink in muddy ground? And, also to see if the ecosystem would sustain them and the cargo he was carrying. So, Noah sent a raven out of the ark to explore for land. And because the raven was not able to stand on solid ground it kept flying back and forth to the ship. Noticing the flight of the raven, Noah sent a dove to see if it could find dry ground to stand on; but the dove came back to the ship. After seven days Noah sent the dove out again to see if it would give a better report. Because the bird did not return that day, Noah's hopes were raised that the dove found dry land; fortunately, it came back in the night with an olive branch in its beak. Encouraged, again Noah waited for another seven days and sent the dove out of the ark to see if the land was dry. Noah and his family waited and waited for a number of days but the bird did not return. Satisfied that the dove was resting on dry land, Noah prayed to the LORD and sought counsel as to what he was to do next.

As Noah waited patiently for the LORD, finally, the huge door of the ark was gently lowered; and the LORD of hosts said, "16 Go forth of the ark, thou [you], and thy [your] wife, and thy sons, and thy sons' wives with thee" [you] (Genesis 8:16). Noah and his family with thankful hearts came out from the ark with their belongings; and after them, the holy angels removed the livestock from the ship and allowed them to go and find their respective habitats to live because now, the earth was going to have four seasons and

Abraham Leaves His Hometown Ur

the residence of the earth had to survive in them.

But, before all of the animals left, in gratitude towards God, Noah and his family built nearby the ship an altar made out of stone to offer sacrifices, as they had done many times before the flood; with thanksgiving hearts, they took a number of the clean animals and birds and offered them in gratitude on the altar of sacrifice to the LORD of hosts.

"21 And the LORD smelled a sweet savour; and the LORD said in His heart, I will not again curse the ground any more for man's sake; for the imagination of man's heart is evil from his youth; neither will I again smite any more every thing living, as I have done. 22 While the earth remaineth, seedtime and harvest, and cold and heat, and summer and winter, and day and night shall not cease."

"1 And God blessed Noah and his sons, and said unto them, Be fruitful, and multiply, and replenish the earth" (Genesis 8:21, 22; 9:1).

After the LORD of hosts blessed Noah and his family, the LORD turned His eye upon the beasts, dragons, and fowls that were lingering around Noah's camp. These predatory animals, beasts, and fowl were ready to tear Noah and his family for lunch; therefore the LORD instilled in them to fear man. All creatures were to fear man whenever man came near them. This instilled fear into the animals caused them to spread further away from the camp of Noah and looked for a suitable habitat for themselves. Therefore Noah and his family did not have to be on guard all of the time and worry of being attacked by the predators.

In addition, in His compassion, the LORD of hosts told the eight persons that it was OK to eat clean animals and fish, since the flood destroyed many of the fruit trees, nuts, and grains. And the LORD further emphasized the point that they were not to eat of the unclean animals and fish, if they wanted to remain healthy and in good stature; otherwise

Abraham Leaves His Hometown Ur

they would degenerate in stature, health, and longevity.

On top of those blessings, the LORD also gave Noah and his family a reminder. He told them that every time they saw a rainbow it would remind them that a world wide flood would not take place again.

In fact, during Isaiah's time, about 730 BC, the LORD of hosts reminded the children of Israel of the flood saying,

"9 for as I have sworn that the waters of Noah should no more go over the earth; so have I sworn that I would not be wroth with thee [you]" (Isaiah 54:9).

To Noah and his family the LORD of hosts said, "13 I do set My bow in the cloud, and it shall be for a token of a covenant between Me and the earth. 14 And it shall come to pass, when I bring a cloud over the earth, that the bow shall be seen in the cloud: 15 And I will remember My covenant, which is between Me and you and every living creature of all flesh; and the waters shall no more become a flood to destroy all flesh. 16 And the bow shall be in the cloud; and I will look upon it, that I may remember the everlasting covenant between God and every living creature of all flesh that is upon the earth. 17 And God said unto Noah, This is the token of the covenant, which I have established between Me and all flesh that is upon the earth" (Genesis 9:13-17).

Comforted in the LORD'S blessings, admonitions, and promises, Noah, Ham, Shem, Japheth, and their wives began to seek out a suitable area to make their camp. From the foot of Mount Ararat, Noah and his family looked for more suitable land to live on. Noah's family lived their lives according to the LORD'S will and bless the LORD of hosts their God for His love and mercy.

After Noah, Shem, Japheth, and Ham chose the land they wanted to live upon, Noah "20 planted a vineyard: 21

Abraham Leaves His Hometown Ur

And he drank of the wine, and was drunken; and he was uncovered within his tent. 22 And Ham, the father of Canaan, saw the nakedness of his father, and told his two brethren without [outside of the tent]. 23 And Shem and Japheth took a garment, and laid it upon both of their shoulders, and went backward, and covered the nakedness of their father; and their faces were backward, and they saw not their father's nakedness. 24 And Noah awoke from his wine, and knew what his younger son had done unto him. 25 And he said, Cursed be Canaan; a servant of servants shall he be unto his brethren. 26 And he said, Blessed be the LORD God of Shem; and Canaan shall be his servant. 27 God shall enlarge Japheth, and he shall dwell in the tents of Shem; and Canaan shall be his servant" (Genesis 9:20-27).

According to the above testimony, Moses tells us that shortly after they had embarked from the ark, Noah planted vineyard; and when the vineyards matured, Noah gathered the grapes and made wine and drank little bit too much and got drunk. And while Noah was inebriated, naked, and lying on the tent's floor, Ham, his youngest son, walked into his father's tent—well, I am not going to tell you what happened, but what is so mind boggling to me is how quickly Ham forgot his deliverance from the flood; and how quickly he drifted away from the LORD of hosts and started to live in sin! And even worse how quickly he influenced his family to drift away from the LORD and refused His blessings?

And after his father's curse, why did he not repent?

Was he that proud of the evil he did to his father?

And even worse, Ham went and bragged to His two brothers of what he did!

How cruel and callous can a person be?

No wonder, after Noah recovered from his inebriation, he cursed Ham and his children that were to follow. "25 And

Abraham Leaves His Hometown Ur

he said, Cursed be Canaan; a servant of servants shall he be
unto his brethren. 26 And he said, Blessed be the LORD
God of Shem; and Canaan shall be his servant. 27 God shall
enlarge Japheth, and he shall dwell in the tents of Shem; and
Canaan shall be his servant" (Genesis 9:25-27).

Although the curse was not fully executed upon Ham
and his son Canaan, the final blow came upon Ham's
descendents eight hundred and ninety-seven years later when
Joshua entered into the land of Canaan with the children of
Israel; there Joshua killed and uprooted the Canaanites from
their homeland. And even then, the children of Israel did
not comply to Moses' directive, when he said that they were
to annihilate the Canaanites if they did not repent and joined
them or leave the country. And because the children of
Israel did not do that, the LORD of hosts said to the
children of Israel and to their leaders that a remnant
(Philistines) of the Canaanites would remain in their land as a
reminder of their failure to execute Moses' command.

And so it was and so it is today, throughout the history
of the children of Israel, a person can readily see how the
Canaanites have become a thorn on the children of Israel's
side. The daily news confirms that fact quite aptly.

Nonetheless, "28 Noah lived after the flood three hundred
and fifty years. 29 And all the days of Noah were nine
hundred and fifty years; and he died" (Genesis 9:28, 29).

But unfortunately, as Noah's family and their children's
families increase and many spread southward from the
vicinity of Mount Ararat and eastward from Mesopotamia
(the rivers of Euphrates and Tigris in modern Iraq), many of
their children drifted away from worshipping the LORD of
hosts. Satan and his evil angels, who live on planet earth
(Revelation 12:9) because they lost the war in heaven and had
nowhere to else to go, worked fervently to grab hold of the
minds of the residence of Mesopotamia away from

Abraham Leaves His Hometown Ur

worshipping the LORD of hosts, by luring them into unnatural sexual acts, sexual dress, flirting, pride, gossip, idols, arrogant self-serving acts, immoral evil behavior, and the list goes on an on, as it goes on and on today. Satan and his evil angels managed to pull many of them away from worshipping the LORD of hosts and convinced them not to believe or rely on the promises of the LORD of hosts.

Thus, in due course, the true evil character could be seen on many of the descendants of Noah. They bragged and plotted evil acts upon each other and upon God's people. And when God's people reminded them of God's mercy, blessing, and of the rainbow, they would defiantly ridicule them. Because of their unbelief, they chose to ignore the evidence of the flood, and the meaning of the rainbow, and chose to build a tower that would reach the heavens in defiance to God's promise that a worldwide flood would not take place again.

Eventually, many who chose to live in the plains of "Shinar," chose to disbelieve the symbol of the rainbow and placed their faith in the satanic influence, saying that the flood was a scientific phenomenon and therefore it would re-occur.

Convinced that a world flood would eventually re-occur, they pooled their resources, and in their pride, they set out to build a tower that would surpass the clouds. The place they chose to build the tower is called "Ur," which is located about one hundred and fifty miles northwest from the mouth of the Persian Gulf and a smidgen west of the Euphrates River, at the south end of Iraq.

As the building of the tower began to sprout, the people became more and more engrossed in their idol worship and paid homage to the gods of their invention. In doing so they began to influence the people throughout the land to a point where it seemed that the God of Noah was slowly

Abraham Leaves His Hometown Ur

diminishing in the minds of the people. Seeing that paganism was spreading rapidly and the tower was poised on reaching its goal, the LORD of hosts decided to put an end to their evil pride and arrogance by confounding their speech.

> He said to His two Associates, "6 Behold, the people is one, and they have all one language; and this they begin to do; and now nothing will be restrained from them, which they have imagined to do. 7 Go to, let us go down, and there confound their language, that they may not understand one another's speech" (Genesis 11:6, 7).

And when the LORD of hosts confused their speech, a complete chaos began to spread up and down the tower.

Abraham Leaves His Hometown Ur

when a worker asked for a load of brick, mortar would be provided; when a worker asked for water, sand would be provided; when a worker asked for a certain tools, straw would be provided; when it was asked to provide more workers in a certain area, that area would be dismantled! And when a person was asked to go for lunch that person would understand that he was not to go to lunch. And when a person was asked to go and help someone that person would go and tell him to stop working.   Eventually, as the misunderstandings began to snowball up and down the tower, and on the ground, confusion began to increase to a point where the people began to fight with each other because each one was blaming the other for not doing what they were suppose to be doing. The riots began to be so intense that eventually they were at war with each other.

Because their animosity grew between each other, the majority finally dispersed from the city of Ur; and moved in other parts of the country in small groups that were able to understand each other to some degree.   Therefore, the original command of the LORD of hosts, to Noah and his family, which was to spread throughout the world, was fulfilled. And regarding the tower and its city, it became to be well known as the "Tower of Babel" (confusion). Later, the expression of the "Tower of Babel" was applied to the city of "Babylon" by the Chaldeans. Furthermore, the term "Babylon," which means confusion, was aptly applied prophetically two thousand years ago to all of the Christian churches, which fail to take heed to Christ's counsel in Revelation 3:15-22. Instead, they have chosen to fall into apostasy by compromising the Gospel doctrine and make it a point to unite with likeminded churches, under one umbrella, on some common points of faith. (See Revelation 14:8; 18:2.)

Unfortunately, prophetically, the Christian churches of

Abraham Leaves His Hometown Ur

today, in their pride, like the tower builders, still want to retain their identity in unity, even though scripturally condemnation falls upon them.

> The prophet of the LORD of hosts says, "9 Whosoever transgresseth, and abideth not in the doctrine of Christ, hath not God. He that abideth in the doctrine of Christ, he hath both the Father and the Son" (2 John 1:9).

So! Why are the Laodiceans (modern day Christian Churches of Revelation 3:14-22) so proud, stiff necked, arrogant, and still refusing Christ's council that He has so patiently given to them in all of these years?

Are the Laodiceans (Christian churches) so bent on fulfilling the prophecies of Revelation chapters 13; 17; 18; and 16 is that the reason why they are not taking heed to Revelation 3:15-22? Or are they like the people of Shinar who were bent on building the Tower of Babel in defiance to the word of the LORD of hosts?

Like the Antediluvians before them, the people of Shinar chose their evil path in defiance to the compassionate call of the LORD of hosts—will all of the Laodiceans do the same today?

Unfortunately, already the Laodiceans are discarding many of the Gospel doctrinal points and forming a bond of unity on common doctrinal ground. Recently (2009), the leaders who have seventy-seven million members in North America of the Anglican Church chose to join the Roman Catholic Church; will others follow? According to the prophecy of Revelation chapters 13 and 17, regrettably, the answer is "Yes!" and when the unity is complete, then the second and third angels messages of Revelation 14:8-11 will predominantly follow.

For more detailed information, please read my book

Abraham Leaves His Hometown Ur

called "Christians Headed Into the Time of Trouble" *By Philip Mitanidis* BeeHive Publishing House Inc. 2007.

Yet, as free moral agents, the Laodiceans (Christian churches) will do what they want; and we should respect their choice of worship even though, in the name of heresy, they will impose the death penalty upon those who will not conform to their political and religious dictates. (See Revelation 13:15.)

As the Antediluvians and Noah's descendants chose to do evil upon God's people in order to discourage them from spreading the Plan of Salvation, the LORD of hosts had to intervene to protect the Plan of Salvation and His people. Only this time, modern day Babylon and her harlots will pay a hefty price by receiving the seven plagues of Revelation chapter 16, and eventually, a total annihilation in the lake of fire, along with Satan and evil angels

Nonetheless, after the irritant confusion at the Tower of Babel, Noah's descendants branched outward from Mesopotamia into other areas. Many of Japheth's descendents kept moving north and east from Mesopotamia. Ham's descendents spread westward and expanded southward from the land of Palestine. Shem's descendents, in the beginning, remained mostly in Mesopotamia; later many of them spread their occupancy north and northwest.

Consequently, through the seed of Noah, the earth was repopulated; and without the Antediluvian's evil influence, the Plan of Salvation was perpetuated; and God the Creator blessed those who preached its message.

Here is the account: "1 And the whole earth was of one language, and of one speech. 2 And it came to pass, as they journeyed from the east, that they found a plain in the land of Shinar; and they dwelt there. 3 And they said one to another, Go to, let us make brick, and burn them

Abraham Leaves His Hometown Ur

throughly. And they had brick for stone, and slime had they for mortar. 4 And they said, Go to, let us build us a city and a tower, whose top may reach unto heaven; and let us make us a name, lest we be scattered abroad upon the face of the whole earth. 5 And the LORD came down to see the city and the tower, which the children of men builded. 6 And the LORD said, Behold, the people is one, and they have all one language; and this they begin to do; and now nothing will be restrained from them, which they have imagined to do. 7 Go to, let us go down, and there confound their language, that they may not understand one another's speech. 8 So the LORD scattered them abroad from thence upon the face of all the earth and they left off to build the city. 9 Therefore is the name of it called Babel; because the LORD did there confound the languages of all the earth; and from thence did the LORD scatter them abroad upon the face of all the earth" (Genesis 11:1-9).

By scattering the people from Ur, the LORD of hosts stopped their evil influence and anarchy, thus allowing the Plan of Salvation to flourish.

The LORD of hosts always had His people in place to lead the citizens of the world into salvation. In an unbroken line, there were Adam, Seth, Enoch, Methuselah, and Noah who ministered to the antediluvians. And after the flood Noah preached for yet three hundred and fifty years before he died; and Shem preached for five hundred years before he died.

But the LORD'S representatives did not end there; out of the lineage of Shem came Nahor who, at the age of nine hundred and twenty years, had a son called Terah. Terah lived seventy years and had a son called Abram (Abraham). And Abram had two brothers whose names are Nahor and

Abraham Leaves His Hometown Ur

Haran. Haran died early in Ur of the Chaldees leaving his son Lot fatherless.

<u>Genesis 11 chronology</u>

Noah begat – Japheth, Shem, and Ham.
Shem begat – Arphasad. Arphasad begat – Cainan. Cainan begat – Salah. Salah begat – Eber. Eber begat – Peleg. Peleg begat – Reu. Rue begat – Serug. Serug begat – Nahor. Nahor begat – Terah. Terah begat - Abram (Abraham)

Although many in Terah's household were idol worshippers, Abraham, Sarai, and Lot remained loyal to the LORD of hosts in spite of the un-relentless evil influence upon them and on many of their servants while they lived in Ur.

But, after the death of Haran, in Ur, the LORD of hosts appeared to Abraham and told him to remove himself from Ur. Hearing the words of the LORD, Abraham revealed the will of the LORD to his father, and the whole family decided to leave their home in Shinar and go with Abraham. Terah, Nahor, Abram (Abraham), Lot (Abraham's nephew), Sarai (Abraham's wife), livestock, servants, possessions, and all of those individuals who chose to go with Terah and his family, left the plains of Shinar and traveled northwest, above Damascus, to a place where they settled near the city of Haran. There, in the vicinity of Haran, the household of Terah remained until Terah died at the age of two hundred and five.

Abraham was seventy-five years old when his father died. At that time, the LORD of hosts said to Abraham,

"1 Get thee [you] out of thy [your] country, and from thy [your] kindred, and from thy father's house, unto a land

Abraham Leaves His Hometown Ur

that I will shew thee [you]: 2 And I will make of thee a
great nation, and I will bless thee, and make thy name
great; and thou shalt be a blessing: 3 And I will bless
them that bless thee [you], and curse him that curseth
thee [you]: and in thee [you] shall all families of the earth
be blessed" (Genesis 12:1-3).

This was the second time the LORD of hosts appeared
to Abraham; the first time was in Shinar, and the second
time was after his father's death. Abraham heeded the call of
the LORD of hosts and told everyone in Haran what the
LORD had said to him. And asked all who were there in
Haran, if they wanted to go with him "unto a land" where
the LORD was going to lead them into. Sarai, Lot, and the
majority of Abraham's servants decided to go with him; but
his brother Nahor and his family decided not to go with
Abraham because many of them still served idols of silver
and gold and the god's of their imaginations.

In fact, later when Sarai (Sarah) died at the age of one
hundred and twenty-seven years, in Canaan, in a place called
Kiriath-arba, or Hebron if you like, Isaac was sad and
remained sad for a long time. Seeing the sadness of his son,
three years later, when Isaac was forty years old, Abraham
sent his trusted servant Eliezer with a caravan to Paddan-
aram, which is not too far from Haran, to take a wife for
Isaac from his brother's household. If you recall, Nahor's
son Bethuel, Abraham's nephew, did consent to give
Rebekah, his daughter, to become a wife to Isaac.

And likewise, when Jacob fled from his twin brother
Esau, he fled to Paddan-aram, which is near Haran to look
for his uncle Laban who is the son of Bethuel. There after
serving for seven years Laban allowed Jacob to marry his
two daughters Leah and Rachel. But after twenty years of
service, Laban still did not want Jacob to leave because

Abraham Leaves His Hometown Ur

Jacob's work made Laban rich. Therefore contrary to the will of Laban, Jacob with his wives, children, servants, and livestock finally fled from serving Laban any further. And on the way back to Canaan, Rachel's father with his warriors, after seven days of pursuit, did catch up with Jacobs's caravan in Mount Gilead to do him harm; but the LORD of hosts appeared in a dream in the night and told him not to harm Jacob or his caravan.

Fearfully, Laban, the following day when he reached Jacob's caravan, he confronted Jacob and demanded that his idols be returned to him that were stolen by his daughter Rachel. The fact that Laban's household in Haran was still steeped in worshipping the gods that were made out of silver and gold gives us the reason why Nahor's family did not want to go with Abraham and Lot to Canaan. But since Nahor and his family made their choice not to follow the God of Abraham, they remained in Haran to serve their gods.

Finally, after all of the preparations were done for their trip, Abraham and Nahor said their goodbyes and then Abraham and his caravan left southward to an uncharted land called Canaan.

> We are told: "₈ By faith Abraham, when he was called to go out into a place which he should after receive for an inheritance, obeyed; and he went out, not knowing whither he went" (Hebrews 11:8).

And when Abraham and his caravan entered and began to travel in the land of Canaan, they noticed the brooks, rivers, fountains of spring water in the hills and valleys, the lush fertile land surrounding them with beautiful trees, flowers, shrubs, fruit trees, olives, honey, vineyards full of grapes, fields full of barley and wheat, and the list went on

Abraham Leaves His Hometown Ur

and on to the beholder's delight.

A good land indeed!

But, what were the natives like?

Abraham and his caravan thrilled with their surroundings, decided to stop and camp in a place called "Sichem," which is located in the plain of "Moreh."

Sichem is commonly referred to by the name of "Shechem," and it is located between the Sea of Galilee and the Salt Sea on the west side of the Jordan River. In fact it's wedged a short distance between Mount Ebal and Mount Gerizim.

To confirm that Abraham was in the right country that he and his offspring were to posses, the LORD of hosts, appeared to Abraham in Shechem and said to him; "Unto your seed (offspring), I will give this land."

This was the third time the LORD of hosts appeared to Abraham, which further strengthened Abraham's faith in the LORD'S promises and leading.

Delighted in the LORD'S promise, Abraham went and gathered rocks and built an altar unto the LORD of hosts. And upon the altar, Abraham and his household offered animal sacrifices for their sins and thanks giving.

After a short stay in Shechem, Abraham moved about twenty miles further south from Shechem to a place called "Bethel." But more precisely Abraham camped near Bethel and the city of "Ai." Ai is located approximately ten miles north of Jerusalem. And if you recall, without the consent of the LORD of hosts, Ai was the first city Joshua went to overthrow without the LORD'S help and what a disaster it turned out to be. Doing things contrary to the will of the LORD and without His help can sometimes turn into more than a disaster—can't they?

Nonetheless, Abraham camped in Bethel; and as his custom was, he built an altar of stone, and there, again,

Abraham Leaves His Hometown Ur

publicly offered thank offerings and sin offerings unto the LORD of hosts.

Building altars and dedicating them to the LORD of hosts and offering sacrificial lambs upon them openly did catch the eyebrows of the Canaanites and made them wonder to what or to whom were those strange offering in the fire directed to? But, Abraham as his custom was did not hide his faith or of the implementation of the ceremonial law that was passed down from his forefathers. He did not falter or become discouraged by the roaming eyes of the Canaanites; he continued to worship the LORD of hosts publicly before them. The altars, the fires, and the billowing of smoke did offer a silent witness for the LORD.

Later on, in need of more pasture, Abraham and his household had to move again into unknown grassy fields. Although Abraham continued to trust in the LORD for his safety, guidance, and food, he still had to make the correct choices as to not provoke the native Canaanites as he moved from one place into another. Thus, again, very carefully, he embarked to move southwards until he found more open space and fertile land for his flock and for his nephew's flock to graze; and that place was the Negeb.

The Negeb—still identified as such today—can be found spanning its land south from Beer-sheba to the Wilderness of Paran; and from the southern part of the Salt Sea to the Mediterranean Sea.

Thus far, the un-turbulent journey of Abraham through the land of the Canaanites was not marred with any great problems that could not be solved. In fact, all seemed well in the Negeb. But that did not last. Abraham did not expect a famine to hit the area. The rains that normally came in November and December failed to appear and replenish the land with water.

The drought took its toll on the crops, animals, birds,

Abraham Leaves His Hometown Ur

man, and beast. Therefore when Abraham heard that there was food and water in Egypt, reluctantly and in his anxiety, he did not want to go there for fear of being killed. On the other hand, if Abraham and his household were to survive, they had to make the journey to Egypt. Consequently, Abraham quickly chose to sin by saying to Sarai, who was about sixty-five years old at this point in time, when she was asked if she was Abraham's wife she was to say that she was Abraham's half sister, which was true, but she was to omit the part that she was also his wife.

The circumstance, which Abraham found himself in, tested his faith in the way the LORD was leading him. Although he was fearful for his life and for his household, he traveled to Egypt.

Realizing his fear, unfortunately for Abraham, when he arrived there, at one point, he found out that the Pharaohs preferred fair-haired women to amass in their realm.

Hoping to avert confrontation, especially with Pharaoh, it was not to be because while Abraham was looking for rations and buying rations, Sarai was spotted by some of the "princes" who were looking to be favored by the Pharaoh. They quickly told Pharaoh about her beauty; and he responded by asking Abraham and his sister to appear before him. And when they did, Pharaoh was well pleased to see her beauty; and when Pharaoh asked Abraham if Sarai was his wife, he lied and said, "She was his sister." Learning that she was his sister, Pharaoh took Sarai and made arrangements for a dowry to be paid to Abraham. Abraham accepted the dowry, and they took Sarai to be prepped for the wedding ceremony.

But, while Pharaoh's servants were preparing Sarai and the wedding ceremony, the LORD of hosts plagued Pharaoh's house and revealed to him that Sarai was already married to Abraham.

Abraham Leaves His Hometown Ur

As a result, Pharaoh was wroth with Abraham and with his deception, saying, I am a just man. If you had told me that she was your wife, I would have not taken her from you. Now, take your wife and go your way.

Here is the record of the agreement between Abraham and Sarai and how the LORD of hosts intervened on his behalf. Abraham said to Sarai: "12 Therefore it shall come to pass, when the Egyptians shall see thee [you], that they shall say, This is his wife and they will kill me, but they will save thee alive. 13 Say, I pray thee, thou [you] art my sister: that it may be well with me for thy [your] sake; and my soul shall live because of thee [you].

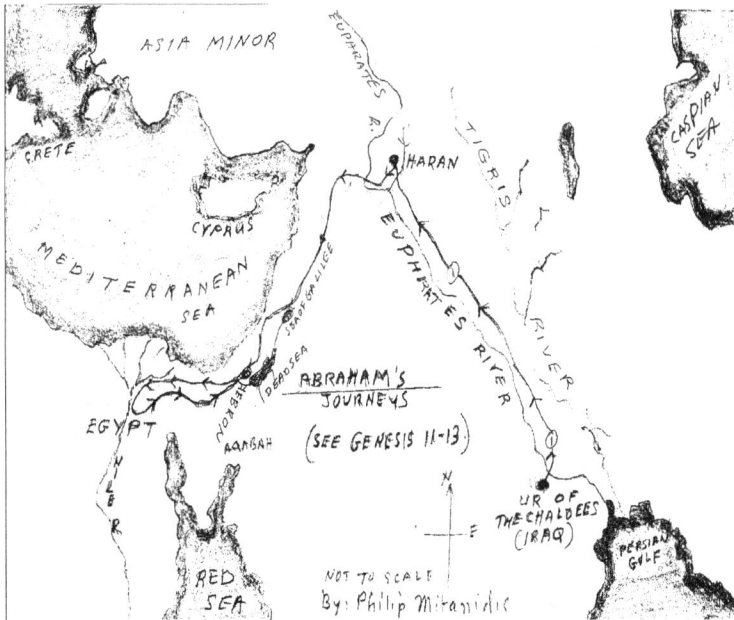

"14 And it came to pass, that, when Abram was come into Egypt, the Egyptians beheld the woman that she was very fair. 15 The princes also of Pharaoh saw her, and commended her before Pharaoh: and the woman was taken

Abraham Leaves His Hometown Ur

into Pharaoh's house. 16 And he entreated Abram well for her sake: and he had sheep, and oxen, and he asses, and menservants, and maidservants, and she asses, and camels. 17 And the LORD plagued Pharaoh and his house with great plagues because of Sarai Abram's wife?

"18 and Pharaoh called Abram, and said, What is this that thou [you] has done unto me? why didst thou not tell me that she was thy [your] wife? 19 Why saidst thou, She is my sister? so I might have taken her to me to wife: now therefore, behold thy wife, take her, and go thy [your] way" (Genesis 12:19).

"Take her and go" was the command indeed by Pharaoh because he did not want to be punished anymore for Abraham's deception. In fact Pharaoh made sure that Abraham, the dowry that Pharaoh gave him, and his caravan made it safely and quickly out of Egypt by commanding his men to make certain they all left Egypt unharmed.

Abraham was made rich by Pharaoh's dowry in silver, gold, servants, and in livestock. But now, he had a greater concern to think about because his livestock needed larger fertile land to graze upon. Therefore he thought about Bethel.

By the grace and love of the LORD of hosts, Abraham was safely removed from Egypt and taken back to the Promised Land—Canaan. There, entering the Negeb, Abraham and his caravan plotted the journey to Bethel. Stopping a number of times in the lush fields and arteries of the three rivers, near and past Beer-sheba; the caravan continued to go northward towards Hebron, past Jerusalem, and onward into Bethel.

Arriving in Bethel, their stay was short lived. Abraham and Lot greatly increased in livestock and servants; and because of lack of grazing land, their servants argued and fought amongst themselves for pasture. Being careful not to

Abraham Leaves His Hometown Ur

aggravate the herdsmen of the Canaanites who lived in walled cities and the Perizzites who lived in open villages, Abraham said to his nephew; "Let there be no strife between you and me; choose the land you want to make your home on and feed your livestock there."

Abraham recognized the peril of strife. If strife and hatred continued between Abraham's servants and Lot's servants, it would definitely cause a misrepresentation of the God they were worshipping to the unbelievers; therefore Abraham wanted to put an end to the riotous behavior between Lot's household and his own household as soon as possible.

Perhaps nothing more effectively would have disrupted, frustrated, derailed, and thwarted the Plan of Salvation for the people of Canaan than the continuous discord between the two families of Lot and Abraham. Misrepresenting God the Creator of heaven and earth, early in their relationship with the natives, would also have created big problems with their residency in Canaan. Therefore Abraham said to Lot, Separate yourself from my household and choose where you want to make your home and where you want to graze your livestock. Abraham gave Lot the first choice; he did not give him a second choice to choose from.

Hearing the offer, Lot immediately took advantage of Abraham and chose the fertile land of the Jordan River. Out of courtesy, Lot did not say to Abraham you choose first and then I will decide where to go; instead, Lot, in greed and without respect or concern for his uncle's livestock proceeded to separate himself towards the Jordan River.

The Jordan River meanders for a distance of about two hundred miles from The Sea of Galilee to the Dead Sea, which in effect, the distance from the Sea of Galilee to the Dead Sea is only about sixty-five miles long as the crow flies.

To its credit, the Jordan fertile valley has a tropical

Abraham Leaves His Hometown Ur

climate all year round, which needless to say, provided a lush fertile land for orchards, farming, and raising livestock. Although Lot made a good choice for the animals, he did not make a good choice to move there for himself and for his family.

The reason I state that Lot did not make a good choice is due to the fact that Lot moved his family too close to the cities of Sodom, Gomorrah, and Zoar; and because eventually, they were drawn to the life style of the cities, and to their detriment, they all ended up dwelling in the city of Sodom.

Regarding Abraham and his household, he trusted in the LORD of hosts for his sustaining hand. Therefore it did not matter so much to Abraham where he was able to go and stay. But the LORD did not leave his faith-full servant stranded; after Lot separated himself from Abraham, the LORD revealed Himself to Abraham again and said to him "Lift up now your eyes" and look around you. Look towards the south; look towards the north; look towards the east; look towards the west; and go walk throughout the land of Canaan and become familiar with it because this land I will give unto you and unto your progeny.

Encouraged by the LORD'S promise and directive, Abraham got up and moved gradually southwards from Bethel to Hebron, which is about twenty-two miles south of Jerusalem. Surveying the breath and width of the land he traveled on, there, near Hebron, in the valley of Mamre, he pitched his tents and built an altar unto the LORD, expressing gratitude and love for the LORD'S mercy, long suffering, promise, and love towards him and his caravan.

The record states: "14 And the LORD said unto Abram, after that Lot was separated from him, Lift up now thine [your] eyes, and look from the place where thou [you] art northward, and southward, and eastward, and westward: 15

Abraham Leaves His Hometown Ur

For all the land which thou [you] seest, to thee [you] will I give it, and to thy [your] seed for ever. 16 And I will make thy [your] seed as the dust of the earth: so that if a man can number the dust of the earth, then shall thy [your] seed also be numbered. 17 Arise, walk through the land in the length of it and in the breath of it; for I will give it unto thee [you]. 18 Then Abram removed his tent, and came and dwelt in the plain of Mamre, which is in Hebron, and built there an altar unto the LORD" (Genesis 13:14-18).

Although Abraham eventually found peace and confederacy with his neighbors, in the valley of Mamre, it did not last because the following kings from the north and from the east of Canaan— Amraphel king of Shinar, Arioch king of Ellasar, Chedorlaomer king of Elam, and Tidal king of nations—revolted against Bera king of Sodom, Birsha king of Gomorah, Shinab king of Admah, and Shemeber king of Zeboiim, and the king of Bela (Zoar) because they decided not to pay homage to King Chedorlaomer who acted as a leader of the coalition of kings.

The five kings of Canaan served Chedorlaomer for twelve years; but on the thirteenth year they rebelled against him and the coalition. And on the fourteenth year Chedorlaomer and his army came south from Hobah, which is not too far northwest from Damascus and traveled on the east side of the Jordan River on the King's Highway. The first strike by Chedorlaomer was unleashed upon the Rephaims that were located on the east side of the Sea of Galilee. The next strike by Chedorlaomer's army was directed upon the Zuzims that were located east of Jericho. The third victims were the Emims that were located near the southern east corner of the Dead Sea. And from there the invaders struck upon the Horites and pushed them southwards past Kadesh. And from there they went northward and invaded the Amalekites and Amorites who

Abraham Leaves His Hometown Ur

lived on top of the Negeb. And when Chedorlaomer came to the valley of Siddim all of the five kings came out to fight the invaders; but because of the onslaught, many were overwhelmed and fled from the invaders to the mountains and many were captured along with their goods and taken with them to the city of Hobah.

After Chedorlaomer and his army defeated the five kings of Siddim and left with the spoils of war, a survivor, who apparently knew that Lot was the nephew of Abraham, went to Mamre and told Abraham that the invaders overthrew the cities of Siddim (Dead Sea), which included Sodom and Gomorrah and took Lot and his family captive from there and left.

Hearing the bad news Abraham gathered three hundred and eighteen of his trained servants, who were born in his household, told them what happened, and armed them. And he also accepted the help of his friends Aner, Eshcol, and Mamre who were confederate with Abraham. They to gathered their armies and joined Abraham's forces.

With their combined manpower they left at night from Hebron to pursue the invaders

They went north from Hebron to Salem and from Salem they went northeast past Jericho, crossed the Jordan River, and then followed the King's Highway northward and passed on the right hand side of the Sea of Galilee.

Passing the Sea of Galilee, Abraham learned that the invaders were headed to the city of Dan, which is located between the Sea of Galilee and Damascus. When they reached Dan, Abraham with his confederates divided their men into small groups and struck Chedorlaomer and his army from all directions, creating panic and confusion throughout camp, and leaving his army vulnerable.

In their disoriented state, Abraham and his confederates struck mercilessly from all directions destroying most of

Abraham Leaves His Hometown Ur

Chedorlaomer's army. But those who remained standing realized that their comrades were quickly falling. A remnant managed to run for safety, leaving the spoils and those that were captured behind.

Seeing that Lot and his family were safe, Abraham did not stop there; he pursued Chedorlaomer and his army all the way up to the city of Hobah; and by the time they reached the city of Hobah, Chedorlaomer's surviving army was fragmented, in shambles, and running for their lives. Confident that Chedorlaomer could not regroup because of lack of manpower, Abraham and his confederates returned

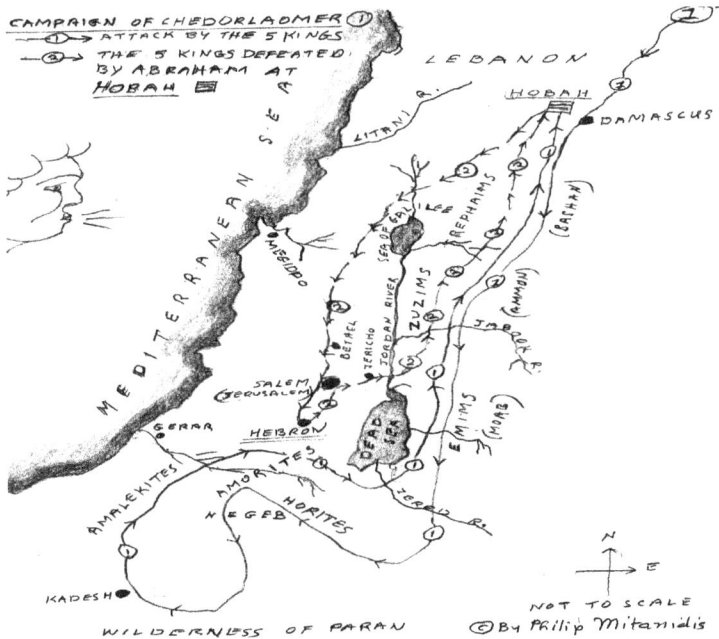

to Dan to pick up Lot and his family, the spoils of war, and the rest of the survivors.

After gathering all of the surviving men, women, children, their belongings, and the spoils of war, Abraham

Abraham Leaves His Hometown Ur

and his confederates started their journey southward on the west side of the Jordan River to go home. But, when they arrived in the Kidron Valley, "17 the king of Sodom" who survived Chedorlaomer's attack, "went out to meet him [Abraham] after his return from the slaughter of Chedorlaomer, and of the kings that were with him, at the valley of Shaveh, which is the king's dale" (Genesis 14:17). If this is the king's dale that is spoken of in 2 Samuel 18:18, the meeting was held in a place that was later known as Kidron valley, which is at the foot of Mount Zion."

With Bera the king of Sodom, was also Melchizedek the king of Salem, and a host of other people who came out to meet the victors. (Salem today is better known as the city of Jerusalem.)

The record states, "18 Melchizedek king of Salem" greeted Abraham and "brought forth bread and wine:" as refreshments, for all of the victors and survivors. Melchizedek "was the priest of the most high God. "19 And he blessed him [Abraham], and said, Blessed be Abram of the most high God, possessor of heaven and earth: 20 And blessed be the most high God, which hath delivered thine [your] enemies into thy hand. And he [Abraham] gave him tithes of all" (Genesis 14:18-20).

As the record indicates, Melchizedek was a priest, which strongly attests to the fact that he was adhering to the ceremonial law that was originally enacted after the fall of Eve and Adam. It must be remembered that the ceremonial law was added to the Ten Commandments because of sin. Therefore the ceremonial law, from day one, when Adam sinned, pointed forward to the supreme sacrifice of Jesus Christ the LORD on Calvary's cross.

And, as the record indicates, like Abraham, Lot, and

Abraham Leaves His Hometown Ur

Melchizedek, God had and has His people scattered throughout the world in all generation to testify of the Plan of Salvation that is in Christ Jesus. (See Isaiah 43:11; Acts 4:12.)

At the same time, it should also be noted, the fact that Abraham did build an altar of stone wherever he went and offered animal sacrifices for his sins and thank offerings, it confirms that Abraham did abide by the Ten Commandments and by the ceremonial law, as previous believers did.

After Melchizedek finished speaking, then Bera "21 the king of Sodom said unto Abram, Give me the persons, and take the goods to thyself.

> "22 And Abram said to the king of Sodom, I have lift up mine hand unto the LORD, the Most High God, the possessor of heaven and earth. 23 That I will not take from a thread even to a shoelatchet, and that I will not take any thing that is thine [yours], lest thou [you] shouldest say, I have made Abram rich: 24 Save only that which the young men have eaten, and the portion of the men which went with me, Aner, Eshcol, and Mamre; let them take their portion" (Genesis 14:21-24).

Abraham refused to take any of the spoils with the exception of what was his own. Abraham did not place some sort of status as being better than anyone else or value in material things. His hopes and desires were not of this world because Abraham looked for a better country—a heavenly. The faith of a believer in Christ the LORD is marked by a lofty mind that transcends all and enables him or her to live above the world and its glittering goods. The hope and faith of a believer is fixed upon Christ the Redeemer and not on the cumbersome material things of the world.

Abraham Leaves His Hometown Ur

Nonetheless, separating his men from his confederates—Lot and his family, and Lot's belongings—Abraham cordially departed from Shaveh and returned to the valley of Mamre.

After the gruesome ordeal with the invading army of Chedorlaomer, Abraham became fearful for his life, not only because the invading army would return in some point of time, but also because of his surrounding pagan kings who resented Abraham's popularity with many of the natives. But even more fearful was the thought of not knowing when death might strike upon him; he began to question the LORD regarding the possession of Canaan? He wondered; how is it possible for him to possess the land from Dan to Kadesh-barnea when there are fearless pagan kings ruling the land all over the place? And since he was getting old and did not have any children, how was the land going to be passed on to them?

Knowing what was in the mind of Abraham, in a vision, the LORD comforted him by saying, "Fear not," and reassured him that He would continue to protect him by saying, "I am your shield." Abraham could relate to those words because before he left to rescue his nephew, Abraham asked the LORD for His protection and for victory over the invaders.

But there was another issue in Abraham's mind. Since he did not have any children, he wanted to have his trusted servant Eliezer from Damascus who was born in Abraham's household to inherit the covenant that was made between himself and the LORD of hosts. Abraham wanted Eliezer to be heir of the covenant because Eliezer was an adopted child. Therefore, under the current civil law, it was proper for Abraham and Sarai to want him to take over their household.

"2 And Abram said, LORD God, what wilt thou [You]

Abraham Leaves His Hometown Ur

give me, seeing I go childless, and the steward of my house is this Eliezer of Damascus? ₃ And Abram said, Behold, to me thou [You] hast given no seed: and, lo, one born in my house is mine heir.

"₄ And, behold, the word of the LORD came unto him, saying, This shall not be thine [your] heir; but he that shall come forth out of thine [your] own bowels shall be thine [your] heir.

"₅ And He brought him forth abroad, and said, Look now toward heaven, and tell the stars, if thou [you] be able to number them: and He said unto him, So shall thy [your] seed be. ₆ And he believed in the LORD; and He counted it to him for righteousness" (Genesis 15:2-6).

And to further ease Abraham's concerns, the LORD reminded Abraham by saying, "₇ I am the LORD that brought thee [you] out of Ur of the Chaldees, to give thee you] this [land to inherit it" (Genesis 15:7).

Then the question came from Abraham saying, "LORD how will I know that I will inherit it?"

How was Abraham going to know?

He was going to know by making a covenant with the LORD of hosts and believe that the covenant would eventually be fulfilled as the LORD of hosts promised.

Therefore to impress upon Abraham's mind that Abraham's offspring would inherit the land, as per the covenant, the LORD of hosts told Abraham to go and prepare for the covenant by bringing a three years old heifer, a three years old she goat, a three years old ram, a turtledove, and a pigeon. And when he had gathered the animals and birds unto one spot, Abraham killed them and sliced the animals from head to toe in half; and regarding the birds, he wrung the birds' necks and left them whole. After that, Abraham took each of the animal's two halves and placed them side-by-side to each other in two rows. And the two

Abraham Leaves His Hometown Ur

birds he placed one at the end of each row. Then, Abraham went and separated each half of the animal's carcasses, leaving enough space in between the two rows of the carcasses, so that he would be able to walk between them.

After the above preparation of the birds and animals was completed, by Abraham, a verbal agreement was to be committed between Abraham and the LORD of hosts. And after the verbal agreement, Abraham and the LORD of hosts were to separately walk in between the two rows of the carcasses in order to bind their verbal agreement.

Therefore, after the above task was done, Abraham waited for the LORD'S response; but the LORD did not respond right away. And as Abraham waited and waited for the LORD, the surrounding birds did not wait; they began to dive from the sky upon the carcasses. Seeing that the birds were picking the flesh of the carcasses, Abraham spent considerable time chasing them away.

Daytime had passed and night fell and still the LORD of hosts did not appear. Abraham was wondering if the LORD would consent to a covenant. Nonetheless Abraham waited patiently, and then a deep sleep fell upon him; and during his deep sleep, Abraham experienced a "great darkness" of "horror" that was impressed upon him by the LORD. And then, the horror and the darkness were explained to Abraham; the LORD said to him, "13 Know of a surety that thy [your] seed shall be a stranger in a land that is not theirs, and shall serve them; and they shall afflict them four hundred years; 14 And also that nation, whom they shall serve, will I judge: and afterward shall they come out with great substance. 15 And thou [you] shalt go to thy [your] fathers in peace; thou shalt be buried in a good old age. 16 but in the fourth generation they shall come hither [here] again: for the iniquity of the Amorites is not yet full" (Genesis 15:13-16).

Abraham Leaves His Hometown Ur

Finally it was revealed to Abraham prophetically what would happen to him and to his progeny. The scene was not too pretty because it revealed for four hundred years Abraham's descendents would be persecuted and the majority would be enslaved in a foreign land.

Isaac was persecuted by his stepbrother Ishmael. Jacob was persecuted by his twin brother Esau and by Laban, his father-in-law. Joseph was persecuted by his step-brothers. The children of Israel (Jacob), while they lived in Goshen, they were persecuted by the natives and Pharaoh for approximately one hundred and forty-four years after the death of Joseph. And, the surrounding pagan kings persecuted the children of Israel, when they inherited the Promised Land.

Therefore the land, which Abraham was standing upon, was a temporary home for him and for his children. But the promise was simple; after four generations the LORD would bring Abraham's offspring back to Canaan to possess the land.

And after the covenant was established between Abraham and the LORD of host, "17 it came to pass, that, when the sun went down, and it was dark, behold a smoking furnace, and a burning lamp that passed between those pieces. 18 In the same day the LORD made a covenant with Abram, saying, Unto thy [your] seed have I given this land, from the river of Egypt unto the great river, the river Euphrates" (Genesis 15:17, 18).

And that included all of the land the kings of Canaan held at the present. They are "19 The Kenites, and the Kenizzites, and the Kadmonites. 20 And the Hittites, and the Perizzites, and the Rephaims. 21 And the Amorites, and the Canaanites, and the Girgashites, and the Jebusites" (Genesis 15:19-21).

God in the above verses reaffirms His promises to

Abraham Leaves His Hometown Ur

Abraham concerning the possession of Canaan. In fact, the LORD of hosts marked the precise landmarks off the amount of land his offspring were going to eventually inherit. These geographic limits were also realized by King David and King Solomon during their reign. (See 1 Kings 4:21; 2 Chronicles 9:26.)

In spite of the precise prophetic revelation to Abraham that his offspring was going to inherit the land, ten years after he left Haran, Abraham was still without any children of his own. Since Sarai was still childless and getting old, she felt that the promise of a son was not going to happen as the LORD had promised because she was unable to become pregnant. Therefore Sarai suggested that Abraham take Hagar, Sarai's servant that was given to her by Pharaoh during the time Abraham and Sarai were in Egypt, and have sex with her, in order to fulfill the promise of the LORD. This method to procreate was a Mesopotamian custom and widely practiced.

Falling into disbelief that the LORD of hosts would grant Sarai children, Abraham fell into disbelief also; therefore, he took Sarai's advice and had sex with Hagar the Egyptian woman.

The faith of Sarai and Abraham was tested and they failed. God does not say one thing and then do something else. God does not lie. He had promised Abraham many times that his own offspring from Sarai would inherit the covenant and not some offspring from another woman. The LORD delayed Sarai's pregnancy in order to strengthen her faith and Abraham's faith; but they failed the test. They went to fulfill the LORD'S promise on their own terms, which created a big problem for both Sarai and Abraham later on.

Abraham was eighty-five years old when Hagar got pregnant. And Hagar, after she became pregnant, began to gradually think of her status as a servant and what privileges

Abraham Leaves His Hometown Ur

she and she and her baby would have after Hagar gave birth. Eventually, Hagar began to be insubordinate to Sarai. And started to act more like the first wife to Abraham. Therefore as the days went by, Hagar became more and more rebellious causing strife and jealousy in Abraham's home.

Finally, Sarai had enough of Hagar's abuses. She regretted the recommendation she made to Abraham when she suggested that he procreate with Hagar. She said to him "5 My wrong be upon thee [you]: I have given my maid into thy [your] bosom; and when she saw that she had conceived, I was despised in her eyes." Therefore Sarai wanted Abraham to solve her problem.

In response, Abraham said to Sarai, "6 Behold, thy [your] maid is in thy [your] hand; do to her as it pleaseth thee [you]" (Genesis 16:5, 6).

Familiar with the Mesopotamian code of slave ownership, section 146 of Hammurabi, it allows for a status change of a slave. It states "if later that female slave has claimed equality with her mistress because she bore children, her mistress may not sell her; she may mark her with the slave-mark and count her among the slaves."

This law permitted the humiliation of an overbearing slave-concubine, but also laid certain restrictions upon her owner of which Abraham was well familiar because he was born, raised, and went to school in Mesopotamia. Therefore Abraham knew that Sarai was permitted to humiliate Hagar for her insubordination but was not allowed to sell her. And because Hagar could not be sold, "Sarai dealt harshly" with her to a point of corporal punishment. And because of that severe corporal punishment, finally Hagar fled from Sarai.

Pregnant and without much substance Hagar ran away from Abraham's household and headed south towards her homeland—Egypt. Actually she was not too far from Egypt because she had reached "Shur," which is near the Egyptian

Abraham Leaves His Hometown Ur

border. And there before she entered her homeland, the LORD confronted Hagar.

Why the LORD waited that long to confront Hagar is a good question?

Nonetheless, "₉ the angel of the LORD said unto her, Return to thy [your] mistress, and submit thyself [yourself] under her hands. ₁₀ And the angel of the LORD said unto her, I will multiply thy [your] seed exceedingly, that it shall not be numbered for multitude. ₁₁ And the angel of the LORD said unto her, Behold, thou [you] art with a child, and shalt bear a son, and shalt call his name Ishmael; because the LORD hath heard thy [your] affliction. ₁₂ And he will be a wild man; his hand will be against every man, and every man's hand against him: and he shall dwell in the presence of all his brethren. ₁₃ And she called the name of the LORD that spake unto her, Thou God seest me: for she said, Have I also here looked after him that seeth me? ₁₄ Wherefore the well was called Beer-la-hai-roi; behold, it is between Kadesh and Bered" (Genesis 16:9-14).

Hagar considered her experience and decided to take the above advice that was given to her and return to Abraham's household and remain a slave under the auspices of Sarai. And when she conceived, Abraham called his son "Ishmael." At the time Ishmael was born, Abraham was eighty-six years old and Sarai was seventy-six years old.

Doing things contrary to the will of the LORD of hosts can prove to be disastrous as Abraham and Sarai found out. And learning from one's mistakes is a valuable characteristic trait. Therefore after that ordeal, very patiently Abraham and Sarai waited for the promise to be fulfilled from his own progeny. But, Abraham and Sarai were getting old; Sarai was eighty-nine years old past the stage where she was able to conceive children. Consequently, after thirteen years, they began to believe that Ishmael was going to be the heir of the

Abraham Leaves His Hometown Ur

covenant.

But that was not to be because the LORD of hosts appeared again to Abraham when he was ninety-nine years old in the plains of Mamre to reinforce the covenant in Abraham's mind, change Abram's name to Abraham, change Sarai's name to Sarah, and to have everybody henceforth circumcised as a token of the covenant between Abraham and the LORD of hosts.

Here is the account: "1 And when Abram was ninety years old and nine, the LORD appeared to Abram, and said unto him, I am the Almighty God; walk before Me, and be thou [you] perfect. 2 And I will make My covenant between Me and thee, and will multiply thee exceedingly. 3 And Abram fell on his face: and God talked with him, saying, 4 As for Me, behold, My covenant is with thee [you], and thou [you] shalt be a father of many nations. 5 Neither shall thy name any more be called Abram, but thy your] name shall be Abraham; for a father of many nations have I made thee. 6 And I will make thee exceeding fruitful, and I will make nations of thee, and kings shall come out of thee. 7 And I will establish My covenant between Me and thee and thy seed after thee in their generations for an everlasting covenant, to be a God unto thee [you] and to thy [your] see after thee. 8 And I will given unto thee, and to thy seed after thee, the land wherein thou [you] art a stranger, all the land of Canaan, for an everlasting possession; and I will be their God" (Genesis 17:1-8).

The LORD of hosts again foretold that the offspring that would come out of Abraham's bowels would eventually possess the land of Canaan; and to impress that fact upon Abraham and Sarai, the LORD added a little ritual that was to be performed by them, upon their children, and their progeny upon their children in all generation. They were to circumcise their children. Therefore, every time they

Abraham Leaves His Hometown Ur

circumcised their children, it would remind them of the covenant that was made between Abraham and God the LORD of hosts that they are His people and that He is their God and that they were to inherit the land of Canaan.

Therefore, circumcision is a token or a sign, if you like, to remind a person of the covenant that was made between Abraham and the LORD of hosts; just as baptism is a token of Christ's death and resurrection; just as the LORD'S supper is a sign of Christ's supreme sacrifice on Calvary's cross; and just as the Sabbath [Saturday] is a symbol for the creation of the heavens and the earth by the LORD of hosts.

Therefore these signs are instituted for our benefit; they are reminders of the LORD of hosts.

But as a consequence, if Abraham and his progeny were to fail compliance to the act of circumcision, it meant that they did not believe in the God of Abraham or that such a covenant ever took place between Abraham and the LORD of hosts.

If that was the attitude of an individual, then that individual was to be cut of from his people.

After receiving the directive, Abraham and all that were in his household were circumcised; and that included Abraham and Ishmael who was thirteen years old at that time. And when everyone in Abraham's household were circumcised and left to heal from their pain, a person would think that it infused an impression upon Abraham's mind that he and Sarai were going to have children of their own.

But the incongruity of unbelief by Abraham and Sarai to the revelation and promises from the LORD of hosts is uncanny.

Why would Abraham and Sarai implement the act of circumcision in their household, if they did not believe in the promises of the covenant?

Could it be because by now they believed that Ishmael

Abraham Leaves His Hometown Ur

was the recipient of the covenant?

It does appear to be the case from the record!

But the LORD told Abraham that Sarai will conceive a son. And to further confirm the fact that she was going to conceive a son, the LORD changed her name to Sarah.

What further evidence did Abraham and Sarah want?

The LORD of hosts was speaking to them personally; wasn't that enough?

Apparently not!

Because Sarah was past the stage of conceiving children, they assumed that there was no hope for Sarah to procreate and fulfill the promise of the LORD; that is why they set their sights on Ishmael.

Therefore, when the LORD told Abraham that Sarah would be the mother of nations, "17 Abraham fell upon his face, and laughed, and said in his heart, Shall a child be born unto him that is an hundred years old? and shall Sarah, that is ninety years old, bear? 18 And Abraham said unto God, O that Ishmael might live before thee [You]! 19 And God said, Sarah thy [your] wife shall bear thee [you] a son indeed; and thou [you] shalt call his name Isaac; and I will establish My covenant with him for an everlasting covenant, and with his seed after him. 20 And as for Ishmael, I have heard thee [you]; Behold, I have blessed him, and will make him fruitful, and will multiply him exceedingly; twelve princes shall he beget, and I will make him a great nation. 21 But My covenant will I establish with Isaac, which Sarah shall bear unto thee at this set time in the next year. 22 And He left off talking with him [Abraham], and God went up from Abraham" (Genesis 17:17-22).

Just before the LORD of hosts stopped talking with Abraham, He told him that Sarah will give birth to a son. Why were Abraham and Sarah still in doubt?

Later on in the year, after the above revelation, the

Abraham Leaves His Hometown Ur

LORD of hosts appeared to Abraham again. This was the sixth time the LORD interacted with Abraham.

As Abraham sat at the tent's door in the heat of the day, in the plains of Mamre, unexpectedly, things began to happen to Abraham and Sarah. Abraham saw three men afar off. And when he saw them he ran to meet them; and as his custom was, he bowed down towards the ground to greet them and offered the travelers food, water, and rest, if they wished.

One individual out of the three came forward and interacted with Abraham. Abraham willing to honor the three strangers with his hospitality said to the one who interacted with him, "If I have found favor in your sight, pass not away? Stay and have some water, wash your dusty feet and rest under the tree while food is prepared for you."

After the invitation was given to the three strangers, they accepted Abraham's hospitality and said to him, "So do, as thou [you] have said."

The three strangers sat under the tree while Abraham went into his tent, which was not too far from the tree and told Sarah to prepare "three measures of fine meal, knead it, and make cakes upon the hearth." And after he told Sarah to prepare the food, he went to the herd, and picked a tender young calf and gave it to a young man to cook the calf.

After the calf and bread were prepared, Abraham took the food to the three strangers; they did eat and drink under the tree. And by the time they finished eating, and talked for a while, it was getting late in the afternoon. And just before the three strangers decided to leave, one of the strangers said to Abraham, "Where is Sarah your wife?" and Abraham replied, "She is in the tent." And then the stranger said to him, "10 I will certainly return unto thee [you] according to the time of life; and, lo, Sarah thy [your] wife shall have a son" (Genesis 18:10).

Abraham Leaves His Hometown Ur

Abraham was stunned to hear these words because he had heard them before and wondered why is this stranger saying this to me?

Who is He?

In the meantime, while Abraham was wondering about the words the stranger had spoken to him. "Sarah heard it in the tent door, which was behind Him." "12 Therefore Sarah laughed within herself, saying, After I am waxed old shall I have pleasure, my lord [Abraham] being old also?"

And to make matters more eerie, the stranger said to Abraham, "13 Wherefore did Sarah laugh, saying, Shall I of a surety bear a child, which am old?" Then the LORD asked Abraham a question; "14 Is any thing too hard for the LORD?"

Again the LORD reaffirmed His promise to Abraham by saying, "14 At the time appointed I will return unto thee [you], according to the time of life, and Sarah shall have a son" (Genesis 18:12-14).

And when Sarah was confronted about her laughter, she denied it because she was afraid. She was afraid because she wondered how did this man know that she laughed within herself?

After that eerie episode, the three men got up to leave. In courtesy, Abraham decided to go with the men a short distance and give them direction, if need be?

But when he found out that they were going to Sodom, Zoar, and Gomorrah, Abraham wanted to know why they were going there?

Then one of the three men began to think by saying, "17 shall I hide from Abraham that thing which I do; 18 Seeing that Abraham shall surely become a great and mighty nation, and all the nations of the earth shall be blessed in him: 19 For I know him, that he will command his children and his household after him, and they shall keep the way of the

Abraham Leaves His Hometown Ur

LORD, to do justice and judgment; that the LORD may bring upon Abraham that which he hath spoken of him."

After thinking upon these things, the LORD of hosts said to Abraham, "20 Because the cry [exceeding wickedness] of Sodom and Gomorrah is great, and because their sin is very grievous; 21 I will go down now, and see whether they have done altogether according to the cry of it, which is come unto Me; and if not, I will know. 22 And the men turned their faced from thence, and went toward Sodom: but Abraham stood yet before the LORD."

Concerned about Lot and his family and realizing that retribution time had come upon Sodom and Gomorrah, Abraham did not make an effort to return to his home; instead, Abraham came near the LORD and said to Him, "23 Wilt thou [You] also destroy the righteous with the wicked?" What if there were "24 fifty righteous within the city: wilt thou [You] also destroy and not spare the place for the fifty righteous that are therein? 25 That be far from thee to do after this manner, to slay the righteous with the wicked: and that the righteous should be as the wicked, that be far from thee: Shall not the judge of all the earth do right?

"26 And the LORD said, If I find in Sodom fifty righteous within the city, then I will spare all the place for their sakes." But, because the other two men (angels) continued to go towards the cities, "27 Abraham answered and said, Behold now, I have taken upon me to speak unto the LORD, which am but dust and ashes: 28 Peradventure there shall lack five of the fifty righteous: wilt thou destroy all the city for lack of five? And He said, If I find there forty and five, I will not destroy it." And the two angels continued to go towards the cities; and again Abraham talked to the LORD and said, "29 Peradventure there shall be forty found there. And He said, I will not do it for forty's sake." And Abraham becoming bolder and concerned for his nephew

Abraham Leaves His Hometown Ur

replied, "30 Oh let not the LORD be angry, and I will speak: Peradventure there shall thirty be found there. And He said I will not do it, if I find thirty there." And Abraham now worried even more about Lot said, "31 Behold now, I have taken upon me to speak unto the LORD: Peradventure there shall be twenty found there. And He said, I will not destroy it for twenty's sake." Pushing the issue even further Abraham said, "32 Oh let not the LORD be angry and I will speak yet but this once: Peradventure ten shall be found there." and the LORD of hosts said again to Abraham, "I will not destroy it for ten's sake" (Genesis 18:17-32).

Disappointed in what Abraham heard, he could not stop the two angels and the LORD of hosts from destroying Sodom, Gomorrah, and the surrounding cities because there were not ten righteous people found in these cities.

Wondering what would happen to Lot and his family, in despair Abraham stopped interacting with the LORD and began his journey homeward slowly; and once in a while stopping and looking anxiously back towards the cities.

Although the cities were about twenty miles southeast from where Abraham's tents were located, Abraham knew that this distance was meaningless to the LORD and to the two angels who were with the LORD of hosts. If they wanted they would be there in a blink of an eye.

Nonetheless, the record states, "33 And the LORD went His way, as soon as he had left communing with Abraham: and Abraham returned unto his place" (Genesis 18:33).

Meanwhile the two angels had already arrived in the plains of Sodom and Gomorrah and waiting for the LORD to finish talking with Abraham. And when the LORD of hosts came to them, He confirmed the wickedness the cities were passionately engaged in. Therefore the cities would not be spared because the LORD could not find ten righteous people in them.

Abraham Leaves His Hometown Ur

Learning that the cities would be destroyed, the two angels changed into human forms and walked towards the city gate of Sodom. And as they were entering the gate, Lot who was sitting there, got up and approached them. And when he came near them, like Abraham, he bowed down towards the ground and offered them his hospitality, by saying to them, come in to your servant's house, and stay the whole night.

They refused Lot's hospitality and told him that they would stay in the street all night.

But Lot would not hear it; the streets were too dangerous. He insisted that they came to his house, wash their feet, eat, and stay there all night; and in the morning, they would go on their way.

Again they refused; but almost insisting that they stay with him, finally the two strangers did go with Lot to his home and stayed there. Lot prepared a feast for his two guests and they did eat and drink and talked for a while. But just before they laid down for the night, the men of the city, young and old, came to Lot's house in droves, gathered around it, and called Lot to come out from his house to talk with them. He came out and asked them what they wanted; and they said that they wanted to meet the two strangers that were in his house so that they would become acquainted with them.

Lot told them that they are his guests therefore he would not bring them out. Hearing Lot's decision, the mob began to be furious with him. Realizing that they would not back down from their demand and do wickedly upon the two strangers, Lot gave them an alternative; he said to them, "I have two virgin daughters in the house, take them instead." But they would not hear of it, they demanded for the strangers to come out and started to push forward towards his front door.

Abraham Leaves His Hometown Ur

Lot tried to hold them back by reasoning with them, but they said to him, "We will deal worse with you than with them, if you don't bring them out." Lot still refused to bring the two men out. And when they saw that he was resisting their demands, they started to push forward in force to a point where they were not only going to crush Lot, but also crush his front door.

Observing the evil frenzy outside the door, the two men (angels) pushed the door open, without hurting Lot, pulled him in the house, and then closed the door. Then the two men (angels) went outside and struck the mob that was outside of the front door with blinding light, which emanated from them. This caused confusion, fear, and bewilderment with the vindictive mob.

Seeing the blinding power of the two men (angels), the rowdy mob gradually dispersed. After the coast was clear, the angels said to Lot, "Go and tell your sons, daughters, and sons-in-law to come out of the city with him because the LORD was going to destroy the cities in the morning." Lot hurried to reach all of his family and their children; but when he talked with them, instead of listening to his words, they mocked him and therefore refused to come out from the cities.

Desperate for his sons and daughters to be saved from their death, Lot thought of ways that he could convince them to flee the cities, but to his dismay, he failed. Therefore before the morning light came, the two angels hurried Lot, his wife, and his two daughters that were with him to get ready to depart quickly.

But Lot, his wife, and his two daughters, could not bring themselves to leave the city without the rest of the family. Therefore they were delaying their exit from the city. Knowing that the rest of the family would not be coming, the two angels grabbed hold of Lot's hand, his wife's hand,

Abraham Leaves His Hometown Ur

and each of his daughter's hands, and pulled them out of the house and led them away from the periphery of the city.

And when they were a distance from the city the angel told Lot and his family to escape in the mountains. They were not to look back at the cities. And they were not to stay in the plain-fields of the cities; if they did, they would be consumed.

But Lot and his wife did not want to go and stay in the mountains; they wanted to stay in the cities. Therefore Lot became adamant to the angel's advice. As stubborn as Lot was, in His mercy, the LORD of hosts allowed Lot and his family to go and stay in the city of Zoar. For Lot's sake the LORD chose to spare the city of Zoar. When the morning light struck the cities, the angels, Lot and his family entered in the small city of Zoar safely. And when the angels left them there,

> "24 The LORD [י ה ו ה] rained upon Sodom and Gomorrah brimstone and fire from the LORD [י ה ו ה] out of heaven." Genesis 19:24

As the brimstone and fire continued to fall from heaven upon Sodom and Gomorrah, the terrifying screams of men, women, and children rose from the inferno in plumes. Insubordinate to the angel's advice, Lot's wife decided to look at the devastation that was taking place upon Sodom, Gomorrah, fields, orchards, and animals in the surrounding area of the cities; and with them she perished by becoming a pillar of salt.

When Lot saw what happened to his wife, in fear he thought that the city of Zoar was also going to be destroyed with its residence. Therefore, Lot and his two daughters ran for the mountains as the angels had told them to go in the first place. And when they arrived on the mountain, they

Abraham Leaves His Hometown Ur

found a cave; and there in the cave they made their home.

While living in the mountain, Lot and the two girls did not see any people for a long time and therefore began to wonder if the human race was coming to an end? While the subject began to preoccupy the two girls, one day the older daughter of Lot said to her younger sister that they should procreate the human race. Eventually, the younger sister agreed; and the older daughter said to the younger, "32 Come, let us make our father drink wine, and we will lie with him, that we may preserve seed of our father. 33 And they made their father drink wine that night: and the firstborn went in, and lay with her father; and he perceived not when she lay down, nor when she arose. 34 And it came to pass on the on the morrow, that the firstborn said unto the younger, Behold, I lay yesternight with my father: let us make him drink wine this night also; and go thou [you] in, and lie with him, that we may preserve seed of out father. 35 And they made their father drink wine that night also; and the younger arose, and lay with him; and he perceived not when she lay down, nor when she arose. 36 Thus were both the daughters of Lot with child by their father. 37 And the firstborn bare a son, and called his name Moab: the same is the father of the Moabites unto this day. 38 And the younger, she also bare a son, and called his name ben-ammi: the same is the father of the children of Ammon unto this day" (Genesis 19:32-38).

In the above scenario, the two sisters revealed the evil influence of the Sodomites. These girls had grown to womanhood in the influence of an immoral society. Lot had been able to protect his two daughters physically from the Sodomites, but he was not able to protect them from their evil influence of sodomy. The principles of right and wrong were not predominant in Lot's family because of the evil satanic environment they were living in. These girls were more to be pitied than blamed for their actions. They

Abraham Leaves His Hometown Ur

thought that was the right thing to do.

Therefore Lot was responsible for the circumstances that led up to their actions; and he was also responsible for drinking the wine they set before him.

The enormous price of losing his family to the sensual pleasures of the cities, for few years, was the loss of his entire family. The vile and idolatrous Moabites and Ammonites were Lot's only posterity.

Meanwhile that morning when fire and brimstone fell upon the cities of Sodom and Gomorrah, Abraham got up and went to the spot where he stood pleading before the LORD of hosts to spare the cities, and see if the destruction did take place or not? When he arrived, "28 he looked toward Sodom and Gomorrah, and toward all the land of the plain, and beheld, and, lo, the smoke of the country went up as the smoke of a furnace" (Genesis 19:28). But for Abraham's sake, the LORD of hosts tried to save Lot and his family from the inferno; unfortunately, they refused the LORD'S salvation.

Wondering what had happened to Lot and his family, Abraham feared the worst because he remembered the words of the LORD—"If I find there ten righteous, I will not destroy it for ten's sake." But obviously, the cities were destroyed; was Lot and his family not righteous?

Seeing the horrible destruction of the cities, life forms, fields, and orchards, in the surrounding area for miles upon miles, Abraham assumed that Lot and his family had perished. With a remorse heart, Abraham began to review the circumstance he found himself in. The destruction of the cities and their kings in Siddim, changed the political landscape. There were new pagan powers coming at play in the region. The Hittites were composed to control the vicinity of the Amorites, which were Abraham's confederates. Not knowing of the political outcome in the

Abraham Leaves His Hometown Ur

region, just in case war broke out, in fear Abraham decided to leave the fields of Mamre and move, further south, near the borders of Egypt.

Collecting his household, Abraham started his journey southward to the Negeb, later called the "Wilderness of Zin," and camped near Kadesh-barnea and Shur. Kadesh is located about eighty miles southwest from Mamre. And Shur and its spring water are located not too far west from the city of Kadesh near the border of Egypt.

Abraham did not stay too long at Kadesh; he wanted a more stable place to pitch his tents in order to avoid moving too often. Therefore he contemplated moving northwest from where he was.

Hearing that the northern kings of the Negeb were reasonably calm, and the grazing land around Kadesh and Shur was dwindling, Abraham decided to move northwest into the Philistine's territory, in the fertile land, near the city of Gerar. Gerar is located about nine miles southwest of the modern day city of Gaza.

Learning that the king (Abimelech) of Gerar summoned all of the unmarried women in whom he felt affection for, Abraham told Sarah again to deny that he was her husband; when asked, she was to say that Abraham was her brother. And likewise when Abraham was asked about Sarah, he was to say that she was his sister.

And sure enough, when Abraham was confronted, he did say to the king of Gerar that Sarah was his sister. Learning that Sarah was Abraham's sister, the king wanted her to be his wife. At the age of about ninety, Sarah was still a beautiful woman; and the king took her.

Abraham failed to believe in the LORD'S protection, even after the LORD of hosts told him that He was going to be his "shield." Failure to believe in the LORD'S promises, Abraham gave his wife to the king in order to save his life

Abraham Leaves His Hometown Ur

that is quite a sacrifice on Sarah's part!

But the relationship between the king and Sarah was not to last. Seeing that Abraham's faith had failed to trust in the LORD of hosts, the LORD had to intervene. And He did. In a dream, the LORD of hosts said to the king, who was dying from a disease that Sarah was Abraham's wife.

But Abimelech, king of Gerar said to the LORD, "Abraham said that she was his sister; and even Sarah said to me that he was her brother. In the integrity of my heart and innocence I took her."

And the LORD said, "I know that you did this in the integrity of your heart, that is why I stopped you from sinning by not touching her. Now therefore restore the man his wife; for he is a prophet, and he will pray for you and restore you to health from your sickness."

The next day, Abraham was brought before the king; and he said to him, "Why have you deceived me?"

In response Abraham said to him, "Because the fear of God was not in this place, I thought that you would slay me and take my wife."

After learning that Sarah was truly Abraham's half-sister and the reason why they lied to him, "14 Abimelech took sheep, and oxen, and menservants, and womenservants, and gave them unto Abraham, and restored him Sarah his wife. 15 And Abimelech said, Behold, my land is before thee: dwell where it pleaseth thee. 16 And unto Sarah he said, Behold, I have given thy [your] brother a thousand pieces of silver: behold, he is to thee [you], a covering of the eyes, unto all that are with thee, and with all other; thus she was reproved.

> "17 So Abraham prayed unto God: and God healed Abimelech, and his wife, and his maidservants; and they bare children" (Genesis 20:14-17).

Abraham Leaves His Hometown Ur

Abraham accepted Abimelech's hospitality and camped beside the lush fields of wheat of Gerar, and finally settling near Beer-sheba amongst the three rivers, which provided abundant pastures and water for his livestock.

Going about their daily chores and unmindful of the promised time of visitation, as the LORD of hosts had promised Sarah and Abraham, Sarah became pregnant! Who would have believed that she would bear a child to Abraham in her old age? She was ninety years old! She was well passed the age of child bearing!

Nonetheless, when Abraham found out that Sarah was pregnant, he was elated. He finally realized, as promised, the LORD'S covenant was fulfilled. First Abraham was told that he was going to have a son; then he was told the name of his son, and finally, Abraham and Sarah were told when Sarah would give birth to a son.

Sarah did give birth to a son. And, as the LORD suggested, Abraham called his son Isaac. And when the name of Isaac is interpreted, it means, "he laughs." The LORD of hosts chose the name "Isaac," in order to remind Sarah and Abraham of the time they laughed when the LORD told them a year ago that Sarah shall give birth to a son.

After eight days, Abraham circumcised Isaac, as per the covenant he made with the LORD of hosts.

Three years later, Isaac was weaned. As per their custom, Abraham gave Isaac a party, revealing that now Isaac's infancy was over.

Although Sarah and Abraham were very happy that the LORD gave them a son, their joy was short lived because Hagar and Ishmael were not happy with Sarah's son. Hagar wanted Ishmael to be the heir of the covenant and not Isaac. As per the custom, the first child was to become the head of the household after Abraham died. But because the LORD

Abraham Leaves His Hometown Ur

of hosts chose Isaac to inherit the covenant, Ishmael lost the inheritance, just as Esau lost the inheritance to Jacob. The LORD picks and chooses with whom He makes a covenant with, and not man, as Abraham did twice or Hagar.

Hagar and Ishmael were creating a hateful discord in Abraham's household because the covenant that was promised to Ishmael by Sarah and Abraham, now, after fourteen years, it was given to Isaac. And, as Isaac grew, the contemptuous attitude, hate, and abuse turned into vicious verbal and physical persecution upon Isaac. It should be remembered, Ishmael was seventeen years older than Isaac at the time Isaac was weaned. And therefore, as Isaac grew, Ishmael continued to taunt Isaac as a reminder that the youngest did not have all of the rights and privileges of the birthright.

Finally, Sarah had enough of Hagar's abuse. Since Hagar was Sarah's slave and Ishmael was the son of a slave one would think that they would be more receptive to the wishes of their masters. Especially after the LORD of hosts told Hagar in the desert of Beer-sheba that she was to go back to Sarah and be subordinate to her. But, since Hagar would not discipline Ishmael for his actions against Isaac, and both of them were becoming more aggravating, Sarah went to Abraham and told him to send Hagar and Ishmael away from their home.

Contemplating Sarah's words, Abraham became very grievous. He wondered why Sarah was not able to contain her slave? And how could she ask of me to send my son Ishmael away from me? Sarah reminded Abraham that Ishmael was not going to be the heir of the covenant and since he and his mother are insubordinate and creating a lot of discord, they had to be expelled from their home.

Finally, Sarah said to Abraham, "Cast out this bondwoman and her son."

Abraham Leaves His Hometown Ur

> Here is the record: "29 But as then he [Ishmael] that
> was born after the flesh persecuted him [Isaac] that
> was born after the Spirit, even so it is now. 30
> Nevertheless what saith the scripture? Cast out the
> bondwoman and her son: for the son of the
> bondwoman shall not be heir with the son of the
> freewoman" (Galatians 4:29, 30).

Abraham contemplated Sarah's request; but because of
the uncertainties as to where Hagar and Ishmael would go,
rested very heavily on his heart, Abraham could not bring
himself to expel Hagar and Ishmael from his home.

Considering the turbulent times in Abraham's
household, and Abraham's concern about Ishmael, the
LORD of hosts intervened and said to Abraham, "12 Let it
not be grievous in thy [your] sight because of the lad, and
because of thy bondwoman; in all that Sarah hath said unto
thee, hearken unto her voice; for in Isaac shall thy [your]
seed be called" (Genesis 21:12).

Confronted with the fact that the LORD was going to
establish the covenant with Isaac and not with Ishmael, and
that the LORD was going to bless Ishmael and make a great
nation out of him, Abraham got up early the next morning
took some rations and water, and went to Hagar and her son
and told them, as much as it pained him, they were to leave
his home and go somewhere else to live.

Furious at the thought that they had to leave,
nonetheless Hagar and Ishmael, after they received the
rations and water, they were compelled to leave Beer-sheba.

Undecided as to where Hagar wanted to go, they found
themselves wandering in the desert of Beer-sheba. And, as
they were wondering where to go, they ran out of water.
Seeing that their situation was hopeless, and on the verge of
dying, Hagar told Ishmael to sit in the shadow of the bush

Abraham Leaves His Hometown Ur

until she came back for him. Unable to find water for herself and her son, Hagar went a distance of a "bow shot" about 300 to 400 feet away from Ishmael and sat there dying in order not to witness her son's death.

Knowing that she and her son were soon to die, she started to think how helpless she was and how vulnerable her son was; at this point, she started to moan and weep. And while she was crying in desperation, Ishmael prayed to the LORD and asked him to help him and his mother.

The LORD heard Ishmael's prayer and confronted Hagar and told her not to despair. God said to her that He was going to make out of Ishmael a great nation, and he will have twelve princes. "Go to your son now," said the LORD, "and take him by the hand to a well not too far from here and quench his thirst and your thirst so that you will be on your way."

After Hagar and Ishmael got their strength, encouraged by the LORD'S promise, they started their journey southward towards the Wilderness of Paran. The Wilderness of Paran is located from the Gulf of Aqabah, which is the northeastern part of the Red Sea and all the way westward to the Mediterranean Sea.

Ishmael lived with his mother in the wilderness and became an archer. Eventually his mother went to her homeland—Egypt, and got Ishmael a wife.

Meanwhile, Abimelech, the Philistinian king of Gerar, heard about Sarah giving a miraculous birth to a son in her old age, and remembered how Abraham had healed him and his family. In fear of the LORD, Abimelech wanted Abraham to commit himself by taking an oath in the name of Abraham's God; that way, Abimelech thought, Abraham would not retaliate by breaking the agreement. Therefore, Abimelech decided to make a treaty with Abraham because of few disputes that were not corrected by Abimelech.

Abraham Leaves His Hometown Ur

Eager to draw a treaty, after Isaac was weaned, Abimelech and Phichol the chief captain of the Philistines came to Abraham and greeted him by acknowledging that God was with Abraham in all that he did.

Knowing the power of the LORD and Abraham's relationship with the LORD, Abimelech said to Abraham, "23 Now therefore swear unto me here by God that thou [you] wilt not deal falsely with me, nor with my son, nor with my son's son: but according to the kindness that I have done unto thee, thou shalt do unto me, and to the land wherein thou [you] hast sojourned. 24 And Abraham said, I will swear: 25 And Abraham reproved Abimelech because of a well of water, which Abimelech's servants had violently taken away. 26 And Abimelech said, I wot not who hath done this thing: neither didst thou [you] tell me, neither yet heard I of it, but to day. 27 And Abraham took sheep and oxen, and gave them unto Abimelech; and both of them made a covenant. 28 And Abraham set seven ewe lambs of the flock by themselves. 29 And Abimelech said unto Abraham, What mean these seven ewe lambs which thou hast set by themselves? 30 And he said, For these seven ewe lambs shalt thou take of my hand, that they may be a witness unto me, that I have digged this well. 31 Wherefore he called that place Beer-sheba [seven]; because there they sware both of them. 32 Thus they made a covenant at Beer-sheba: then Abimelech rose up, and Phichol the chief captain of his host, and they returned into the land of the Philistines 33 And Abraham planted a grove in Beer-sheba, and called there on the name of the LORD, the everlasting God" (Genesis 21:23-33).

After making a covenant with Abimelech, Abraham spent seventeen years around Beer-sheba without any major problems arising from his neighbors. And his worries about Ishmael had calmed down because Ishmael had settled in the Wilderness of Paran, and the LORD'S blessing was upon

Abraham Leaves His Hometown Ur

him as the LORD promised Abraham and Hagar.

But this calm was soon to end because the LORD was going to test Abraham's faith to what appeared to be an extreme test of trust upon the LORD of hosts.

When Isaac reached the age of twenty, the LORD said to Abraham,

> "2 Take now thy [your] son, thine only son Isaac, whom thou [you] lovest, and get thee into the land of Moriah; and offer him there for a burnt offering upon one of the mountains which I will tell thee [you] of" (Genesis 22:2).

Hearing the command of the LORD, Abraham was devastated. He could not believe what he was hearing!

How could God ask him to offer Isaac on the altar of sacrifice? This cannot be the command from the LORD? Why, if I offer Isaac on the altar of sacrifice, how is the promise of the covenant going to be fulfilled? How was the land of Canaan going to be occupied by his descendants? What would the circumcised think about the covenant? And the list of questions went on and on in Abraham's mind. The anxiety because of the lack of answers created havoc in Abraham's mind. Abraham prayed and prayed but there was no answer from the LORD.

Wrapped up in his thoughts, the night finally passed away and the morning light was dimly breaking in the sky. Abraham got up; and, as per the LORD'S command, began to gather rations, water, and fire; and then, he went and called couple of his servant and told them to get ready to leave on a journey as soon as possible.

Abraham went and got Isaac and then told Sarah that he and Isaac were going for a short journey. Abraham did not disclose to Sarah the real nature of his departure with Isaac;

Abraham Leaves His Hometown Ur

but she still wondered where they were going?

After they all got ready, Abraham left with his son Isaac on the heartbreaking journey to Mount Moriah.

The spot where Abraham was led by the LORD of hosts to offer his son Isaac was on Mount Moriah, which is the same spot where King David bought the field from King Araunah the Jebusite and offered sacrifices unto the LORD of hosts in order to stop the plagues. And it is the very same spot where his son Solomon later built the Sanctuary for the LORD of hosts, better known today as the second hill of Jerusalem. (See 2 Chronicles 3:1.) And perhaps the second hill can better be visualized by thinking that the Sanctuary, during Solomon's time, was built a smidgen north of "The Lower City" of Jerusalem and west of Kidron Valley.

ABRAHAM'S 3 DAYS JOURNEY TO MT. MORIAH (JERUSALEM) FROM BEER-SHEBA (SEE GENESIS 22)

NOT TO SCALE
©By Philip Mitanidis

Abraham Leaves His Hometown Ur

Wrapped up in his anxiety, fear, and awe, Abraham left Beer-sheba through the Philistine territory called" Shephelah," which is located west of the mountain range of Judah and all the way to the Mediterranean Sea. Abraham more likely took this ancient caravan route to Jerusalem not only because he would be traveling in friendly territory, but also because this route was easier to travel on in comparison to the route to Jerusalem through the mountains of Judah.

The route to Jerusalem through the Philistine territory was about sixty miles long in comparison to the route through the rugged mountains of Judah, which is about forty-eight miles long.

Silently and slowly and still struggling, not whether he should obey the LORD'S command, but rather for the intervention of divine assurance that his senses and reasoning were not deceiving him. His silence and tardiness was quite apparent to his two young servants and to Isaac; they wondered what was wrong with him? Isaac and the servants full of energy had to periodically slow down in order for Abraham to catch up with them.

Realizing Abraham's actions, Isaac asked him if he was all right? Abraham responded by saying that he was just tired. Unfortunately, Abraham's demeanor did not get any livelier day after day because of lack of sleep, his two trusted servants and his son Isaac began to worry about him. But, on the third day, they had arrived to Mount Moriah. Abraham looked for the site where he was going to build the altar of sacrifice. He prayed for guidance from the LORD and the LORD guided Abraham to the spot where he was to offer Isaac.

Gathering his thoughts, Abraham came to the conclusion; since it was God's will that he sacrifice Isaac, it meant that Isaac would be raised from the dead in order to fulfill the promise. Therefore in confidence Abraham told

Abraham Leaves His Hometown Ur

his two servants to stay where they were with the donkey while they went a short distance to worship; and then Abraham said, "We will return."

Abraham took the wood and gave it to Isaac to carry. Likewise, Abraham took the fire from his servant and both of them left the servants with the animal behind.

In silence and in prayer, Abraham led the way to the spot where Isaac was to be offered. But when they reached the site, and Abraham asked Isaac to help him gather whole stones to build an altar, Isaac noticed the obvious; they had the altar, the wood, and the fire, but where is the sacrifice? Therefore Isaac said, "My father, where is the lamb?"

Hearing the words "My father" coming from Isaac's lips in the moment of trying times cut deep in Abraham's heart. In response, Abraham said to Isaac, "The LORD will provide."

Confident that the LORD had a plan for Isaac; when all was complete, apart from the placing of the sacrifice upon the altar, Abraham finally told Isaac what the LORD had said to him.

Hearing the words of his father, it is hard to express Isaac's emotional perplexity of his father's intent to kill him. Isaac was twenty years old, he could have very easily declined and even overtake his father in a struggle; but because of his faith in the LORD, Isaac not only understood the command of the LORD, but also wanted to do the will of the LORD of hosts. Therefore Isaac submitted to his father. They said their good byes; and then, Abraham tied Isaac—as if it was necessary—and placed him on the altar of sacrifice.

Offering a sacrificial lamb on the altar was oh, so easy; but now, Abraham was staring down upon his son who did not scurry, offered no complaint, scream for mercy, or for help; he just laid there waiting for the last act to take place.

Finally Abraham made his decision. He picked up the

Abraham Leaves His Hometown Ur

knife to slay his son; and as he made ready to thrust his knife into Isaac's body, the angel of the LORD, from heaven, said to Abraham,

> "12 Lay not thine [your] hand upon the lad, neither do thou [you] any thing unto him: for now I know that thou [you] fearest God, seeing thou [you] hast not withheld thy [your] son, thine only son from Me" (Genesis 22:12).

In relief and with thankful heart, Abraham untied Isaac and helped him up from the altar. Overjoyed for sparing Isaac's life and sparing him from the ordeal of slaying his son, Abraham went and brought a ram that was entangled by the horns in a near by thicket and offered it as a thank offering to the LORD of hosts.

ISAAC AND ABRAHAM ON MT. MORIAH (JERUSALEM)

©by: PHILIP MITANIDIS

"The LORD will provide" indeed. Abraham's heart and Isaac's heart were full of thanks giving to the LORD for their faith and steadfastness in the LORD of hosts. "14 And Abraham called the name of that place Jehovah-jireh: as it is

Abraham Leaves His Hometown Ur

said to this day, In the mount of the LORD it shall be seen."
Genesis 22:14

And just before Abraham and Isaac left the area, the
LORD called upon Abraham the second time and said to
him,

> "16 By Myself have I sworn, saith the LORD." The
> reason the LORD of hosts sworn by Himself is due to
> the fact that there is no one greater than Himself to
> swear by. And the LORD of hosts added, "for because
> thou [you] hast done this thing, and hast not withheld
> thy [your] son, thine [your] only son: 17 That in blessing
> I will bless thee [you], and in multiplying I will multiply
> thy [your] seed as the stars of the heaven, and as the sand
> which is upon the sea shore; and thy [your] seed shall
> possess the gate of his enemies; 18 And in thy [your] seed
> shall all the nations of the earth be blessed; because thou
> [you] hast [have] obeyed My voice" (Genesis 22:16-18).

As you have read, in the above verses, the LORD of
hosts reassures Abraham that "in blessing I will bless thee
[you], and in multiplying I will multiply thy [your] seed as the
stars of the heaven, and as the sand which is upon the sea
shore."

And so it was, Abraham had Isaac; Isaac had Jacob, and
Jacob had twelve sons. And when the twelve sons of Jacob
grew and had their own families, they were better known as
the twelve tribes of Israel (Jacob). These tribes inherited the
Promised Land, which spanned from the city of Dan that is
located north of the Sea of Galilee to Beer-sheba, which is
south of the Salt Sea in the Negeb. There, the children of
Israel continued to prosper and multiply, as the LORD of
hosts had promised Abraham.

But the blessing was not to stop with the increase of the

Abraham Leaves His Hometown Ur

children of Israel; the LORD of hosts added that through
Abraham's seed, "all the nations of the earth be blessed."

Therefore the seed that was to give the blessing to all
nations of the world had to come through one of the sons of
Israel (Jacob). And that son, according Jacob and the pen of
Moses is Jacob's son Judah. Just before Jacob died in Zoan,
he was foretelling the future of his sons; and when he came
to his son Judah, Jacob said to him,

> "10 The sceptre shall not depart from Judah, nor a
> lawgiver from between his feet, until Shiloh come;
> and unto Him shall the gathering of the people be"
> (Genesis 49:10).

So, who is "Shiloh" that was to come and gather His
people to Himself?

According 1 Samuel 1:17, 14, and 4:4, "Shiloh" is the
LORD God of Israel. And according to the Torah and the
rest of the prophets, "Shiloh" is also identified as the God
of Israel, more on this point later.

Nonetheless, I would like to leave one more point with
you for your consideration, and that is, the offering of Isaac
on the altar.

It should be noted that the offering of Isaac on the altar
was personal and a secluded event; an event that was acted
amongst the LORD of hosts, Abraham, and Isaac. It had
nothing to do with the pagan practices of offering their
children openly to their gods for appeasement.

This private event was not only to strengthen Abraham
and Isaac in their relationship with the LORD of hosts, but
also to reveal to Abraham and Isaac that the LORD they
were worshiping was the seed that the nations of the world
would be blessed by. Therefore, by assuring them that
salvation would be secured in the future, for the faithful, by

Abraham Leaves His Hometown Ur

the death of their LORD God on Calvary's cross, Abraham was "glad" to see Christ's day, in fulfillment of the promise the LORD of hosts had made to him.

Their experience on Mount Moriah was paramount. It drew them closer to each other, and more importantly, to the LORD of hosts; and it prepared Isaac to not only receive the covenant, but to also, continue to trust in the LORD of hosts and in the way He would lead him.

With thankful hearts, reverently, Isaac and Abraham left their secluded spot.

Coming around the corner, the two young servants saw a deferent Isaac and a deferent Abraham in comparison to the demeanor they departed with. Both Abraham and Isaac were beaming with joy and full of energy. Their servants wondered what happened to them?

They refreshed themselves, gathered their belongings, and returned to Beer-sheba.

How would Abraham or Isaac begin to explain to Sarah of their experience with the LORD of hosts, and what He had promised them and their progeny? And what will Sarah's reaction be after she hears what Abraham was going to do and what happened on Mount Moriah?

For over thirty years Abraham dwelt south from Hebron, in the Negeb; but most of the time his tents were pitched in the area of Beer-sheba. From there, he moved northwest to a familiar ground in Kirjath-arba, or the city of Arba if you like. It was found by one of the giant Anakims. Afterward, Arba became better known by the name of Hebron.

Previously, when Sodom and Gomorrah were destroyed, Abraham dwelt in Mamre. At that time, the Amorites were in control of the region; now it appeared that the Hittites were in control.

Nonetheless, shortly after Abraham moved to Kirjath-

Abraham Leaves His Hometown Ur

arba, Sarah died at the age of one hundred and twenty-seven.

There, Abraham and Isaac mourned their loss, and prepared for her burial. But Abraham did not want to bury her just anywhere. Since Canaan was promised to him and to his seed after him, Abraham decided to have a fixed place to bury his progeny. Therefore he chose a place, which was located at the end of a field called Machpelah.

Although Abraham wanted to bury his wife there, he did not want to bury her there without buying the property first. Therefore he went to talk with the residents of the region, who identified themselves by the name of Hittites. They derived their name from the ruler of the area whose name was Heth. Abraham spoke to the sons of Ephron, who owned the field with a cave at the end of it, called Machpelah, by cordially saying to them that he was a sojourner and made no claim to their land. Instead Abraham made it clear that he wanted to buy Machpelah. But because the Hittites recognized Abraham as a mighty prince, they offered him access to their burial ground. In fact they even said to Abraham bury your dead at the choice sepulchers. But because Abraham preferred to secure the property, he cordially requested that they speak to Ephron the son of Zohar and see if he would permit him to buy the field.

Ephron responded to Abraham and said that he would gladly give Abraham the cave and the field; but Abraham insisted that he pay for it. Knowing that Abraham preferred to bury his wife as soon as possible on his own property, it appears that Ephron took advantage of Abraham and overcharged him for the property. From the Babylonian records, a fertile field sold for forty shekels where as an average field sold for four shekels. To avoid any hard feelings or animosity towards Abraham, Abraham did not reject Ephron's asking price; he paid the four hundred shekels Ephron was asking for the property.

Abraham Leaves His Hometown Ur

Once the money was exchanged, Abraham received the deed to the field and to the cave, which included whatever was growing on the land, minerals, and water.

Finally, Abraham buried his wife in the cave of the field of Machpelah, which was located in Mamre.

Isaac was thirty-seven years old when his mother died. His love for his mother was so great that he grieved for her continuously. In fact, three years after his mother death, Isaac continued to be depressed. Seeing that Isaac was sad, Abraham thought I t best they move from the area. They packed their belongings and headed south from Mamre and ended in the Negeb, near the well of Lahai-roi. There they pitched their tents; but changing locations did not cure Isaac from his sadness. He was still miserable three years after his mother death.

Finally, Abraham decided to find him a wife. Not only because Isaac was sad, but because Abraham was getting quite old; he was about one hundred and forty years old at this point of time.

Therefore, in a sense of urgency, Abraham approached Eliezer, his trusted old friend, and asked him to go on a mission for him. But before Eliezer accepted the mission, he had to swear to Abraham that he would do exactly as he was asked, by placing his hand under Abraham's thigh and take a solemn oath.

Since Abraham was aware of the Canaanites entrenched idolatrous worship, growing licentiousness, and the pending of their imminent doom, Abraham did not want to make the same mistake as he did with Hagar who was of a heathen background.

Therefore Abraham made Eliezer to take an oath that he would not bring a Canaanite woman to be a wife for Isaac. Instead, Eliezer was instructed to go to Haran and bring someone from his brother's household because to some

Abraham Leaves His Hometown Ur

degree, at least, some of his relatives still worshipped the God of Abraham, even though many in the family still bowed down to their idols.

Then Eliezer said to Abraham, "What if no woman wanted to become the wife of Isaac?"

"If that is the case," Abraham said, "don't bring him one." But Abraham was confident that the LORD would supply a wife of His choice for Isaac in order to fulfill the covenant in Isaac. Therefore Abraham said to Eliezer, "He shall sent His angel before you; and help you to take a wife for Isaac."

Comforted by those words, Eliezer made the oath, took ten camels; and prepared the caravan for his 1,100 miles journey. He started his expedition by going northward from Lahai-roi and traveling on the west side of the River Jordan.

Finally, Eliezer arrived with his caravan at a well near the city of Nahor, which is a smidgen west of the city of Haran. There he stopped to refresh himself, the servants, and the camels. But before he did that, he wanted to make certain that he did not pick the woman for Isaac without the LORD'S help. Eliezer remembered Abraham's words that the angel of the LORD would help him choose a wife for Isaac; therefore he knelt down and asked for a sign.

He said; "12 O LORD God of my master Abraham, I pray thee [You], send me good speed this day, and shew kindness unto my master Abraham. 13 Behold, I stand here by the well of water; and the daughters of the men of the city come out to draw water: 14 And let it come to pass, that the damsel to whom I shall say, Let down thy [your] pitcher, I pray thee [you], that I may drink; and she shall say, Drink, and I will give thy [your] camels drink also: let the same be she that thou [You] hast appointed for thy [Your] servant Isaac; and thereby shall I know that thou [Your] hast shewed kindness unto my master.

Abraham Leaves His Hometown Ur

"15 And it came to pass, before he had done speaking, that, behold, Rebekah came out, who was born to Bethuel, son Milcah, the wife of Nahor, Abraham's brother, with her pitcher upon her shoulder. 16 And the damsel was very fair to look upon, a virgin, neither had any man known her: and she went down to the well, and filled her pitcher, and came up. 17 And the servant [Eliezer] ran to meet her, and said, Let me, I pray thee [you], drink a little water of thy [your] pitcher. 18 And she said, Drink, my lord; and she hasted, and let down her pitcher upon her hand, and gave him drink. 19 And when she had done giving him drink, she said, I will draw water for thy [your] camels also, until they have done drinking" (Genesis 24:12-19).

This was music to Eliezer's ears!

Rebekah, who had been asked only for a drink of water for a weary traveler, immediately manifested her kindly disposition. Her offer to draw water for the camels was voluntary and not a requirement of custom. It demonstrated a genuine desire to help those who were in need of assistance. It should not be forgotten that Rebekah's kindness was utilized in the divine intervention of God as evidence to Eliezer that He had chosen her to be Isaac's wife.

Eliezer was so fascinated by Rebekah's unaffected willingness to be of help that he allowed her to draw water for his ten camels without as much as offering assistance. Eliezer was startled momentarily by the precision and dispatch with which the LORD of hosts answered his prayer.

While Rebekah was providing water for the camels, Eliezer, went and got couple of presents to reward her for her help. Though suspecting that she was to become Isaac's wife, Eliezer did not know her name; in fact, he did not know if Rebekah or her family was related to Abraham.

Abraham Leaves His Hometown Ur

After Rebekah finished providing water for the ten camels, Eliezer gave her a golden earring and two golden bracelets by putting the earring on her face and the bracelets on her hands. And asked her, "Whose daughter are you?" And almost instantly he asked her again, "Is there enough room in your house for us to lodge in?"

Rebekah replied, "We have both straw and provender enough, and room to lodge in."

Hearing that Rebekah was from the family of Abraham's brother and her words of hospitality, Eliezer bowed down his head and gave thanks to the LORD God of Abraham for answering his prayer.

Eliezer said; "27 Blessed be the LORD God of my master Abraham, who hath not left destitute my master of his mercy and his truth: I being in the way, the LORD led me to the house of my master's brethren" (Genesis 24:27).

Rebekah led Eliezer and his caravan to her father's house, and went in the house to tell the family that she brought guests to their home, and told them what happened and how Eliezer gave her the expensive bracelets and ring. When her brother Laban (meaning the blond one) saw the expensive gifts, he ran out to greet the guests and find out who they were and what they were doing in these parts of the city?

But first, Laban greeted them by saying, "Come in, you blessed of the LORD; why are you standing outside? I have prepared the house, and room for the camels."

Eliezer came into the house, saw the prepared food, but he was not interested in the food; he was anxious to accomplish his errand first before he partook of the festivities. Therefore, feeling confident that Rebekah was the one that he should take back to his master, he said that he wanted to talk to them about Rebekah first before he took the time to eat.

Abraham Leaves His Hometown Ur

After recounting the events of Abraham's prosperity in Canaan, the miraculous birth of Isaac, of his own oath to Abraham to seek a wife for Isaac among his relatives, the way the LORD of hosts gave him a sign, and the way the LORD had led him to Rebekah's home, Eliezer, with solemn earnestness, pressed for an immediate decision from Laban and Bethuel.

Hearing Eliezer's words, Laban and Bethuel knew how the LORD called Abraham to leave his father's home and go to Canaan. Therefore they recognized and accepted the sign Eliezer asked for and how Rebekah fulfilled it. Therefore, they reasoned, they could not say, "Yes or No" against the will of the LORD. The decision of the LORD was not a subject for debate; Eliezer was to take Rebekah and bring her to Isaac.

Therefore they said to Eliezer; "51 Behold, Rebekah is before thee [you], take her, and go, and let her be thy [your] master's son's wife, as the LORD hath spoken.

"52 And it came to pass, that, when Abraham's servant heard their words, he worshipped the LORD, bowing himself to the earth. 53 And the servant [Eliezer] brought forth jewels of silver, and jewels of gold, and raiment, and gave them to Rebekah: he gave also to her brother and to her mother precious things. 54 And they did eat and drink, he and the men that were with him, and tarried all night; and they rose up in the morning, and he [Eliezer] said, Send me away unto my master. 55 And her brother and her mother said, Let the damsel abide with us a few days, at the least ten; after that she shall go. 56 And he [Eliezer] said unto them, Hinder me not, seeing the LORD hath prospered my way; send me away that I may go to my master. 57 And they said, We will call the damsel, and enquire at her mouth. 58 And they called Rebekah, and said unto her, Wilt thou go with this man? And she said, I will go. 59 And they sent away

Abraham Leaves His Hometown Ur

Rebekah their sister, and her nurse, and Abraham's servant, and his men. 60 And they blessed Rebekah, and said unto her, Thou [you] art our sister, be thou the mother of thousands of million, and let thy [your] seed possess the gate of those which hate them. 61 And Rebekah arose, and her damsels, and they rode upon the camels, and followed the man [Eliezer]: and the servant took Rebekah, and went his way" (Genesis 24:51-61).

Happy with the accomplishment of his errand, Eliezer and the caravan, headed with the precious cargo for home in Lahai-roi, which is in the Negeb.

As the caravan approached Isaac's home, Isaac came out of his tent and started to walk in the vicinity of the well. As he was meditating, he noticed the caravan coming towards his camp. He stopped meditating and started to go towards the caravan to greet it. And as the caravan got closer, Rebekah called upon Eliezer and asked him who was the man that was approaching them?

Eliezer told Rebekah that it was Isaac his master. Then Rebekah got down from the camel, covered her face with a vail, and started to walk with Eliezer towards Isaac.

Eliezer conferred with Isaac for a short while telling him about the trip and how Rebekah was chosen by the LORD of hosts for him and how she consented to become his wife.

Hearing how the LORD of hosts chose Rebekah to be his wife, Isaac thanked Eliezer for bringing her to him; and then, Eliezer went to meet with Abraham to tell him that he accomplished the errand with the LORD'S help. Meanwhile, Isaac took Rebekah into his tent, signifying that he had accepted Rebekah to be his wife. Isaac was forty years old when he accepted Rebekah as his wife.

After Isaac's and Rebekah's marriage union, Abraham and his household celebrated the wedding festivities.

Abraham was one hundred and thirty-seven years old

Abraham Leaves His Hometown Ur

when Sarah died. And he was one hundred and forty years old when Isaac got married.

Shortly after Isaac and Rebekah settled in their marriage, Abraham became lonely; therefore he took one of his concubines for a wife, whose name was "Keturah," meaning "incense." And to Abraham's blessings, she bare him six children whose names are: Zimran, and Jokshan, and Medan, and Midian, and Ishbak, and Shuah.

Abraham was very happy with Keturah and with his children. But he was even happier when his children got married and had their own children.

"3 Jokshan begat Sheba, and Dedan. And the sons of Dedan were Asshurim, and Letushim, and Leummim 4 And the sons of Midian; Ephah, and Epher, and Hanoch, and Abidah, and Eldaah. All these were the children of Keturah.

"5 And Abraham gave all that he had unto Isaac, 6 But unto the sons of the concubines, which Abraham had, Abraham gave gifts, and sent them away from Isaac his son, while he yet lived, eastward, unto the east country" (Genesis 25:3-6).

As you have read, Abraham separated from his son Isaac, by moving his camp eastward from Isaac. And there, Abraham dwelt for approximately thirty-five years during his twilight years. Abraham lived for one hundred and seventy-five years and died.

Hearing of his death, Ishmael came to Isaac and they both buried their father at Mamre in the cave of Machpelah where his wife lay sleeping (dead).

Isaac and Jacob

"11 And it came to pass after the death of Abraham, that God blessed his son Isaac; and Isaac dwelt by the well Lahai-roi." "19 And these are the generations of Isaac, Abraham's son: Abraham begat Isaac: 20 And Isaac was forty years old when he took Rebekah to wife, the daughter of Bethuel the Syrian of Padan-aram, the sister to Laban the Syrian. 21 And Isaac intreated the LORD for his wife, because she was barren: and the LORD was intreated of him, and Rebekah his wife conceived. 22 And the children struggled together within her; and she said, If it be so, why am I thus? And she went to enquire of the LORD. 23 And the LORD said unto her, Two nations are in thy [your] womb, and two manner of people shall be separated from thy [your] bowels; and the one people shall be stronger than the other people; and the elder shall serve the younger. 24 And when her days to be delivered were fulfilled, behold, there were twins in her womb. 25 And the first came out red, all over like an hairy garment; and they called his name Esau. 26 And after that came his brother out, and his hand took hold on Esau's heel; and his name was called Jacob: and Isaac was threescore years old when she bare them. 27 And the boys grew: and Esau was a cunning hunter, a man of the field; and Jacob was a plain man, dwelling in tents. 28 And Isaac loved Esau, because he did eat of his venison but Rebekah loved Jacob. 29 And Jacob sod pottage; and Esau came from the field, and he was faint: 30 And Esau said to Jacob, Feed me, I pray thee [you], with that same red pottage; for I am faint: therefore was his name called Edom. 31 And Jacob said, Sell me this day thy [your] birthright, 32 And Esau said, Behold, I am at the point to die: and what profit shall this birthright do to me? 33 And Jacob said, Swear to me this day; and he swear unto him: and he sold his birthright unto Jacob. 34 Then Jacob gave Esau bread and pottage of lentils; and he did eat and drink, and rose up, and went his way: thus Esau despised his birthright" (Genesis 25:11, 19-34).

Isaac and Jacob

When Jacob was seventy-five years old, he ran away from home because his twin brother threatened to kill him. Therefore Jacob headed into his mother's relatives in Padan-aram. And when he got there he fell in love with Rachel and offered her father seven years of labor, as a dowry, so that he could marry her. Laban, Rachel's father, consented to the offer and Jacob worked for seven years and then asked

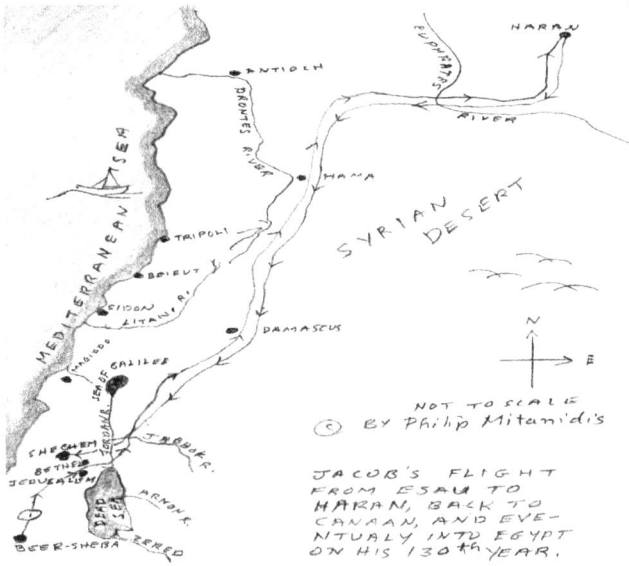

JACOB'S FLIGHT FROM ESAU TO HARAN, BACK TO CANAAN, AND EVENTUALLY INTO EGYPT ON HIS 130th YEAR.

Laban if Rachel could become his wife? Laban agreed and arranged for the wedding ceremony. And when Jacob removed the veil from her face, to his surprise, it was not Rachel; it was Leah her older sister!

Furious with Laban's deception, Jacob stormed in the presence of Laban and demanded an explanation. His father-in-law said to him, here we don't marry the youngest first; we marry the oldest first then the younger. But if you want Rachel the youngest, then you have to work for another seven years before you can have her. Annoyed with Laban's

Isaac and Jacob

deceptive games, Jacob was not going to fall for another trick. He said to Laban give me Rachel now, or else the deal is off.

Laban realizing that Jacob had brought him prosperity and wealth, he though about it for a bit and said to him, all right you can have her now, but only if you promise me that you will work another seven years for me.

Jacob did not want to wait for another seven years for Rachel. He wanted Rachel so bad that he consented to work for another seven years. And when Jacob consented, Laban gave Rachel to him after a week was past. Although Jacob loved Rachel, more than Leah, Leah made Jacob happy because she conceived him a son; and she called him "Reuben." And Leah conceived again a son, and called him "Simeon." And again, Leah gave birth to another son, and she called Him "Levi." And Leah blessed Jacob with another son, and she called Him "Judah."

And when Rachel realized that she could not have any children, she demanded from Jacob to give her children. So Rachel brought her maid, whose name was Bilhah, and asked that she become his wife, and when Jacob accepted her, Rachel said to Jacob "Go into her so that I may have children by her." "5 And Bilhah conceived, and bare Jacob a son. 6 And Rachel said, God hath judged me, and hath also heard my voice, and hath given me a son: therefore called she his name Dan. 7 And Bilhah Rachel's maid conceived again, and bare Jacob a second son. 8 And Rachel said, With great wrestlings have I wrestled with my sister, and I have prevailed: and she called his name Naphtali.

"9 When Leah saw that she had left bearing, she took Zilpah her maid, and gave her Jacob to wife. 10 And Zilpah Leah's maid bare Jacob a son. 11 And Leah said, A troop cometh: and she called his name Gad. 12 And Zilpah Leah's maid bare Jacob a second son. 13 And Leah said, Happy am

Isaac and Jacob

I, for the daughters will call me blessed: and she called his name Asher." "16 And Jacob came out of the field in the evening, and Leah went out to meet him, and said, Thou [you] must come in unto me; for surely I have hired thee with my son's mandrakes. And he lay with her that night. 17 And God hearkened unto Leah, and she conceived, and bare Jacob the fifth son, 18 And Leah said, God hath given me my hire, because I have given my maiden to my husband: and she called his name Issachar. 19 And Leah conceive again, and bare Jacob the sixth son. 20 And Leah said, God hath endued me with a good dowry; now will my husband dwell with me, because I have born him six sons: and she called his name Zebulun. 21 And afterwards she bare a daughter, and called her name Dinah.

"22 And God remembered Rachel, and God hearkened to her, and opened her womb. 23 And she conceived, and bare a son; and said, God hath taken away my reproach: 24 And she called his name Joseph; and said, The LORD shall add to me another son. 25 And it came to pass, Rachel had born Joseph, that Jacob said unto Laban, Send me away, that I may go unto mine own place, and to my country." Genesis 30:5-13, 16-25

And when Laban heard those words, Laban was devastated. Jacob was making him wealthy, how could he let him go. Laban made all sorts of excuses to keep Jacob there, but none of the excuses worked. Jacob wanted to take his belongings and his wives and leave.

Seeing that Jacob was serious, Laban began to offer Jacob all manner of enticing proposals. And finally said to Jacob, "31 What shall I give thee [you]? And Jacob said, Thou [you] shalt not give me any thing: if thou wilt do this thing for me [let him go], I well again feed and keep thy [your] flock."

Hearing that Jacob was willing to stay a little bit longer,

Isaac and Jacob

Laban agreed to Jacob's proposal and said to him, "34 Behold, I would it might be according to thy [your] word." Gene 30:31, 34

After awhile the LORD of hosts got involved with the affairs of Laban and Jacob; the LORD blessed Jacob more so than Laban. Seeing that Jacob's livestock was healthy and growing and Laban's livestock was feeble, the sons of Laban began to make all manner of accusations against Jacob. Notably, Laban's attitude changed towards Jacob. And when Jacob saw that Laban and his household were not as receptive to him as before, Jacob went to his wives and told them that their father was not being fair to him. Jacob also told them that the LORD had appeared in a dream last night and told him that he should return to his father's house in Canaan.

"14 Rachel and Leah answered and said unto him, Is there yet any portion or inheritance for us in our father's house? 15 Are we not counted of him strangers? for he hath sold us, and hath quite devoured also our money. 16 For all the riches which God hath taken from our father, that is our's, and our children's: now then, whatsoever God hath said unto thee do" (Genesis 31:14-16).

After his wives agreed that he should return to his homeland, Jacob discreetly began to prepare for the move. And when he saw that Laban was going to be gone for few days, Jacob told his servants to prepare a caravan by placing certain groups at the front of the caravan and Leah and Rachel at the back. The servants were to gather everyone's belongings, his wives, eleven sons, Dinah his daughter, the livestock, and when they were ready, finally, after twenty years, Jacob went at the front of the caravan and started the voyage westward towards the land of Canaan.

After three days, when Laban got home and saw that his livestock was astray and Jacob with his belongings gone, he

Isaac and Jacob

went throughout his house looking if anything was stolen, got his servants mounted and went after Jacob.

After seven days journey southwest to Canaan, Laban was given a message in a dream from the LORD, telling him that he was not to harm Jacob and his caravan. Fearful of the message, when Laban overtook Jacob's caravan on Mount Gilead, he down played his approach towards Jacob and his caravan.

Laban said to Jacob, "26 What hast thou [you] done, that thou hast stolen away unawares to me, and carried away my daughters, as captives taken with the sword? 27 Wherefore didst thou flee away secretly, and steal away from me; and didst not tell me, that I might have sent thee [you] away with mirth, and with songs, with tabret, and with harp? 28 And hast not suffered me to kiss my sons and my daughters? thou hast now done foolishly in so doing. 29 It is in the power of my hand to do you hurt: but the God of your father spake unto me yesternight, saying, Take thou heed that thou speak not to Jacob either good or bad. 30 And now, though thou [you] wouldest needs be gone, because thou sore longedst after thy [your] father's house, yet wherefore hast thou stolen my gods?

"31 And Jacob answered and said to Laban, Because I was afraid: for I said, Peradventure thou [you] wouldest take by force thy [your] daughters from me. 32 With whomsoever thou [you] findest thy [your] gods, let him not live: before our brethren discern thou what is thine [yours] with me, and take it to thee [you], For Jacob knew not that Rachel had stolen them." Genesis 31:26-32

Laban, nonetheless, did not believe Jacob, so he went into their tents and looked everywhere for stolen goods, but he found none because apparently, the only things that Rachel had stolen were Laban's precious gods.

It makes a person wonder, how can Laban still cling to

Isaac and Jacob

his man made gods after he was confronted by the God of
the universe in the previous night? You would think, having
being confronted so vividly by the God of Abraham that
Laban would give up his false gods. But, as you have
observed, Laban was persistent. He knew that his gods were
missing; so who had them?

Well, the only place Laban did not look was under
Rachel's seat where she was sitting on top of the camel. And
the reason her father did not look in the camel's load was do
to the fact that their custom was that a woman must not be
disturbed when she was sitting on top of an animal.
Therefore, Laban resigned from his search and went to
console with Jacob.

After few heated words between Jacob and Laban, they
settled down and had a cordial stay overnight. And the
following day, they made a covenant between them by
putting a heap of rocks in a configuration, as witness, and
swearing by the God of their fathers that they would not
harm each other.

After Jacob and Laban made the covenant before all the
witnesses, Jacob made a feast. And after everyone had drank
and eaten, Laban kissed his daughters and sons and blessed
them, then he departed.

Jacob after few trying events, reached Canaan in a place
called Shechem and stayed there because the land was fertile
and the natives appeared to be friendly.

But, all was not well at Shechem, Dinah was raped by
Shechem, Hamor's son; and in retaliation Simon and Levi,
the Brothers of Dinah killed all of the males in their city, "26
And they slew Hamor and Shechem his son with the edge of
the sword, and took Dinah out of Shechem's house, and
went out. 27 The sons of Jacob came upon the slain, and
spoiled the city, because they had defiled their sister. 28 They
took their sheep, and their oxen, and their asses, and that

Isaac and Jacob

which was in the city, and that which was in the field, 29 And all their wealth, and all their little ones, and their wives took they captive, and spoiled even all that was in the house.

"30 And Jacob said to Simeon and Levi, Ye [all of you] have troubled me to make me to stink among the inhabitants of the land, among the Canaanites and the Perizzites: and I being few in number, they shall gather themselves together against me, and slay me; and I shall be destroyed, I and my house." Genesis 34:26-30

But the LORD of hosts had his eye over Jacob, he said to him to gather his belongings and move to Bethel. And when Jacob arrived there, he gathered everyone's idols and that included the idols from his pregnant wife Rachel and took them near one of the oak trees and buried them all there. Then Jacob built an altar, which he named "El-bethel" and offered sin offerings and thank offerings to the LORD of hosts on the altar of sacrifice. And the LORD of hosts appeared to Jacob again, and said to him "10 thy [your] name shall not be called any more Jacob, but Israel shall be thy [your] name: and He called his name Israel. 11 And God said unto him, I am God Almighty be fruitful and multiply; a nation and a company of nations shall be of thee, and kings shall come out of thy loins; 12 And the land which I gave Abraham and Isaac, to thee I will give it, and to thy

Isaac and Jacob

seed after thee will I give the land. 13 And God went up from him in the place where He talked with him." Genesis 35:10-13

After, Jacob (Israel) moved from Bethel and went on his way to his father's house at Mamre. But, as they were traveling southward and arrived not too far from Ephrath (Bethlehem), Rachel went into a complicated labor. The midwife assured her that she was going to have the baby, therefore he was not to worry. Although Rachel gave birth to a son it left her feeble and dying. In her last dying breath, Rachel named her baby Benoni. But later, Israel (Jacob) changed the baby's name to Benjamin.

Finally, Israel's caravan reached Isaac's home at Mamre, and there Israel (Jacob) united with his father.

Isaac lived for one hundred and eighty years and fell asleep —died. His sons Esau and Israel buried their father.

After Isaac's death Esau continued to live in mount Seir with his three wives. And Jacob lived in the plains of Canaan.

Meanwhile, as you probably know only too well the story of Joseph, therefore I will not dwell on the forthcoming events in large detail. Joseph was hated by his brothers because he told them that they would bow down before him. Therefore they tried to get rid of him. And they did. Joseph landed in Egypt and was sold to Potiphar and became his servant. Eventually, Joseph at the age of thirty became second to Pharaoh because Joseph foretold of the famine that was to come for seven years.

And when the famine came it also affected the land of Canaan. There Jacob sent his sons to Egypt to buy food; and when they came before Joseph to buy the corn, they did not recognize him. They bowed down before him and requested to buy food. Joseph did give them food under the condition they prove that they were not spies by bringing Benjamin to him. In the mean time, he was going to hold one of their

Isaac and Jacob

brother's ransom until they brought Benjamin to him.

When the food ran out from Jacob's home, he suggested to his sons to go to Egypt and buy some more food. But there was one huge snag; and that was the governor of Egypt wanted to see Benjamin to prove that they were not lying to him.

Finally, out of necessity, Jacob was forced to send Benjamin with his brothers to Egypt. And when they appeared before the governor, they bowed down before him and requested to buy corn. Instead he had the authorities take them to his house. And there Joseph the second most powerful person in Egypt revealed himself to them and told them to go home and bring his father and his whole household to Egypt because the famine was to continue for another five years.

They went home with the corn and told their father what happened. But he was dumbfounded in what his sons were saying to him about Joseph. How can Joseph be alive; he wondered. Nevertheless, he prayed about the move and the God of his fathers told him to go to Egypt with all of his possessions.

Jacob was one hundred and thirty years old when he arrived in Goshen. There he met his son Joseph and seventeen years later, just before he took his last breath, he gathered his sons around him and prophesied what would happen to each of his sons. And after he finished revealing to them what would happen, he curled up in his bed and died.

There in Goshen, the children of Israel (Jacob) continued to multiply and prosper. But after Joseph died at the age of one hundred and ten a new dynasty came to power and feared the multitude of the children of Israel; so they enslaved them and killed their male babies to prevent their increase. And Pharaoh put taskmasters over them to make sure they did not join forces with another foreign power and rebel against Egypt. And since the children of Israel could not bring another power to liberate them from the hand of Pharaoh, they remained miserably enslaved in Egypt.

Thus during the covenant that was made between Abraham and God in Genesis chapter fifteen, the LORD did tell him that his seed would be enslaved. But, after telling him that, God also told him that they would be liberated at the end of the forth generation and brought to Canaan to inherit the land.

The Children of Israel

If you recall, in Genesis chapter fifteen Abraham and God made a covenant that his descendents were going to inherit the land that he was standing on, at the end of the fourth generation.

And, as the God of Abraham had promised, at the end of the fourth generation, He came down to Moses, where he was hiding from the Egyptians, amongst his relatives—the Midianites. The Midianites were the descendants of Abraham. If you recall, they are the children of Keturah, Abraham's second wife.

Nonetheless, there in the desert of Sinai the God of Abraham drew Moses' attention to what appeared to be a burning bush. And when Moses came near the burning bush, the God of Abraham started to talk to him. And after a short introduction, He asked Moses to go to Egypt to bring the children of Israel out of Egypt, and lead them into the Promised Land.

The God of Abraham said to Moses, "8 I am come down to deliver them [the children of Israel] out of the hand of the Egyptians, and to bring them up out of that land unto a good land and a large, unto a land flowing with milk and honey; unto the place of the Canaanites, and the Hittites, and the Amorites, and the Perizzites, and the Hivites, and

The Children of Israel

the Jebusites. 9 Now therefore, behold, the cry of the children of Israel is come unto Me: and I have also seen the oppression wherewith the Egyptians oppress them. 10 Come now therefore, and I will send thee [you] unto Pharaoh, that thou [you] mayest bring forth My people the children of Israel out of Egypt" (Exodus 3:8-10).

Moses was eighty years old at this point in time, when God asked him to go on an errand. But because Moses had not only lost his eloquent speech to a degree; but also mostly forgot the Egyptian language that he was so fluent in; thus he felt inadequate to take the mission, and therefore he did not want to go to Egypt. One of the reasons why his language skills were degenerated was due to the fact that after he married his Midianite wife Zipporah, Moses remained with his father-in-law Jethro and shepherded the animals on the east side of Mount Sinai. Spending his time day in and day out with the animals, Moses had no one to talk too for forty years; therefore he felt inadequate to take on the LORD'S mission.

But the God of Abraham wanted Moses to go on the mission. Therefore He said unto him; "16 Go, and gather the elders of Israel together, and say unto them, The LORD God of your fathers, the God of Abraham, of Isaac, and of Jacob, appeared unto me, saying, I have surely visited you, and seen that which is done to you in Egypt: 17 And I have said, I will bring you up out of the affliction of Egypt unto the land of the Canaanites, and the Hittites, and the Amorites, and the Perizzites, and the Hivites, and the Jebusites, unto a land flowing with milk and honey" (Exodus 3:16, 17).

"10 And Moses said unto the LORD, O my LORD, I am not eloquent, neither heretofore, nor since thou [you] hast spoken unto thy [your] servant: but am slow of speech, and of a slow tongue."

The Children of Israel

"14 And the anger of the LORD was kindled against Moses, and He said, Is not Aaron the Levite thy [your] brother? I know that he can speak well. And also, behold, he cometh forth to meet thee [you]: and when he seeth thee [you], he will be glad in his heart. 15 And thou [you] shalt speak unto him, and put words in his mouth: and I will be with thy mouth, and with his mouth, and will teach you what ye [all of you] shall do" (Exodus 4:10, 14, 15).

Finally, Moses agreed to go to Egypt and lead the children of Israel to the Promised Land. Meanwhile, knowing that Moses was going to accept the mission, God already had sent Aaron from Egypt to come to Moses and prepare for the errand.

After Moses and the God of Abraham finished with their meeting, Moses went home and told Zipporah, His wife, of the incident. And how the LORD God of Abraham had contacted his older brother Aaron to come and meet him and discuss what God had said and then go to Egypt to bring the children of Israel out of their bondage from the Egyptians.

Zipporah acknowledged Moses' mission and in turn Moses also told his father-in-law that he was going to leave his home for an unknown period of time and therefore he had to make arrangements with someone to take care of the livestock while he was gone.

Moses got ready; Zipporah his wife took their two sons with them, and went a short distance from their home to see Moses off on his journey.

But, at one point of the journey, the God of Abraham intervened and was ready to kill Moses. The reason the LORD God of Abraham was going to remove Moses from the mission was due to the fact that he had not circumcised his youngest son.

Realizing what the problem was, Zipporah took a sharp

The Children of Israel

stone and cut her son's foreskin and threw it at the feet of Moses. And as her child was bleeding, it appears that Zipporah did not have any sympathy for Moses; she called him "a bloody husband" because she did not approve of the circumcision.

Anyway, they said their goodbyes, Zipporah and her two children returned to her father's house very, very slowly because of the pain. And Moses went on his way to Egypt as God had asked him.

On his way to Egypt, while Moses was traveling westward in the Sinai Peninsula, as per GOD'S directions, Aaron his brother met him there, and from there, they both continued to Egypt.

When Moses and Aaron finally arrived in Egypt, at a place called Goshen (Goshen is located west of the Nile River at the northern end of Egypt), they went and gathered all the elders of the children of Israel so that they could tell them why they came to meet with them?

Aaron told them what the LORD God of their fathers had said to Moses. But the elders of Israel were not convinced that they were sent by the God of Abraham to them; therefore Aaron "30 did the signs" as God had instructed him, "in the sight of the people. 31 And the people believed: and when they heard that the LORD had visited the children of Israel, and that He had looked upon their affliction, then they bowed their heads and worshipped" (Exodus 4:30, 31).

After the children of Israel and their elders agreed to leave Egypt and go with Moses and Aaron to the Promised Land, as the LORD God had directed them "1 Moses and Aaron went in, and told Pharaoh, Thus saith the LORD God of Israel, Let My people go, that they may hold a feast unto Me in the wilderness. 2 And Pharaoh said, Who is the LORD, that I should obey His voice to let Israel go? I know

The Children of Israel

not the LORD, neither will I let Israel go." "4 And the king of Egypt said unto them, Wherefore do ye [all of you], Moses and Aaron, let the people from their works? get you unto your burdens" (Exodus 5:1, 2, 4).

In retaliation, Pharaoh increased the workload upon the children of Israel. He commanded the taskmasters the same day to increase the workload on the children of Israel by making them gather their own straw from the fields and bring it to the site so that they could make the bricks. In fact, Pharaoh wanted more work to be laid upon the children of Israel so that they would stop listening to Moses and Aaron and to the promises of their God.

The workload was so cumbersome that the children of Israel were not able to keep up with the quota that was set before them. Therefore Pharaoh was wroth with them and with the taskmasters. He beat the taskmasters for not making the children of Israel work hard enough. And in turn, the taskmasters beat the children of Israel in order to make them work harder and longer. Their punishment was so great and so unreasonable that the children of Israel finally went to Moses and Aaron and said to them, "21 The LORD look upon you, and judge; because ye [all of you] have made our savour to be abhorred in the eyes of Pharaoh, and in the eyes of his servants, to put a sword in their hand to slay us.

"22 And Moses returned unto the LORD, and said, LORD, wherefore hast thou [You] so evil entreated this people? why is it that thou hast sent me? 23 For since I came to Pharaoh to speak in thy name, he hath done evil to this people; neither hast thou delivered thy people at all" (Exodus 5:21-23).

Then the LORD God of Abraham replied by saying, "5 I have also heard the groaning of the children of Israel, whom the Egyptians keep in bondage; and I have

The Children of Israel

remembered My covenant. 6 Wherefore say unto the children of Israel, I am the LORD, and I will bring you out from under the burdens of the Egyptians, and I will rid you out of their bondage, and I will redeem you with a stretched out arm, and with great judgments:

"7 And I will take you to Me for a people, and I will be to you a God: and ye [all of you] shall know that I am the LORD your God, which bringeth you out from under the burdens of the Egyptians.

"8 And I will bring you in unto the land, concerning the which I did swear to give it to Abraham, to Isaac, and to Jacob; and I will give it you for an heritage: I am the LORD" (Exodus 6:5-8).

Moses and Aaron were asked by the LORD God of Abraham to return to Pharaoh and ask him to let the children of Israel (Jacob) leave Egypt; and if he would not let them go, then Moses and Aaron were to perform signs and wonders before Pharaoh and before the people of Egypt.

Needless to say, Pharaoh would not let the children of Israel (Jacob) go; therefore Aaron was forced to perform the signs and wonders before Pharaoh. The first sign that was performed before Pharaoh was to turn Aaron's staff into a serpent. Seeing that the serpent was slithering towards Pharaoh, Pharaoh's sorcerers threw their staffs on the floor and they to formed into serpents. But, Aaron's serpent swallowed all of the sorcerers' serpents; and then, Aaron took the serpent by the tail and it returned into a staff again.

Seeing that Pharaoh's sorcerers could not outdo Aaron's serpent and get their staff's back, Pharaoh's heart became bitter and therefore more adamant not to let the children of Israel go with Moses and Aaron. (See Exodus 7:10-13)

The second sign that Aaron did before Pharaoh and his

The Children of Israel

sorcerers was to stretch his rod over the water so that the water of the pools of the streams of their jugs of the ponds of the rivers etc., etc., turned into blood. And so did Pharaoh's sorcerers do the same; but, the water that was turned into blood by Aaron's command remained bloody and the fish died and all the life forms died that were in the water and stunk the rivers and the ponds. And when the Egyptians got thirsty, they started to dig for wells; but everywhere they dug, they found the water undrinkable because it had turned into blood. For seven days, the Egyptians were not able to drink water or to find water for themselves or for their animals.

Furious and thirsty because Pharaoh's sorcerers and his magicians could not undo what Aaron had done to the waters of Egypt, he hardened his heart and refused to let God's people go. (See Exodus 7:19-25)

Although Moses knew that Pharaoh would not let the children of Israel go from their bondage until the last plague was performed, he continued with the signs and wonders through Aaron before Pharaoh and his people, in order to impress upon their hearts that their magicians and sorcerer's illusions were futile. And at the same time, impress upon their hearts that the God of the children of Israel is the true God of the heavens and the earth, and His power is inexhaustible. Therefore Moses and Aaron continued with their mission as the LORD God of their fathers had commanded them.

> Serpents - Exodus 7:10-13
> River turned into blood - Exodus 7:19-25
> Frogs - Exodus 8:1-15
> Swarms of lice – Flies - Ex. 8:17, 20-32
> Cattle of Egypt died - Exodus 9:1-7
> Dust in all the land - Exodus 9:8-12

The Children of Israel

> Fire mingled with hail - Exodus 9:22-35:
> Locust - Exodus 10:4-20
> Darkness - Exodus 10:21-29

The last plague that was to befall Egypt was the one that the LORD God of Abraham already had said to Moses, before he came to Egypt, would be the one that would cause Pharaoh to let the children of Israel go from their bondage. And this plague was to be a memorial to all of the children of Israel in all generations. They were to celebrate it once a year, on the first month of the year (April) for seven days starting from day fourteen to the twenty-first.

The preparation for the final plague was as follows:

"1 And the LORD spake unto Moses and Aaron in the land of Egypt, saying, 2 This month [Abib-April] shall be unto you the beginning of months: it shall be the first month of the year to you.

"3 Speak ye [all of you] unto all the congregation of Israel, saying, In the tenth day of this month they shall take to them every man a lamb, according to the house of their fathers, a lamb for an house: 4 And if the household be too little for the lamb, let him and his neighbour next unto his house take it according to the number of the souls; every man according to his eating shall make your count for the lamb. 5 Your lamb shall be without blemish, a male of the first year: ye shall take it out from the sheep, or from the goats: 6 And ye shall keep it up until the fourteenth day of the same month: and the whole assembly of the congregation of Israel shall kill it in the evening. 7 And they shall take of the blood, and strike it on the two side posts and on the upper door post of the houses, wherein they shall eat it. 8 And they shall eat the flesh in that night, roast with fire, and unleavened bread; and with bitter herbs they shall eat it. 9 Eat not of it raw, nor sodden at all with water, but

The Children of Israel

roast with fire; his head with his legs, and with the purtenance thereof. 10 And ye shall let nothing of it remain until the morning; and that which remaineth of it until the morning ye shall burn with fire.

"11 And thus shall ye eat it; with your loins girded, your shoes on your feet, and your staff in your hand; and ye shall eat it in haste: it is the LORD'S passover. 12 For I will pass through the land of Egypt this night, and will smite all the firstborn in the land of Egypt, both man and beast; and against all the gods of Egypt I will execute judgment: I am the LORD. 13 And the blood shall be to you for a token upon the houses where ye are: and when I see the blood, I will pass over you, and the plague shall not be upon you to destroy you, when I smite the land of Egypt. 14 And this day shall be unto you for a memorial; and ye shall keep it a feast to the LORD throughout your generations; ye shall keep it a feast by an ordinance for ever. 15 Seven days shall ye eat unleavened bread; even the first day ye shall put away leaven out of your houses: for whosoever eateth leavened bread from the first day until the seventh day, that soul shall be cut off from Israel. 16 And in the first day there shall be an holy convocation, and in the seventh day there shall be an holy convocation to you; no manner of work shall be done in them, save that which every man must eat, that only may be done of you. 17 And ye shall observe the feast of unleavened bread; for in this selfsame day have I brought your armies out of the land of Egypt: therefore shall ye observe this day in your generations by an ordinance for ever.

"18 In the first month, on the fourteenth day of the month at even, ye shall eat unleavened bread, until the one and twentieth day of the month at even. 19 Seven days shall there be no leaven found in your houses: for whosoever eateth that which is leavened, even that soul shall be cut off from the congregation of Israel, whether he be a stranger, or

The Children of Israel

born in the land. 20 Ye shall eat nothing leavened; in all your habitations shall ye eat unleavened bread.

"21 Then Moses called for all the elders of Israel, and said unto them, Draw out and take you a lamb according to your families, and kill the passover. 22 And ye shall take a bunch of hyssop, and dip it in the blood that is in the bason, and strike the lintel and the two side posts with the blood that is in the bason; and none of you shall go out at the door of his house until the morning. 23 For the LORD will pass through to smite the Egyptians; and when he seeth the blood upon the lintel, and on the two side posts, the LORD will pass over the door, and will not suffer the destroyer to come in unto your houses to smite you. 24 And ye shall observe this thing for an ordinance to thee [you] and to thy [your] sons for ever. 25 And it shall come to pass, when ye be come to the land which the LORD will give you, according as He hath promised, that ye shall keep this service. 26 And it shall come to pass, when your children shall say unto you, What mean ye by this service? 27 That ye shall say, It is the sacrifice of the LORD'S passover, who passed over the houses of the children of Israel in Egypt, when He smote the Egyptians, and delivered our houses. And the people bowed the head and worshipped. 28 And the children of Israel went away, and did as the LORD had commanded Moses and Aaron, so did they.

"29 And it came to pass, that at midnight the LORD smote all the firstborn in the land of Egypt, from the firstborn of Pharaoh that sat on his throne unto the firstborn of the captive that was in the dungeon; and all the firstborn of cattle. 30 And Pharaoh rose up in the night, he, and all his servants, and all the Egyptians: and there was a great cry in Egypt; for there was not a house where there was not one dead.

"31 And he [Pharaoh] called forth Moses and Aaron by

The Children of Israel

night, and said, Rise up, and get you forth from among my people, both ye and the children of Israel; and go, serve the LORD, as ye have said. 32 Also take your flocks and your herds, as ye have said, and be gone; and bless me also. 33 And the Egyptians were urgent upon the people, that they might send them out of the land in haste; for they said, We be all dead men.

"34 And the people took their dough before it was leavened, their kneadingtroughs being bound up in their clothes upon their shoulders. 35 And the children of Israel did according to the word of Moses; and they borrowed of the Egyptians jewels of silver, and jewels of gold, and raiment: 36 And the LORD gave the people favour in the sight of the Egyptians, so that they lent unto them much things as they required. And they spoiled the Egyptians.

"37 And the children of Israel journeyed from Rameses [Raamses] [in 1447 BC] to Succoth, about six hundred thousand on foot that were men, beside children. 38 And a mixed multitude went up also with them; and flocks, and herds, even very much cattle. 39 And they baked unleavened cakes of the dough which they brought forth out of Egypt, for it was not leavened; because they were thrust out of Egypt, and could not tarry, neither had they prepared for themselves any victual.

"40 Now the sojourning of the children of Israel, who dwelt in Egypt, was four hundred and thirty years. 41 And it came to pass at the end of the four hundred and thirty years, even the selfsame day it came to pass, that all the host of the LORD went out from the land of Egypt. 42 It is a night to be much observed unto the LORD for bringing them out from the land of Egypt: this is that night of the LORD to be observed of all the children of Israel in their generations."
Exodus 12:1-42

All of these signs were performed by the God of

The Children of Israel

Abraham, not only for the Egyptians, but also, for the children of Israel. They were to remember the way they were brought forth out of the land of Egypt. And they were to tell their children of these events.

"17 And it came to pass, when Pharaoh had let the people go, that God led them not through the way of the land of the Philistines, although that was near; for God said, Lest peradventure the people repent when they see war, and they return to Egypt: 18 But God led the people about, through the way of the wilderness of the Red sea: and the children of Israel went up harnessed out of the land of Egypt. 19 And Moses took the bones of Joseph with him: for he had straitly sworn the children of Israel, saying, God will surely visit you; and ye shall carry up my bones away hence with you.

"20 And they took their journey from Succoth, and encamped in Etham, in the edge of the wilderness. 21 And the LORD went before them by day in a pillar of cloud, to lead them the way; and by night in a pillar of fire, to give them light; to go by day and night" (Exodus 13:17-22).

"1 And the LORD spake unto Moses, saying, 2 Speak unto the children of Israel, that they turn and encamp before Pihahiroth, between Migdol and the sea, over against Baal-zephon: before it shall ye encamp by the sea. 3 For Pharaoh will say of the children of Israel, They are entangled in the land, the wilderness hath shut them in. 4 And I will harden Pharaoh's heart, that he shall follow after them; and I will be honoured upon Pharaoh, and upon all his host; that the Egyptians may know that I am the LORD."

"8 And the LORD hardened the heart of Pharaoh king of Egypt, and he pursued after the children of Israel:" "10 And when Pharaoh drew nigh, the children of Israel lifted up their eyes, and, behold, the Egyptians marched after them; and they were sore afraid: and the children of Israel cried out

The Children of Israel

unto the LORD. 11 And they said unto Moses, Because there were no graves in Egypt, hast thou taken us away to die in the wilderness? wherefore hast thou dealt thus with us, to carry us forth out of Egypt? 12 Is not this the word that we did tell thee in Egypt, saying, Let us alone, that we may serve the Egyptians? For it had been better for us to serve the Egyptians, than that we should die in the wilderness.

"13 And Moses said unto the people, Fear ye not, stand still, and see the salvation of the LORD, which He will shew to you to day: for the Egyptians whom ye have seen to day, ye shall see them again no more for ever."

"21 And Moses stretched out his hand over the sea; and the LORD caused the sea to go back by a strong east wind all that night, and made the sea dry land, and the waters were divided. 22 And the children of Israel went into the midst of the sea upon the dry ground: and the waters were a wall unto them on their right hand, and on their left. 23 And the Egyptians pursued, and went in after them to the midst of the sea, even all Pharaoh's horses, his chariots, and his horsemen."

"26 And the LORD said unto Moses, Stretch out thine hand over the sea, that the waters may come again upon the Egyptians, upon their chariots, and upon their horsemen." Exodus 14:1-4, 8, 10-13, 21-23, 26

And when they were delivered, "22 Moses brought Israel from the Red sea, and they went out into the wilderness of Shur; and they went three days in the wilderness, and found no water. 23 And when they came to Marah, they could not drink of the waters of Marah, for they were bitter: therefore the name of it was called Marah. 24 And the people murmured against Moses, saying, What shall we drink? 25 And he cried unto the LORD; and the LORD shewed him a tree, which when he had cast into the waters, the waters were made sweet:" "26 And said, If thou [you] wilt diligently

The Children of Israel

hearken to the voice of the LORD thy God, and wilt do that which is right in His sight, and wilt give ear to His commandments, and keep all His states, I will put none of these diseases upon thee [you], which I have brought upon the Egyptians: for I am the LORD that healeth thee [you]. 27 And they came to Elim, where were twelve wells of water, and threescore and ten [70] palm trees: and they camped there by the waters." Exodus 15:22-27

"1 And they took their journey from Elim, and all the congregation of the children of Israel came unto the wilderness of Sin, which is between Elim and Sinai, on the fifteenth day of the second month after their departing out of the land of Egypt. 2 And the whole congregation of the children of Israel murmured against Moses and Aaron in the wilderness: 3 And the children of Israel [Jacob] said unto them, Would to God we had died by the hand of the LORD in the land of Egypt, when we sat by the flesh pots, and when we did eat bread to the full; for ye [all of you] have brought us forth into this wilderness, to kill this whole assembly with hunger." Exodus 16:1-3

"11 And the LORD spake unto Moses saying, 12 I have heard the murmurings of the children of Israel: speak unto them, saying, At even ye [all of you] shall eat flesh, and in the morning ye shall be filled with bread; and ye shall know that I am the LORD your God. 13 And it came to pass, that at even the quails came up, and covered the camp: and in the morning the dew lay round about the host. 14 And when the dew that lay was gone up, behold, upon the face of the wilderness there lay a small round thing, as small as the hoar frost on the ground. 15 And when the children of Israel saw it, they said one to another, It is manna: for they wist not what it was. And Moses said unto them, This is the bread which the LORD hath given you to eat." "21 And they gathered it every morning, every man according to his eating:

The Children of Israel

and when the sun waxed hot, it melted." Exodus 16:11-15, 21

In addition, the children of Israel were reminded that in "26 Six days shall ye gather it; but on the seventh day [Saturday], which is the sabbath, in it there shall be none." Exodus 16:26

So what did this manna taste like?

Here is the answer; "31 it was like coriander seed, white; and the taste of it was like wafers made with honey" (Exodus 16:31).

"1 And all the congregation of the children of Israel journeyed from the wilderness of Sin, after their journeys, according to the commandment of the LORD, and pitched in Rephidim: and there was no water for the people to drink. 2 Wherefore the people did chide with Moses, and said, Give us water that we may drink. And Moses said unto them, Why chide ye with me? wherefore do ye tempt the LORD? 3 And the people thirsted there for water; and the people murmured against Moses, and said, Wherefore is this that thou [you] hast brought us up out of Egypt, to kill us and our children and our cattle with thirst?

"4 And Moses cried unto the LORD, saying, What shall I do unto this people? they be almost ready to stone me. 5 And the LORD said unto Moses, Go on before the people, and take with thee [you] of the elders of Israel; and thy

The Children of Israel

[your] rod, wherewith thou smotest the river, take in thine hand, and go. 6 Behold, I will stand before thee [you] there upon the rock in Horeb; and thou shalt smite the rock, and there shall come water out of it, that the people may drink. And Moses did so in the sight of the elders of Israel. 7 And he called the name of the place Massah, and Meribah, because of the chiding of the children of Israel, and because they tempted the LORD, saying, Is the LORD among us, or not?" Exodus 17:1-7

"1 In the third month, when the children of Israel were gone forth out of the land of Egypt, the same day came they into the wilderness of Sinai. 2 For they were departed from Rephidim, and were come to the desert of Sinai, and had pitched in the wilderness; and there Israel camped before the mount. 3 And Moses went up unto God, and the LORD called unto him out of the mountain, saying, Thus shalt thou say to the house of Jacob, and tell the children of Israel; 4 Ye have seen what I did unto the Egyptians, and how I bare you on eagles' wings, and brought you unto Myself. 5 Now therefore, if ye will obey My voice indeed, and keep My covenant, then ye shall be a peculiar treasure unto Me above all people: for all the earth is mine: 6 And ye shall be unto Me a kingdom of priests, and an holy nation. These are the words which thou shalt speak unto the children of Israel.

"7 And Moses came and called for the elders of the people, and laid before their faces all these words which the LORD commanded him. "8 And all the people answered together, and said, All that the LORD hath spoken we will do. And Moses returned the words of the people unto the LORD.

"9 And the LORD said unto Moses, Lo, I come unto thee in a thick cloud, that the people may hear when I speak with thee, and believe thee for ever. And Moses told the words of the people unto the LORD. 10 And the LORD said

The Children of Israel

unto Moses, Go unto the people, and sanctify them to day and to morrow, and let them wash their clothes, 11 And be ready against the third day: for the third day the LORD will come down in the sight of all the people upon mount Sinai." Exodus 19:1-11

And on the third day, the people gathered before the LORD God of Abraham, at the foot of Mount Sinai as He had requested; "1 And God spake all these words, saying, 2 I am the LORD thy [your] God, which have brought thee out of the land of Egypt, out of the house of bondage.

i

"3 Thou [you] shalt have no other gods before Me.

ii

"4 Thou [you] shalt not make unto thee any graven image, or any likeness of any thing that is in heaven above, or that is in the earth beneath, or that is in the water under the earth: 5 Thou [you] shalt not bow down thyself to them, nor serve them: for I the LORD thy God am a jealous God, visiting the iniquity of the fathers upon the children unto the third and fourth generation of them that hate Me; 6 And shewing mercy unto thousands of them that love Me, and keep My commandments.

iii

"7 Thou [you] shalt not take the name of the LORD thy God in vain; for the LORD will not hold him guiltless that taketh His name in vain.

iv

"8 Remember the sabbath day, to keep it holy. 9 Six days shalt thou [you] labour, and do all thy work: 10 But the seventh day is the sabbath of the LORD thy God: in it thou [you] shalt not do any work, thou, nor thy son, nor thy daughter, thy manservant, nor thy maidservant, nor thy cattle, nor thy stranger that is within thy gates: 11 For

The Children of Israel

in six days the LORD made heaven and earth, the sea, and all that in them is, and rested the seventh day: wherefore the LORD blessed the Sabbath day, and hallowed it.

v

"12 Honour thy [your] father and they [your] mother: that thy days may be long upon the land which the LORD thy God giveth thee.

vi

"13 Thou [you] shalt not kill.

vii

"14 Thou [you] shalt not commit adultery.

viii

"15 Thou [you] shalt not steal.

ix

"16 Thou [you] shalt not bear false witness against thy neighbour.

x

"17 Thou [you] shalt not covet thy [your] neighbour's house, thou shalt not covet thy neighbour's wife, nor his manservant, nor his maidservant, nor his ox, nor his ass, nor any thing that is thy neighbour's." Exodus 20:1-17

While hearing the Ten Commandments and the earth shaking beneath their feet and the lightning and the thunder and the noise and the smoke bellowing on the mount, the children of Israel panicked because their sins were revealed and thought they were going to perish. Therefore they ran away from the mountain yelling to Moses, "19 Speak thou [you] with us, and we will hear: but let not God speak with us, lest we die." Exodus 20:19

Calming their fears down, the children of Israel agreed to abide by the covenant.

"1 And he said unto Moses, Come up unto the LORD,

The Children of Israel

thou, and Aaron, Nadab, and Abihu, and seventy of the elders of Israel; and worship ye afar off. 2 And Moses alone shall come near the LORD: but they shall not come nigh; neither shall the people go up with him. 3 And Moses came and told the people all the words of the LORD, and all the judgments: and all the people answered with one voice, and said, All the words which the LORD hath said will we do. 4 And Moses wrote all the words of the LORD, and rose up early in the morning, and builded an altar under the hill, and twelve pillars, according to the twelve tribes of Israel. 5 And he sent young men of the children of Israel, which offered burnt offerings, and sacrificed peace offerings of oxen unto the LORD. 6 And Moses took half of the blood, and put it in basons; and half of the blood he sprinkled on the altar. 7 And he took the book of the covenant, and read in the audience of the people: and they said, All that the LORD hath said will we do, and be obedient. 8 And Moses took the blood, and sprinkled it on the people, and said, Behold the blood of the covenant, which the LORD hath made with you concerning all these words." Exodus 24:1-8

After the covenant was ratified at the foot of Mount Sinai, the LORD God of Abraham said to Moses,

"8 let them make Me a sanctuary; that I may dwell among them. "9 According to all that I shew thee, after the pattern of the tabernacle, and the pattern all the instruments thereof, even so shall ye [all of you] make it." Exodus 25:8, 9

After the LORD of hosts asked Moses to build a Sanctuary for Him, Moses called upon the people to give of their materials in order to accomplish the task. And those who gave begrudgingly, Moses turned them and their gifts away. And when the materials were evaluated, it was

The Children of Israel

observed that they had more than it was needed; therefore Moses asked the people to stop giving any more.

Glad of the outcome, Moses started to look for people that were capable of making the furniture for the Sanctuary, the tent (tabernacle), the altar of sacrifice, and the fence that was to encamp the tent.

To his surprise, Moses could not fined people that were capable of performing the intricate work to make the Sanctuary and the furniture for the Sanctuary, after the pattern that was revealed to Moses, at the mount! It required people with very highly specialized skills. And since there were not found any highly skilled persons for the jobs, Moses went to the God of Abraham and asked Him for help; "1 And the LORD spake unto Moses saying, 2 See, I have called by name Bezaleel the son of Uri, the son of Hur, of the tribe of Judah: 3 And I have filled him with the spirit of God, in wisdom, and in understanding, and in knowledge, and in all manner of workmanship. 4 To devise cunning works, to work in gold, and in silver, and in brass. 5 And in cutting of stones, to set them, and in carving of timber, to work in all manner of workmanship. 6 And I, behold, I have given with him Aholiah, the son of Ahisamach, of the tribe of Dan: and in the hearts of all that are wise hearted I have put wisdom, that they may make all that I have commanded thee [you];" Exodus 31:1-6

After the LORD God of Abraham revealed to Moses who was capable of doing the intricate work, Moses gave them their respective work and told them to accomplish their work to perfection according to the pattern that was given to him.

Regarding the construction of the tent (tabernacle), God said to Moses, "1 thou [you] shalt make the tabernacle [tent] with ten curtains of fine twined linen, and blue, and purple, and scarlet: with cherubims of cunning work shalt thou

The Children of Israel

make them. 2 The length of one curtain shalt be eight and twenty cubits, and the breadth of one curtain four cubits: and every one of the curtains shall have one measure. 3 The five curtains shall be coupled together one to another; and other five curtains shall be coupled one to another. 4 And thou [you] shall make loops of blue upon the edge of the one curtain from the selvedge in the coupling; and likewise shalt thou make in the uttermost edge of another curtain, in the coupling of the second. 5 Fifty loops shalt thou make in the one curtain, and fifty loops shalt thou make in the edge of the curtain that is in the coupling of the second; that the loops may take hold one of another. 6 And thou [you] shalt make fifty taches of gold, and couple the curtains together with the taches: and it shall be one tabernacle.

"7 And thou [you] shalt make curtains of goats' hair to be a covering upon the tabernacle: eleven curtains shalt thou make. 8 The length of one curtain shall be thirty cubits, and the breadth of one curtain four cubits: and the eleven curtains shall be all of one measure. 9 And thou [you] shalt couple five curtains by themselves, and six curtains by themselves, and shalt double the sixth curtain in the forefront of the tabernacle. 10 And thou shalt make fifty loops on the edge of the one curtain that is outmost in the coupling, and fifty loops in the edge of the curtain which coupleth the second. 11 And thou [you] shalt make fifty taches of brass, and put the taches into the loops, and couple the tent together, that it may be one. 12 And the remnant that remaineth of the curtains of the tent, the half curtain that remaineth, shall hang over the backside of the tabernacle. 13 And a cubit on the one side, and a cubit on the other side of that which remaineth in the length of the curtains of the tent, it shall hang over the sides of the tabernacle on this side and on that side, to cover it. 14 And thou shalt make a covering for the tent of rams' skins dyed red, and a covering

The Children of Israel

above of badgers' skins.

"15 And thou [you] shalt make boards for the tabernacle of shittim wood standing up. 16 Ten cubits shall be the length of a board, and a cubit and a half shall be the breadth of one board. 17 Two tenons shall there be in one board, set in order one against another: thus shalt thou make for all the boards of the tabernacle. 18 And thou shalt make the boards for the tabernacle, twenty boards on the south side southward. 19 And thou shalt make forty sockets of silver under the twenty boards; two sockets under one board for his two tenons, and two sockets under another board for his two tenons. 20 And for the second side of the tabernacle on the north side there shall be twenty boards: 21 And their forty sockets of silver; two sockets under one board, and two sockets under another board. 22 And for the sides of the tabernacle westward thou [you] shalt make six boards. 23 And two boards shalt thou make for the corners of the tabernacle in the two sides. 24 And they shall be coupled together beneath, and they shall be coupled together above the head of it unto one ring: thus shall it be for them both; they shall be for the two corners. 25 And they shall be eight boards, and their sockets of silver, sixteen sockets; two sockets under one hoard, and two sockets under another board.

"26 And thou [you] shalt make bars of shittim wood; five for the boards of the one side of the tabernacle. 27 And five bars for the boards of the other side of the tabernacle, and five bars for the boards of the side of the tabernacle, for the two sides westward. 28 And the middle bar in the midst of the boards shall reach from end to end. 29 And thou [you] shalt overlay the boards with gold, and make their rings of gold for places for the bars: and thou shalt overlay the bars with gold. 30 And thou shalt rear up the tabernacle according to the fashion thereof which was shewed thee [you] in the mount." Exodus 26:1-30

The Children of Israel

And regarding the production of the fence that had a
front entrance on the east side of the Sanctuary and the rest
of the fence that encamped the tent (tabernacle) and the altar
for the animal sacrificial offering, you will find the pattern in
the following references: Exodus 27:9-19

Regarding the production of the altar of sacrifice, which
was placed in the eastern courtyard of the Sanctuary, you will
find the pattern in the following references: Exodus 27:1-8

And regarding the production of the Ark of the
Covenant that was placed in the "most holy place" (second
room of the tent), you will find the pattern in the following
references: Exodus 25:10-21

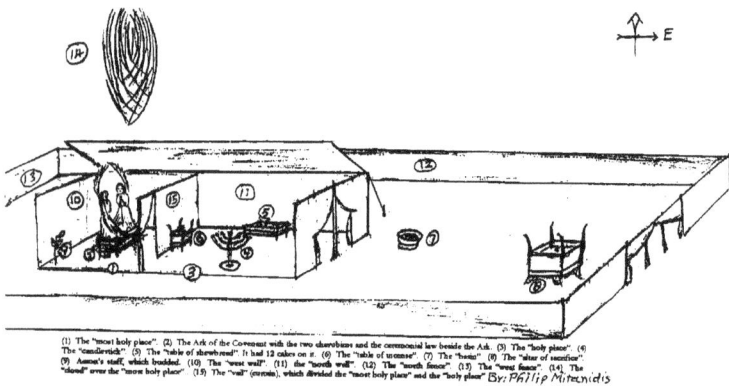

(1) The "most holy place". (2) The Ark of the Covenant with the two cherubims and the ceremonial law beside the Ark. (3) The "holy place". (4) The "candlestick". (5) The "table of shewbread". It had 12 cakes on it. (6) The "table of incense". (7) The "basin". (8) The "altar of sacrifice". (9) Aaron's staff, which budded. (10) The "west wall". (11) the "north wall". (12) The "north fence". (13) The "west fence". (14) The "cloud" over the "most holy place". (15) The "veil" (curtain), which divided the "most holy place" and the "holy place" By: *Philip Mitanidis*

And regarding the production of the table of incense,
which was placed in the first room ("holy place") against the
curtain that divided the first room and the smaller second
room of the tent, you will find the pattern in the following
references: Exodus 30:1-10.

And regarding the construction of the table of
shewbread (for the 12 cakes) that was placed on the
northern side of "the holy place" (the first room), you will
find the pattern in the following references: Exodus 25:23-30

And regarding the manufacturing of the stand with

The Children of Israel

seven candlesticks, which was placed on the south side of the first room ("holy place"), you will find the pattern in the following references: Exodus 25:31-39

When the parts of the Sanctuary for the LORD God of Abraham were completed, Moses gave the responsibility of the Sanctuary and its furniture to the tribe of Levi. Moses delegated the responsibility to the tribe of Levi for the care of the Sanctuary, for the assembly, and disassembly of the Sanctuary; and who would carry the parts of the Sanctuary and who would carry the Ark of the Covenant in and out of the "most holy" place of the Sanctuary.

Therefore, when all of the pieces were produced, the Levites erected the Sanctuary according to the pattern and placed the furniture in the appropriate rooms. The construction of the Sanctuary was completed on the first day of the first month (April) of the second year of their stay at the foot of Mount Sinai.

And, after they finished placing the furniture in the Sanctuary, they dedicated the Sanctuary to the God of Abraham. And when the dedication took place, "34 Then a cloud covered the tent of the congregation, and the glory of the LORD filled the tabernacle. 35 And Moses was not able to enter into the tent of the congregation, because the cloud abode thereon, and the glory of the LORD filled the tabernacle." Exodus 40:34, 35

The Sanctuary was complete and dedicated to the God of Abraham on the first day of the second year of their stay at the foot of Mount Sinai.

Now that the Sanctuary was built and dedicated to the God of Abraham, the God of Abraham dwelt in "the most holy place" of the tabernacle above the mercy seat and in between the two cherubims that were on each end of the Ark of the Covenant.

The LORD God of Abraham said to Moses; "22 And

The Children of Israel

there I will meet with thee [you], and I will commune with thee from above the mercy seat, from between the two cherubims which are upon the ark of the testimony, of all things which I will give thee [you] in commandment unto the children of Israel" (Exodus 25:22).

From there—the mercy seat—the God of Abraham communicated with Moses. From there, twice a day, in the morning and at dusk, the sinner's sins were covered, after the sacrificial offering took place in the eastern courtyard of the Sanctuary. And from there, once a year on the Day of Atonement, all of the sins of the children of Israel were removed from the camp, via a scapegoat.

As you have read, the LORD God of Israel had moved into the tabernacle, above the mercy seat, and the shekinah glory of the LORD was present there. Now Moses could talk with the LORD God of Abraham face to face, whereas before the Sanctuary was constructed, all Moses could see was a cloud over the camp of Israel.

And then, to their surprise, the LORD God of Abraham, who appeared in the form of a cloud above the tabernacle, signified by moving from above the tent (tabernacle) a distance away from the Sanctuary in a northeast direction. That meant that the children of Israel were to pack up their things, dismantle the camp, and get ready to move from the area, and follow the LORD God of Abraham who appeared in the form of a cloud.

We are told: "36 when the cloud was taken up from over the tabernacle [tent], the children of Israel went onward in all their journeys: 37 But if the cloud were not taken up, then they journeyed not till the day that it was taken up. 38 For the cloud of the LORD was upon the tabernacle by day, and fire was on it by night, in the sight of all the house of Israel, throughout all their journeys." Exodus 40:36-38

From mount Sinai, on the first month of the second

The Children of Israel

year, the LORD God of Abraham took the children of Israel on an eleven days journey to Kadish-barnea, which is located about one hundred and fifty miles slightly northeast from Sinai. And when they got there, the LORD God of Abraham told them to go and possess the Promised Land. Unfortunately, the children of Israel did not want to go into Canaan to possess the land. To their detriment, they wandered for thirty-eight years in the deserts of the Negeb and of the Sinai Peninsula.

And forty years after they left the field of Goshen, Moses, on the eastside of the River Jordan, at a place called "Shittem," reminded the children of Israel how thirty-eight years and eleven months ago, they were camped at Kadish-barnea. Moses said, "6 The LORD our God spake unto us in Horib, saying, Ye have dwelt long enough in this mount: 7 Turn you, and take your journey, and go to the mount of the Amorites, and unto all the places nigh thereunto, in the plain, in the hills, and in the vale, and in the south, and by the sea side, to the land of the Canaanites, and unto Lebanon, unto the great river, the river Euphrates, 8 Behold, I have set the land before you: go in and possess the land which the LORD sware unto your fathers, Abraham, Isaac, and Jacob, to give unto them and to their seed after them." Deuteronomy 1:6-8

And Moses added, "22 And ye came near unto me every one of you, and said, We will send men before us, and they shall search us out the land, and bring us word again by what way we must go up, and into what cities we shall come. 23 And the saying pleased me well: and I took twelve men of you, one of a tribe: 24 And they turned and went up into the mountain, and came unto the valley of Eshcol, and searched it out. 25 And they took of the fruit of the land in their hands, and brought it down unto us, and brought us word again, and said, It is a good land which the LORD our God

The Children of Israel

doth give us.

"26 Notwithstanding ye would not go up, but rebelled against the commandment of the LORD your God: 27 And ye murmured in your tents, and said, Because the LORD hated us, He hath brought us forth out of the land of Egypt, to deliver us into the hand of the Amorites, to destroy us. 28 Whither shall we go up? our brethren have discouraged our heart, saying, The people is greater and taller than we; the cities are great and walled up to heaven; and moreover we have seen the sons of the Anakims there."

"34 And the LORD heard the voice of your words, and was wroth, and sware, saying, 35 Surely there shall not one of these men of this evil generation see that good land, which I sware to give unto your fathers, 36 Save Caleb the son of Jephunneh; he shall see it, and to him will I give the land that he hath trodden upon, and to his children, because he hath wholly followed the LORD. 37 Also the LORD was angry with me for your sakes, saying, Thou also shalt not go in thither. 38 But Joshua the son of Nun, which standeth before thee [you], he shall go in thither: encourage him: for he shall cause Israel to inherit it. 39 Moreover your little ones, which ye said should be a prey, and your children, which in that day had no knowledge between good and evil, they shall go in thither, and unto them will I give it, and they shall possess it. 40 But as for you, turn you, and take your journey into the wilderness by the way of the Red Sea." Deuteronomy 1:22-28, 34-40

Because the children of Israel refused to go and inherit the Promised Land of Canaan, the LORD allowed them to return to Egypt. But, when they could not find captains to guide them, protect them, feed them, or give them water to drink, they stopped wanting to go back to Egypt; and even worse, if they somehow managed to go back to Egypt, would the Egyptians want them there?

The Children of Israel

Anyway, the LORD God of Abraham in His mercy allowed the children of Israel to wander for thirty-eight years in the wilderness of Sinai, Shur, Paran, and the wilderness of Zin, until their children grew up. They were more willing to go and inherit the land.

Therefore on their fortieth year, the LORD God of Abraham took the children of Israel northward from Ezion-geber (the northeastern tip of the Red Sea), along Mount Seir, where Esau's descendants lived, and towards the south end of the Salt Sea; but because they tempted the LORD God of Abraham along the way and said all manner of things, the LORD God of Abraham left His Sanctuary and departed from the camp of Israel. At the same time, the LORD God of Abraham removed His protection from the camp of Israel and left them in their own devices. And when the adversary (Satan) and his evil angels observed the LORD'S divine protection was removed from the children of Israel, they coerced the snakes and scorpions to attack the children of Israel. In a perpetual fierce and horrifying attack, in one day, twenty three thousand of the children of Israel died from the venom of the snakes and scorpions.

We are told; "4 And they [the children of Israel] journeyed from mount Hor by the way of the Red Sea, to compass the land of Edom: and the soul of the people was much discouraged because of the way. 5 And the people spake against God, and against Moses, Wherefore have ye [all of you] brought us up out of Egypt to die in the wilderness? for there is no bread, neither is there any water; and our soul loatheth this light bread. 6 And the LORD sent fiery serpents among the people, and they bit the people; and much people of Israel died." Numbers 21:4-6

After the children of Israel repented, the LORD God of Abraham came back into the camp. He dispersed Satan and his evil angels from the camp of Israel; and at the same time,

The Children of Israel

He caused the snakes and scorpions to depart from the camp of Israel.

After the dead bodies were removed from the camp and buried, the LORD God of Abraham took the children of Israel North; and just before they ran into the southern tip of the Dead Sea, the LORD took the children of Israel eastward across the Brook of Zered. From there the children of Israel dethroned all of the kings that were east of the Salt Sea, east of the Jordan River, east of the Sea of Galilee, and settled east of the River Jordan in a place called Shittim, which is about eight miles east of Jericho.

From there the LORD God of Abraham took Moses to the top of Mount Nebo. And from there Moses saw all of the Promised Land. After he saw it, Moses died and the LORD God of Abraham buried him in an unknown place.

After Moses' death, Joshua took over the leadership; and eventually, on the 41st year crossed from the east side of the Jordan River to the west side of the river and camped temporary at Gilgal. There at Gilgal Joshua circumcised the children of Israel and pitched the Sanctuary of the LORD God of Abraham amongst them. Later, when the Promised Land was divided amongst the children of Israel, Joshua pitched the Sanctuary of the LORD of hosts in a place called "Shiloh." Shiloh is a short distance (about 20 miles) north of Jerusalem.

And because the children of Israel (twelve tribes) worshipped the God of their fathers at "Shiloh," the name "Shiloh" became synonymous with the God of Israel.

The God of Israel

As you probably know Christians, Muslims, and Jews believe that the God of Abraham and Jesus Christ the LORD of hosts are two different Individuals; and, perhaps, you like them believe likewise.

If you do, I have a question for you.

Here is the question, "Who is the God of Abraham?"

If you said that the God of Abraham is God the Father, as we know him now in the New Testament, which is a common belief by the Christians, Muslim, and Jewish religious denominations, then I would like to ask you to go in the Old Testament and gather about twenty references of God the Father. But, if you were unable to find twenty references, would you at least find five references of God the Father!

How did you make out?

Did you say that you have dozens of references!

Can I ask how you came to that conclusion?

You know, if you were to stop and think for a moment, you would realize that in all of your dozens of verses that you have sighted, they do not reveal a specific person; all you have done is to provide me with someone's name in the form of LORD God or LORD or God. By sighting someone's name and saying that it refers to God the Father is only an assumption because without qualifying your assumption you or I can assume that it refers to whom ever we want.

Let me give you an example in the following verse:

"1 And he shewed me Joshua the high priest standing before the angel of the LORD, and Satan standing at his right hand to resist him. 2 And the LORD said unto Satan, The LORD rebuke thee, O Satan; even the LORD that hath chosen Jerusalem rebuke thee." Zechariah 3:1, 2

Now I ask you, who is the LORD in verse two?

The God of Israel

Who spoke to Satan? And who is the LORD that is to rebuke Satan?

The answer is given in verse two.

In another example, King David was referring to his own LORD and to another LORD who talked to his own LORD.

Here is the reference:

"1 The LORD said unto my LORD, Sit thou [You] at my right hand, until I make thine [Your] enemies thy [Your] footstool." Psalms 110:1

So! Who is David's LORD? And who is talking to David's LORD?

Furthermore, in the following example, God is saying that he is going to save the house of Judah "by the LORD their God."

"6 And she conceived again, and bare a daughter. And God said unto him, Call her name Loruhamah: for I will no more have mercy upon the house of Israel; but I will utterly take them away. 7 But I will have mercy upon the house of Judah, and will save them by the LORD their God," Hosea 1:6, 7

Who is this God of verse six that is going to save the house of Judah "by the LORD their God"? And who is the LORD God of the house of Judah or Jews if you like?

The point that I am making, by giving you the above three examples, is to reveal to you that by somebody telling me your last name, as an example, I would not know to whom he or she is referring to, especially if there is more than one individual in your family with the same last name. But, if that person also provided me with your given name,

The God of Israel

then I would know to whom he or she was referring to.

Likewise, since God the Father and God the Christ have the same name (LORD God), last name if you like, it makes it hard to identify who is who by referring to Them by their last name; but when we use their character names, or given names if you like, then it is easier to know to whom the prophets of old are referring to.

So! As per verses six and seven above (Hosea 1:6, 7), after the house of Israel (ten tribes) was scattered, who was "the LORD God" of "the house of Judah" (two tribes)? And who was the LORD God of "the house of Israel" before they were dislodged? By the way, the reason the house of Israel was dislodged and abandoned by Christ the God of Israel was due to the ungodly acts King Jeroboam made the children of Israel do. If you recall, Jeroboam the king of the house of Israel plunged them into idol worship by building one shrine for their idols at "Bethel" and the other shrine for their idols in the tribe of "Dan"?

The last king of "the house of Israel" was Hoshea and that kingdom was terminated in 722 BC.

Nonetheless, seeing that there is more than one Individual mentioned in the above three verses by the name of LORD God, can you differentiate who is who?

Therefore to clarify who is who in the above verses, and like verses, consider this and the following chapters.

The first statement that is made by Moses in the Torah (five books of Moses) is in reference to the name of God and this reference is found in the first book, in the first chapter, and in the first verse.

The verse reads as follows: "1 In the beginning God created the heaven and the earth." In that verse we are given the partial name of the all-powerful God. But, the full name of God does not appear until we reach Genesis 2:4. It reads, "4 These are the generations of the heavens and of the earth

The God of Israel

when they were created, in the day that the LORD God created and made." Therefore the full name of God the Creator is "LORD God."

The Hebrew name for the word "God" reads as follows: *alohim* . א ל ה י ם   And the Hebrew name for the word "LORD" reads: *yhwh* . י ה ו ה   Together, the full name "LORD God" in the Hebrew language will read, from left to right, *hwhy mihola* .(א ל ה י ם   י ה ו ה)

The word God (א ל ה י ם) is referred to over three thousand times in the Bible. And the word LORD (י ה ו ה) is referred to over six thousand times in the Bible. But most of the time, the full name of the LORD God of Abraham is not used as much. The words LORD and God are used independently throughout the inspired Scriptures most of the time.

Although most Bibles in the market place have translated the Hebrew word י ה ו ה (yhwh) to read "LORD" which is correct; unfortunately, a handful of Bible translators have chosen to translate the Hebrew word י ה ו ה (yhwh) to read "Jehovah" in their Bibles, which is one hundred percent in error. The word "Jehovah" appears only in seven places in the entire Bible. It does not appear over six thousand times as they have done so erroneously in their Bibles. (As example: the NIV Bible and the NWT Bible.)

In addition, there are a handful of individuals who have gone on the limb and have stated that the word "Jehovah" exists eight times and not seven times. I will refrain from becoming entangled in their dispute at this time; but if you are interested in the subject, you can look into the matter a little bit closer. It will be quite an exercise for you that is, if you feel like taking up the task.

Anyway, as it was stated before, the full name of God was revealed by the God of Abraham to Moses; and it was acknowledged by Moses, just before Moses made up his

The God of Israel

mind to go to Egypt to bring the children of Israel into the Promised Land.

> "13 And Moses said unto God, Behold, when I come unto the children of Israel [Jacob], and shall say unto them, The God of your fathers hath sent me unto you; and they shall say to me, What is His name? what shall I say unto them? 14 And God said unto Moses, I AM THAT I AM: and He said, Thus shalt thou [you] say unto the children of Israel, I AM hath sent me unto you.

> "15 And God said moreover unto Moses, Thus thou [you] shalt say unto the children of Israel, The LORD God of your fathers, the God of Abraham, the God of Isaac, and the God of Jacob, hath sent me unto you: this is My name for ever, and this is my memorial unto all generation" (Exodus 3:13-15

In response to Moses' question, did you notice what the God of Abraham said to Moses regarding His name? He said to Moses to say to the children of Israel, "The LORD God of your fathers...hath sent me unto you." And then God added, "this is My name for ever."

Therefore, if you were to go and read the entire Torah, or better still, go and read the entire sixty-six books of the Bible, and when you do, you will find the name of the God of Abraham, LORD God or LORD and God running like a thread throughout the sixty-six books of the Bible.

Now we can ask, "Who is the God of the children of Israel? Who led them by a cloud, fed them, gave them water to drink, protected them, and brought them into the Promised Land to live?"

As per the Torah, it was the God of Abraham better known in the New Testament by His character name of

The God of Israel

"Messiah" (Christ) (John 1:41; 1 Corinthians 10:1-4). He led the children of Israel *in a cloud* in the way that they should go. In confirmation, the references read as follows:

> "20 And they [the children of Israel] took their journey from Succoth, and encamped in Etham, in the edge of the wilderness. 21 And the LORD went before them by day in a pillar of a cloud, to lead them the way; and by night in a pillar of fire, to give them light; to go by day and night: 22 He took not away the pillar of the cloud by day, nor the pillar of fire by night, from before the people." Exodus 13:20-22

And the cross-reference, which identifies the God of Abraham by the character name of "Christ" (Χριστος), it reads as follows:

> "1 Moreover brethren, I [Apostle Paul] would not that ye [all of you] should be ignorant, how that all our fathers were under the cloud, and all passed though the sea;" 1 Corinthians 10:1

The identity: And that "Rock that followed them:…was Christ [Χριστος]." 1 Corinthians 10:4

In addition, we can also conclude, as per the Torah, it was Christ (Χριστος) the God of Abraham who led the children of Israel *through the Red Sea* and crossed to the other side.

Here is the reference: "21 And Moses stretched out his hand over the sea; and the LORD caused the sea to go back by a strong east wind all that night, and made the sea dry land, and the waters were divided. 22 And the children of Israel went into the midst of the sea upon the

The God of Israel

dry ground: and the waters were a wall unto them on their right hand, and on their left." Exodus 14:21, 22

Here is the cross reference, which identifies the God of Abraham by the character name of Christ (Χριστος):

"1 Moreover brethren, I would not that ye [all of you] should be ignorant, how that all our fathers…all passed though the sea; 2 And were all baptized unto Moses in the cloud and in the sea;" 1 Corinthians 10:1, 2

And that "Rock that followed them" and allowed the children of Israel to "passed through the sea" "was Christ [Χριστος]." 1 Corinthians 10:1, 2, 4

In addition, we can also conclude, as per the Torah, it was Christ (Χριστος) the God of Abraham who led the children of Israel and *fed them*. Moses said:

"14 And when the dew that lay was gone up, behold, upon the face of the wilderness there lay a small round thing, as small as the hoar frost on the ground. 15 And when the children of Israel saw it, they said one to another, It is manna: for they wist not what it was. And Moses said unto them, This is the bread which the LORD hath given you to eat." "35 And the children of Israel did eat manna forty years, until they came to a land inhabited; they did eat manna, until they came unto the borders of the land of Canaan." "31 And the house of Israel called the name thereof Manna: and it was like coriander seed, white; and the taste of it was like wafers made with honey." Exodus 16:14, 15, 35, 31

Here is the cross reference, which identifies the God of

The God of Israel

Abraham by the character name of Christ (Χριστος):

"3 And did all eat the same spiritual meat;" 1 Corinthians 10:3

"and that…Rock that followed them" and allowed the children of Israel to "passed through the sea" and "did all eat the same spiritual meat [food]," was provided by "Christ [Χριστος]." 1 Corinthians 10:1, 2, 3, 4

In addition, we can also conclude, as per the Torah, it was Christ (Χριστος) the God of Abraham who led the children of Israel and gave them *water to drink from rocks*.

:

The reference reads: "1 And all the congregation of the children of Israel journeyed from the wilderness of Sin, after their journeys, according to the commandment of the LORD, and pitched in Rephidim: and there was no water for the people to drink. 2 Wherefore the people did chide with Moses, and said, Give us water that we may drink. And Moses said unto them, Why chide ye with me? wherefore do ye tempt the LORD? 3 And the people thirsted there for water; and the people murmured against Moses, and said, Wherefore is this that thou [you] hast brought us up out of Egypt, to kill us and our children and our cattle with thirst?

"4 And Moses cried unto the LORD, saying, What shall I do unto this people? they be almost ready to stone me. 5 And the LORD said unto Moses, Go on before the people, and take with thee [you] of the elders of Israel; and thy [your] rod, wherewith thou smotest the river, take in thine hand, and go. 6 Behold, I will stand before thee [you] there upon the rock in Horeb; and thou shalt smite the rock, and there shall come water out of it, that

The God of Israel

the people may drink. And Moses did so in the sight of the elders if Israel. 7 And he called the name of the place Massah, and Meribah, because of the chiding of the children of Israel, and because they tempted the LORD, saying, Is the LORD among us, or not?" Exodus 17:1-7

Here is the cross reference, which identifies the God of Abraham by the character name of Christ (Χριστος):

"4 And did all drink the same spiritual drink: for they drank of that spiritual Rock that followed them: and that Rock was Christ [Χριστος]. 1 Corinthians 10:4

So, as per the above verses, the LORD God of Abraham was the One who led the children of Israel in a cloud from the fields of Raamses through the Red Sea, fed them, and gave them water to drink from rocks. And according to the prophet of the LORD, the God of Abraham is identified by the name of Christ (Χριστος), as we know Him now in the New Testament.

And to further confirm the fact that the God of Abraham is Christ the LORD God of Israel who is referred to in 1 Corinthians 10:1-4, here is the Greek text. Notice Christ's name: "Χριστος" (Christ.)

"4 και παντες το αυτο πνευματικον ποτον επιον διοτι επινον απο πνευματικης πετρας [Exodus 17:1-6] ακολουθουσης η δε πετρα [Rock] ητο ο Χριστος [Christ]" (Α Κορινθιου 10:4 (Βιβλικη Εταιρεια)

And the Old King James Version of the above verse reads as follows:

"4 And did all drink the same spiritual drink; for they

The God of Israel

drank of that spiritual Rock [Exodus 17:1-6] that followed them: and that Rock [πετρα] was Christ [Χριστος]" (1 Corinthians 10:4).

In addition, we can also conclude, as per the Torah, it was Christ (Χριστος) the God of Abraham who led the children of Israel and delivered them from *the poisonous snakes*. Moses wrote:

"4 And they [the children of Israel] journeyed from mount Hor by the way of the Red Sea, to compass the land of Edom: and the soul of the people was much discouraged because of the way. 5 And the people spake against God, and against Moses, Wherefore have ye [all of you] brought us up out of Egypt to die into the wilderness? for there is no bread, neither is there any water; and our soul loatheth this light bread. 6 And the LORD sent fiery serpents among the people, and they bit the people; and much people of Israel died." Numbers 21:4-6

Here is the cross reference, which identifies the God of Abraham by the character name of Christ (Χριστον):

"8 Neither let us commit fornication, as some of them committed, and fell in one day three and twenty thousand. 9 Neither let us tempt Christ [Χριστον], as some of them also tempted; and were destroyed of serpents." 1 Corinthians 10:8, 9

As you have read, the children of Israel tempted Christ the God of Abraham and of Israel; and when Christ departed from amongst them and removed His divine protection from the camp of Israel, Satan and his evil angels coerced the scorpions and the venomous snakes to sink their

The God of Israel

fangs into the children of Israel creating terror, havoc, confusion, and death in the camp of Israel.

Again, to confirm the fact that it was the God of Abraham, better known in the New Testament by the name of Christ (Χριστον), who was tempted by the children of Israel, here is the Greek text:

"9 Μηδε ας πειραζωμεν τον Χριστον [Christ], καθως και τινες αυτων επειρασαν,   και απωλεσθησαν υπο των οφεων." Α Κορινθιους 10:9 (Βιβλικη Εταιρεια)

And here is the Old King James Version (OKJV).

"9 Neither let us tempt Christ [Χριστον], as some of them also tempted; and were destroyed of serpents." 1 Corinthians 10:9

If you were to read the Torah (five books of Moses) and summarize the events of the children of Israel, from Egypt and all the way into the Promised Land, you would probably summarize them as the Psalmist had done in Psalms seventy-eight or you would compress their activities as Nehemiah had done in Nehemiah chapter nine or you would condense the events even further as Apostle Paul did in first Corinthians chapter ten.

And in those three summaries of the Torah, you would have noticed, the Scripture references reveal to us how the God of Abraham (Genesis 3:14, 15) went to Egypt with Moses and Aaron (Exodus 3:8), to free the children of Israel (Jacob) from their bondage, how He became the God of Israel (Exodus 6:7), and how the God of Israel lead the children of Israel in a cloud, fed them, gave them water to drink, and protected them all the way into the Promised Land.

In addition, the above cross references that are provided by Apostle Paul, from the Torah, also reveal to us that the God of Israel of the Old Testament is the same God of Israel in the New Testament who is identified by Apostle Paul in 1 Corinthians 10:1-9 by the names of "Rock," "God," and "Christ" which means "Messiah" (John 1:41).

Therefore, as per Apostle Paul's revelation, in 1 Corinthians 10:1-9, the God of Israel and the God of Abraham is the same person whose name is Christ (Χριστος); and that, as per Scripture (vs. 4, 5, 9), is an unavoidable fact.

* Therefore as per the above Scriptures, we can refer to Jesus Christ by the following names, "the God of Abraham, Isaac, and Jacob," "the God of Israel," and by the name of "the Rock" because Christ brought water from rocks to quench the thirst of the children of Israel and their livestock.

Where was the God of Israel Worshipped?

After the children of Israel removed the majority of the pagan tribes from the Promised Land, Joshua erected the Sanctuary of Christ (Χριστος) the LORD God of Israel in a place called "Shiloh." And from there, the elders of the children of Israel made many decisions. And one of those decisions was the inheritance of the land. And when the Promised Land was divided and given to each tribe of Israel, with the exception of the tribe of Levi, the children of Israel possessed their inheritance and began to settle down in their homes.

At the beginning of their settlement in their inheritance, especially those who were in the fringe of the Promised Land, they were very concerned about their peripheral enemies who were eager to kill them or enslave them, as past experience had revealed.

Where was the God of Israel Worshipped?

But, their worries were further compounded because Christ the God of Israel expected the children of Israel to worship Him by attending the festivities three times a year before Him in a place called "Shiloh" where His Sanctuary was erected.

How could the children of Israel leave their homes unattended, unprotected by human souls, and for some, travel for five to six days to Shiloh in order to attend the special feast days?

What would happen to their homes, livestock, and land?

Although Joshua and the priests had ensured them that Christ the God of Israel had made the children of Israel repulsive to their enemies and therefore they would not attack their homes, it was still very hard to pack up and leave their homes during those three festive occasions and travel to Shiloh to worship Christ the God of Israel who resided in His Sanctuary above the "mercy seat."

You must remember; the children of Israel were surrounded by fierce pagan tribes and especially those pagan tribes that were dislodged from their land on which the children of Israel were sitting on.

And even more worrisome was the fact that while the children of Israel went to Shiloh, three times during the year to worship Christ the God of Israel, what was to prevent their enemies from attacking them. They would be at their most vulnerable state during those festive days?

As I stated before, at the beginning of their inheritance, it was very hard for the children of Israel to leave their homes unprotected and unattended. They did because that was the directive from the Levi priests. They told the people what Christ the God of Israel had promised. Christ the God of Israel said,

"24 I will cast out the nations before

Where was the God of Israel Worshipped?

> thee [you], and enlarge thy [your] borders:
> neither shall any man desire thy [your] land,
> when thou [you] shalt go up to appear before
> the LORD thy [your] God thrice in the year."
> Exodus 34:24

Even when the children of Israel heard the LORD'S promise, many were still very skeptical; nonetheless, they did leave their homes and did attend the solemn holy days in Shiloh before Christ the God of Israel.

And when the children of Israel returned to their homes, they found everything intact the way they left them! After experiencing couple of years of the LORD'S protection upon their homes, the children of Israel rejoiced, and it became easier to attend the festivities in Shiloh, each successive year.

The Passover, the Pentecost, and the Day of Atonement, which was followed very closely by the Feast of Tabernacles, were the main events.

The Passover commemorated the solemn deliverance from the yoke of bondage by the hand of Pharaoh. It was celebrated on the fourteenth day of the first month (April), followed by the wave offering. (Exodus 12; Numbers 9:1-14.)

The Pentecost took place fifty days after the wave offering was celebrated, which followed the Passover (Leviticus 23:15-21).

The wave offering consisted of omer of barley or wave sheaf that was waved before Christ the God of Israel (Leviticus 23:10-14).

The Day of Atonement took place in the seventh month (October) and on the fourteenth day of that month. It was the most solemn occasion because it was the time when the sins of the children of Israel were covered; and the Sanctuary was cleansed by placing the sins on a scapegoat and sending

Where was the God of Israel Worshipped?

it in the wilderness to die. (See Leviticus 16; 23:27-32.)

The Feast of the Tabernacles was celebrated as a continuation of the Day of Atonement (Leviticus 23:34-43; Numbers 29:12-34).

It was during the above festivities where the following events took place, which reveal where the children of Israel worshipped the God of Israel. But more precisely, during the administration of Eli the high priest who was a descendant from Aaron's youngest son Ithamar. It was during the end of the Judges that Eli had become the high priest of the tabernacle (Sanctuary) that was placed in a place called "Shiloh" by Joshua.

The events, which follow take place about a year before Hannah gave birth to Samuel. The narrative is as follows: There was a man from the tribe of Ephraim who lived in a city with an Egyptian name of "Ramathaimzophim"—quite a mouthful don't you think? —you can call the city "Ramah" if you prefer?

Nonetheless, this man whose name was Elkanah, had two wives; and one of his wives was childless. Her name was Hannah. This man came yearly from his home, which was in the territory of Ephraim, "to worship and to sacrifice unto the LORD of hosts in Shiloh" (v.3). Shiloh is about twenty miles north of Jerusalem. "And her adversary [Satan] also provoked her sore, for to make her fret, because the LORD had shut up her womb" (6).

"10 And she was in bitterness of soul, and prayed unto the LORD, and wept sore. 11 And she vowed a vow, and said, O LORD of hosts, if thou [You] wilt indeed look on the affliction of thine [your] handmaid, and remember me, and not forget thine [your] handmaid, but wilt give unto thine handmaid a man child, then I will give him unto the LORD all the days of his life, and there shall no razor come upon his head" (1 Samuel 1:10, 11).

Where was the God of Israel Worshipped?

"12 And it came to pass, as she continued praying before the LORD, that Eli marked her mouth. 13 Now Hannah, she spake in her heart; only her lips moved, but her voice was not heard: therefore Eli thought she had been drunken. 14 And Eli said unto her, How long wilt thou [you] be drunken? put away thy [your] wine from thee [you]. 15 And Hannah answered and said, No, my lord, I am a woman of a sorrowful spirit; I have drunk neither wine nor strong drink, but have poured out my soul before the LORD. 16 Count not thine [your] handmaid for a daughter of Belial; for out of the abundance of my complaint and grief have I spoken hitherto. 17 Then Eli answered and said, Go in peace; and the God of Israel grant thee thy [your] petition that thou [you] hast asked of Him" (1 Samuel 1:12-17).

To make the story short, a year later Hannah conceived a son; and she named him Samuel. And when Samuel was weaned, "24 she took him up with her, with three bullocks, and one ephah of flour, and a bottle of wine, and brought him [Samuel] unto the house of the LORD in Shiloh: and the child was young. 25 And they slew a bullock, and brought the child to Eli." And Hannah said to Eli the priest, "28 I have lent him [Samuel] to the LORD; as long as he liveth he shall be lent to the LORD. And he worshipped the LORD there" (1 Samuel 1:24, 25, 28).

"11 And Elkanah [Hannah's husband] went to Ramah to his house. And the child did minister unto the LORD before Eli the priest" (1 Samuel 2:11). Ramah is about seven miles northwest of Jerusalem.

"19 And Samuel grew, and the LORD was with him, and did let none of His words fall to the ground. 20 And all Israel from Dan even to Beer-sheba knew that Samuel was established to be a prophet of the LORD" (1 Samuel 3:19, 20).

Where was the God of Israel Worshipped?

The area that is mentioned in the above verses that the children of Israel occupied, "from Dan even to Beer-sheba," refers to the area north of the Sea of Galilee and all the way down on both sides of the River Jordan to the Negeb, which is south of the Dead Sea. And from this area, the children of Israel came to Shiloh to worship and sacrifice to Christ the God of Israel who dwelt in "between the two cherubims," above "the mercy seat," in His Sanctuary, which was pitched in a place called "Shiloh" (1 Samuel 1:3; 4:4).

Furthermore, as you have observed in the above presentation, the children of Israel also knew Christ "the God of Israel" (1 Samuel 1:17) by the name of "the LORD of hosts" and referred to Him as such (1 Samuel 1:3; 4:4; 15:2).

Thus, for nearly three hundred and thirty years, the children of Israel came to the Sanctuary in Shiloh for all of the festivities that took place there during the year, and worshipped in the presence of Christ the LORD of hosts who "4 dwelleth between the cherubims" (1 Samuel 4:4), in a place called "Shiloh."

And because Christ the LORD of hosts was worshipped by the children of Israel in a place called Shiloh, the name of "the LORD of hosts" became synonymous with the name of "Shiloh."

In fact, Christ the God of Israel was identified by Jacob by the name of "Shiloh" over two hundred and thirty years before Joshua erected Christ's Sanctuary in Shiloh—quite astonishing revelation don't you think!

Jacob said to his son Judah,

"10 The scepter shall not depart from Judah, nor a lawgiver from between his feet, until Shiloh come; and unto Him shall the gathering of the people be. 11 Binding His foal unto the vine, and His ass's colt unto the choice vine." Genesis 49:10, 11 (See Matthew 21:5 for the cross reference where Shiloh is identified by the name of Christ.)

Therefore, Christ's character name (the LORD of hosts) was synonymous with the name of "Shiloh" because Christ the LORD of hosts was worshipped in His Sanctuary in a place called Shiloh.

*   Therefore as per Scripture, we can refer to Jesus Christ by the following names, "the God of Abraham, Isaac, and Jacob," "the God of Israel," "the Rock," "the LORD of hosts," and by the name of "Shiloh" because Christ was worshipped by the children of Israel, in the Promised Land, in a place called "Shiloh."

The King of Israel Rejected

Shortly after the activities in the previous chapter, almost all of the children of Israel fell into apostasy, which was in the middle of the 11th century B.C., due to the influence of the surrounding pagan nations and because of the unrestrained evil acts of the leaders and the priests of Israel. And because of their apostate condition, the children of Israel did not want to reform or give up their evil ways; therefore, Christ the LORD of hosts removed the restraint from the Philistines and the divine protection from the children of Israel, and when that occurred, the Philistines declared war on the children of Israel by killing four thousand foot soldiers on their first strike.

But before the Philistines killed thirty thousand Hebrews, took the Ark of the Covenant, burnt the Sanctuary in Shiloh, and the city of Shiloh, the children of Israel in their apostate condition did not realize when Hophni and Phinehas prayed for victory over the Philistine army that there was no response from Christ the LORD of hosts before they took the Ark of the Covenant to the battlefield.

The King of Israel Rejected

They simply assumed that Christ the LORD of hosts would be with them as He was with their forefathers. Therefore, in confidence they took the Ark of the Covenant to the battlefield. "5 And when the ark of the covenant of the LORD came into the camp, all Israel shouted with a great shout, so that the earth rang again. 6 And when the Philistines heard the noise of the shout, they said, What meaneth the noise of this great shout in the camp of the Hebrews? And they understood that the ark of the LORD was come into the camp. 7 And the Philistines were afraid, for they said, God is come into the camp. And they said, Woe unto us! for there hath not been such a thing heretofore. 8 Woe unto us! who shall deliver us out of the hand of these mighty Gods? these are the Gods that smote the Egyptians with all the plagues in the wilderness." 1 Samuel 4:5-8

And the leaders of the Philistines said to their solders, "9 Be strong, and quit yourselves like men, O ye Philistines, that ye be not servants unto the Hebrews, as they have been to you: quit yourselves like men, and fight.

"10 And the Philistines fought, and Israel was smitten, and they fled every man into this tent: and there was a very great slaughter: for there fell of Israel thirty thousand footmen. 11 And the ark of God was taken" by the Philistines. 1 Samuel 4:9-11

As the men of Israel fell right and left in the battlefield and their men dwindled, many foot soldiers fled the scene and escaped the slaughter. One such man, a Benjemite, came into Shiloh and told the survivors what happened. And when Eli the priest heard about the commotion, he wanted the report to be brought to him. And when the man arrived in Eli's house in Ramah, he told Eli that the Ark of the Covenant was taken by the Philistines and his two sons, Hophni and Phinehas were killed; Eli, in his overweight

The King of Israel Rejected

condition, when he tried to get up abruptly from his chair, he fell backwards, broke his neck, and died.

Eli was ninety-eight years old when he died

Meanwhile Christ the LORD of hosts plagued the Philistine people and their gods in the areas where the Ark of the Covenant was taken. The record says, "1 And the Philistines took the ark of God, and brought it from Ebenezer as unto Ashdod. 2 When the Philistines took the ark of God, they brought it into the houses of Dagon, and set it by Dagon.

"3 And when they of Ashdod arose early on the morrow, behold, Dagon [their fish god] was fallen upon his face to the earth before the ark of the LORD. And they took Dagon, and set him in his place again. 4 And when they arose early on the morrow morning, behold, Dagon was fallen upon his face to the ground before the ark of the LORD; and the head of Dagon and both the palms of his hands were cut off upon the threshold; only the stump of Dagon was left to him. 5 Therefore neither the priests of Dagon, nor any that come into Dagon's house, tread on the threshold of Dagon in Ashdod unto this day. 6 But the hand of the LORD was heavy upon them of Ashdod, and He destroyed them, and smote them with emerods, even Ashdod and the coasts thereof. 7 And when the men of Ashdod saw that it was so, they said, The ark of the God of Israel shall not abide with us: for His hand is sore upon us, and upon Dagon our god. 8 They sent therefore and gathered all the lords of the Philistines unto them, and said, What shall we do with the ark of the God of Israel? And they answered, Let the ark of the God of Israel be carried about into Gath. And they carried the ark of the God of Israel about thither. 9 And it was so, that, after they had carried it about, the hand of the LORD was against the city with a very great destruction: and He smote the men of the

The King of Israel Rejected

city, both small and great, and they had emerods in their secret parts.

"10 Therefore they sent the ark of God to Ekron. And it came to pass, as the ark of God came to Ekron, that the Ekronites cried out, saying, They have brought about the ark of the God of Israel to us, to slay us and our people. 11 So they sent and gathered together all the lords of the Philistines, and said, Send away the ark of the God of Israel, and let it go again to his own place, that it slay us not, and our people: for there was a deadly destruction throughout all the city; the hand of God was very heavy there. 12 And the men that died not were smitten with the emerods: and the cry of the city went up to heaven." 1 Samuel 5:1-12

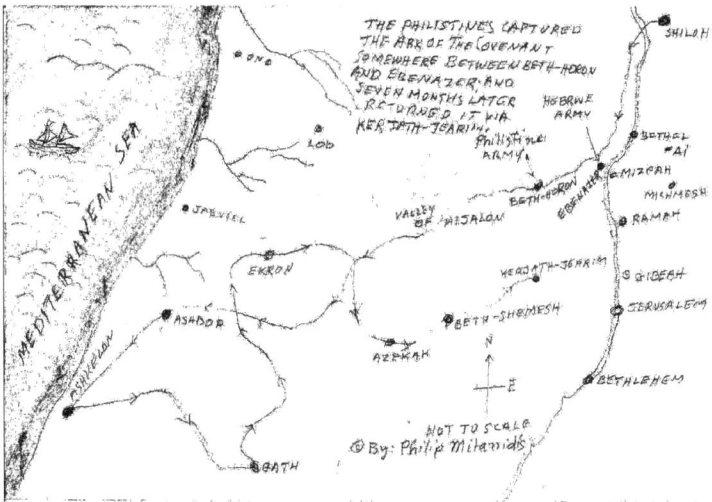

After seven months of excruciating plagues and death in all of the areas where the Ark of the Covenant was taken, finally the Philistine authorities consulted with their pagan priests and asked them what they should do to stop the plagues and the deaths of their people?

The Philistine pagan priests recommended to the

The King of Israel Rejected

Philistine leaders that they should return the Ark of the Covenant by placing it on a new cart and pulled by two cows that have not had a yoke on them and recently gave birth to their calfs and a trespass offering consisting of "4 Five golden emerods, and five golden mice, according to the number of the lords of the Philistines: for one plague was on you all, and on your lords. 5 Wherefore ye [all of you] shall make images of your emerods, and images of your mice that mar the land; and ye shall give glory unto the God of Israel: peradventure He will lighten His hand from off you, and from off your gods, and from off your land." 1 Samuel 6:4, 5

But the Philistine leaders, when they heard the proposal by their pagan priests, they were furious because they did not want to acknowledge the God of Israel or give Him a trespass offering for taking the Ark of the Covenant.

Then the pagan priests said to the Philistine leaders, "6 Wherefore then do ye harden your hearts, as the Egyptians and Pharaoh hardened their hearts? when He had wrought wonderfully among them, did they not let the people go, and they departed?" 1 Samuel 6:6

Realizing that the Philistines, like the Egyptians, could not win a battle with Christ the God of Israel, they finally returned the Ark of the Covenant as their pagan priests suggested and discontinued the war temporarily with the Hebrews. The Ark of the Covenant was placed in Abinidabs house because the Sanctuary of Christ the LORD of hosts was destroyed in Shiloh.

Meanwhile, after Eli's death, Samuel took over his duties. Eventually, he was recognized as the prophet of Christ the LORD of hosts and became the judge of Israel. Samuel judged Israel mainly from his house, which was in Ramah, but did travel from place to place in the Promised Land to look after the affairs of the children of Israel. And when Samuel became old, he placed his two sons in charge, but

The King of Israel Rejected

the people of Israel did not approve of Samuel's decision because his two sons were evil and therefore they did not want to be judged by them.

They said to Samuel, "5 Behold, thou art old, and thy [your] sons walk not in thy ways: now make us a king to judge us like all the nations.

"6 But the thing displeased Samuel, when they said, Give us a king to judge us. And Samuel prayed unto the LORD. 7 And the LORD said unto Samuel, Hearken unto the voice of the people in all that they say unto thee [you]: for they have not rejected thee [you], but they have rejected Me, that I should not reign over them. 8 According to all the works which they have done since the day that I brought them up out of Egypt even unto this day, wherewith they have forsaken Me, and served other gods, so do they also unto thee [you]." 1 Samuel 8:5-8

Christ the God of Israel was rejected as their King long before this incident took place, therefore Samuel was assured that the rejection was not about him; it was an excuse, which they used to get a human king like the pagan nations that were around them. They said to Samuel, it did not matter what he thought or said, they were still going to appoint a king over them.

Although the apostate hearts of the children of Israel rejected Christ the LORD of hosts as their King, Christ told Samuel to go ahead and give them their king.

Finally, the children of Israel chose Saul the Benjemite whose stature was fair to look at and his shoulders stood taller than the heads of the rest of the people in Israel. But because Saul was not chosen by Christ the LORD of hosts, Samuel privately approached Saul, poured oil over his head, kissed him, and said to him, "1 It is not because the LORD hath anointed thee [you] to be captain over His inheritance?" 1 Samuel 10:1; it is because the people hath chosen you.

The King of Israel Rejected

But, in order to make Saul a king over the children of
Israel officially, he requested that all of the leaders of Israel
tell their people of the crowning that is going to take place in
Gilgal. "15 And all the people went to Gilgal; and there they
made Saul king before the LORD in Gilgal; and there they
sacrificed sacrifices of the peace offerings before the LORD;
and there Saul and all the men of Israel rejoiced greatly." 1
Samuel 11:15

"1 And Samuel said unto all Israel, Behold, I have
hearkened unto your voice in all that ye said unto me, and
have made a king over you. 2 And now, behold, the king
walketh before you: and I am old and grayheaded; and,
behold, my sons are with you: and I have walked before you
from my childhood unto this day. 3 Behold, here I am:
witness against me before the LORD, and before His
anointed: whose ox have I taken? or whose ass have I taken?
or whom have I defrauded? whom have I oppressed? or of
whose hand have I received any bribe to blind mine eyes
therewith? and I will restore it you. 4 And they said, Thou
[you] hast not defrauded us, nor oppressed us, neither hast
thou taken ought of any man's hand.

"5 And he said unto them, The LORD is witness against
you, and His anointed is witness this day, that ye [all of you]
have not found ought in my hand. And they answered; He is
witness.

"6 And Samuel said unto the people, It is the LORD that
advanced Moses and Aaron, and that brought your fathers
up out of the land of Egypt. 7 Now therefore stand still, that
I may reason with you before the LORD of all the righteous
acts of the LORD, which He did to you and to your fathers.
8 When Jacob was come into Egypt, and your fathers cried
unto the LORD, then the LORD sent Moses and Aaron,
which brought forth your fathers out of Egypt, and made
them dwell in this place. 9 And when they forgat the LORD

The King of Israel Rejected

their God, He sold them into the hand of Sisera, captain of the host of Hazor, and into the hand of the Philistines, and into the hand of the king of Moab, and they fought against them. 10 And they cried unto the LORD, and said, We have sinned, because we have forsaken the LORD, and have served Baalim and Ashtaroth: but now deliver us out of the hand of our enemies, and we will serve thee. 11 And the LORD sent Jerubbaal, and Bedan, and Jephthah, and Samuel, and delivered you out of the hand of your enemies, on every side, and ye dwelled safe.

"12 And when ye saw that Nahash the king of the children of Ammon came against you, ye said unto me, Nay; but a king shall reign over us: when the LORD your God was your King.

"13 Now therefore behold the king whom ye have chosen, and whom ye have desired! and, behold, the LORD hath set a king over you. 14 If ye [all of you] will fear the LORD, and serve Him, and obey His voice, and not rebel against the commandment of the LORD, then shall both ye and also the king that reigneth over you continue following the LORD your God: 15 But if ye will not obey the voice of the LORD, but rebel against the commandment of the LORD, then shall the hand of the LORD be against you, as it was against your fathers." 1 Samuel 12:1-15

As you probably already know, Saul fell into apostasy. He had a problem completing the assignments that were given to him by Christ the LORD of hosts. Saul would say that he would accomplish the assignment as the LORD of hosts requested, but to only do the opposite. Although Saul was forgiven over and over again, his promissory word finally reached a point where Saul could not be trusted any more.

The King of Israel Rejected

But another chance was given to King Saul to redeem himself and start doing what Christ the LORD of hosts wanted him to do. Samuel said to Saul, "2 Thus saith the LORD of hosts, I remember that which Amalek did to Israel, how he laid wait for him in the way, when he came up from Egypt. 3 Now go and smite Amalek, and utterly destroy all that they have, and spare them not; but slay both man and woman, infant and suckling, ox and sheep, camel and ass." 1 Samuel 15:2, 3

Well King Saul promised to execute the LORD'S command, but when he saw some of the animals in such a healthy condition he not only spared them but also took them and the king with him. And when Samuel asked him what was the meaning of his insubordinate acts, Saul said to him that he took the animals for an offering unto the LORD.

Then Samuel said to Saul, "22 Hath the LORD as great delight in burnt offerings and sacrifices, as in obeying the voice of the LORD? Behold, to obey is better than sacrifice, and to hearken than the fat of rams. 23 For rebellion is as the sin of witchcraft, and stubbornness is as iniquity and idolatry." Then Samuel had the unpleasant task of telling King Saul,

> "23 Because thou [you] hast rejected the word of the LORD, He hath also rejected thee [you] from being king." 1 Samuel 15:22, 23

"27 And Samuel turned about to go away, he [Saul] laid hold upon the [Samuel's] skirt of his mantle, and it rent. 28 And Samuel said unto him [Saul], The LORD hath rent the kingdom of Israel from thee [you] this day, and hath given it to a neighbour of thine, that is better than thou [you]." "35 And Samuel came no more to see Saul until the day of his death: nevertheless Samuel mourned for Saul: and the

LORD repented that He had made Saul king over Israel." 1 Samuel 15:27-35

The children of Israel could have averted all of the horrible ordeals that they went through with their chosen king; if they had retained Christ the LORD of hosts as their King; or if they asked Christ the LORD of hosts to set a king over them. But an apostate heart wants what it wants and that is what it got an apostate king.

In the previous chapters, Apostle Paul identified Christ by the name of "the God of Israel," and then, Samuel identified Christ by the names of "the LORD of hosts" and "Shiloh"; now Samuel identifies Christ the LORD of hosts as the rejected "King of Israel" (1 Samuel 8:7; 15:2; 12:12) who use to dwelt above "the mercy seat" and "in between the two cherubims" of the Ark of the Covenant (1 Samuel 4:4).

* Therefore as per Scripture, we can refer to Jesus Christ by the following names, "the God of Abraham, Isaac, and Jacob," "the God of Israel," "the Rock," "the LORD of hosts," "Shiloh" and by the name of "the King of Israel" who dwelt in between the two cherubims of the Ark of the Covenant.

David Crowned a King

After King Saul was rejected by Christ the LORD of hosts as the king of Israel, instead of repenting, he continued in his insubordinate actions by pleasing his subjects instead of Christ the LORD of hosts. And when the Philistines came by the thousands to eradicate Israel, Saul instead of repenting, he stooped so low that he did the unthinkable by seeking counsel from a devil-possessed woman in Endor.

After meeting with the witch of Endor, the following day Saul and his three sons were killed in the battle with the Philistines.

It did not have to be that way; but a proud heart, it appears, it rarely wants to admit that it is wrong and therefore the need to repent is rejected at any cost.

David Crowned a King

But before King Saul died on the battlefield, Christ the LORD of hosts told Samuel to go and anoint David to be the king of Israel. Samuel went and did as Christ the LORD of hosts requested and made David the king of Israel. But, Saul did not want to give up his throne and therefore continued to persecute David his son-in-law. In fact Saul made it a point to hunt David in order to kill him because he thought that David was trying to kill him and take his throne. But the protective hand of Christ the LORD of hosts was upon David, until finally, just before Samuel died, Saul said to David, "21 Swear now therefore unto me by the LORD, that thou [you] wilt not cut off my seed after me, and that thou wilt not destroy my name out of my father's house. 22 And David sware unto Saul. And Saul went home; but David and his men gat them up unto the hold." 1 Samuel 24:21, 22

Although David kept his word, Saul did not; therefore after Samuel's death, David left Hebron and went to the wilderness of Paran, which was in the Negeb. And when David returned from Paran "1 David said in his heart, I shall now perish one day by the hand of Saul: there is nothing better for me than that I should speedily escape into the land of the Philistines; and Saul shall despair of me, to seek me any more in any coast of Israel: so shall I escape out of his hand. 2 And David arose, and he passed over with the six hundred men that were with him unto Achish, the son of Maoch, king of Gath. 3 And David dwelt with Achish at Gath, he and his men, every man with his household, even David with his two wives, Ahinoam the Jezreelitess, and Abigail the Carmelitess, Nabal's wife. 4 And it was told Saul that David was fled to Gath: and he sought no more again for him.

"5 And David said unto Achish, If I have now found grace in thine eyes, let them give me a place in some town in

David Crowned a King

the country, that I may dwell there: for why should thy [your] servant dwell in the royal city with thee [you]? 6 Then Achish gave him Ziklag that day; wherefore Ziklag pertaineth unto the kings of Judah unto this day." 1 Samuel 27:1-6

But David's troubles were not over yet; after few bumps on the way, the Philistines gathered themselves in a place called Shunem to go to war with the children of Israel. And since Achish was a Philistine, he was summond to gather his forces and meet with the rest of the leaders of Philistine to get ready for war. And when the Philistine leaders saw Achish with David and his men with him, they questioned Achish why he had brought David with him? He said to them that David and his men are going to fight the Hebrews with me. But the Philistines were very uncomfortable because they feared that maybe David might change his mind and fight against them. Therefore the princes of the Philistines told Achish to send David and his men back to their homes.

Achish went to David and told him what the princes of the Philistines said to him. The next morning, the Philistine army went and gathered in Jezreel; and David and his men, got ready for their three days trip to Ziklag. When they arrived to their homes in Ziklag, to their surprise, they found the town invaded and burnt by the Amalekites.

Meanwhile because of the sheer numbers of the Philistines, Saul was afraid of losing the war and his life. In desperation, Saul inquired of the LORD of hosts as to what he should do? But Christ the LORD of hosts would not respond to Saul's prayers because he would not repent. In extreme anxiety, King Saul turned to Satan for advice. Contrary to Christ's will, Saul went to see the witch of Endor. And when he arrived there, he was given the bad news. He was told by the satanic spirit, who impersonated

David Crowned a King

Samuel that tomorrow the Philistines are going to win the war over Israel, and his three sons are going to die in the war with him, and "be with me," added the evil satanic spirit.

The devastating news left King Saul helpless and weak and refused to eat and drink in order to replenish his strength.

Eventually after continuous coaxing, Saul did eat; but in his stubborn pride, he irrationally went to war with the Philistines; and as the evil spirit had said to him, he and his three sons were killed and Israel lost the war.

Learning that Israel lost their king and the war to the Philistines, David and his men left Ziklag and went to Hebron to live. There the men of Judah made David to be their king. And eventually, the children of Israel decided to acknowledge David as their king also. And after seven years, David moved to Jerusalem, built a palace of cedar wood for himself and started to reign over the children of Israel from there.

But David felt uncomfortable living in his palace. He called Nathan the prophet of the LORD of hosts and said to him, "2 See now, I dwell in an house of cedar, but the ark of God dwelleth within curtains. 3 And Nathan said to the king, Go, do all that is in thine heart; for the LORD is with thee [you].

"4 And it came to pass that night, that the word of the LORD came unto Nathan, saying, 5 Go and tell my servant David, Thus saith the LORD, Shalt thou [you] build Me an house for Me to dwell in? 6 Whereas I have not dwelt in any house since the time that I brought up the children of Israel

David Crowned a King

out of Egypt, even to this day, but have walked in a tent and in a tabernacle. 7 In all the places wherein I have walked with all the children of Israel spake I a word with any of the tribes of Israel, whom I commanded to feed My people Israel, saying, Why build ye [all of you] not Me an house of cedar? 8 Now therefore so shalt thou say unto My servant David, Thus saith the LORD of hosts, I took thee from the sheepcote, from following the sheep, to be ruler over My people, over Israel:"

Then, the unexpected was told to King David by Christ the LORD of hosts. "12 And when thy [your] days be fulfilled, and thou [you] shalt sleep [die] with thy [your] fathers, I will set up thy seed after thee, which shall proceed out of thy [your] bowels, and I will establish his kingdom. 13 He shall build an house for My name" (2 Samuel 7:2-8, 12, 13).

Seeing that King David was not allowed to build the Sanctuary for Christ the LORD of hosts, he had a tent built for the Ark of the Covenant to house it in Jerusalem. So he set out to bring the Ark of the Covenant from Abinadab's house to Jerusalem. Unfortunately, on the way to Jerusalem, Uzzah touched the Ark and died. In fear King David diverted the Ark of the Covenant away from Jerusalem to Obededom's house the Gittite, which was between Kiriath-jearim and Jerusalem and stayed there for three months. And when David was told that Obededom was blessed because of the Ark, King David decided to bring it into Jerusalem and put it into the tent, which he had built for it. And just before the Ark of the Covenant, with its procession, entered through Jerusalem's gates, King David said,

"7 Left up your heads, O ye gates; and be ye lift up, ye everlasting doors; and the King of glory shall come in. 8 Who is this King of glory? The LORD strong and mighty, the LORD mighty in battle. 9 Lift up your

David Crowned a King

heads, O ye gates; even lift them up, ye everlasting doors; and the King of glory shall come in."

Then David asked, "10 Who is this King of glory?" David answered, "The LORD of hosts, He is the King of glory. Selah." Psalms 24:7-10

As you have read in verse ten above, King David identifies the Individual who dwelt in between the two cherubims of the Ark of the Covenant by the name of "the King of Israel." And David also identified "the King of Israel" by the name of "the LORD of hosts."

David shouted, "10 Who is this King of glory?" And then, David declared, "The LORD of hosts, He is the King of glory. Selah" (Psalms 24:10).

As per the above Scripture reference, "the King of glory" is "the LORD of hosts." And as per the previous chapters, Christ is identified by the name of "the LORD of hosts." Therefore, Christ the LORD of hosts, who was rejected up until the death of King Saul, as the King of Israel, now since David became the King of Israel, he accepted and reinstated Christ as the King of Israel (Psalm 5:2) by declaring Him before the children of Israel by the name of "the King of glory." And when King David declared Christ the LORD of hosts as their King, the Ark of the Covenant went through the gates of Jerusalem with the Levite priests and was placed in a tent, which King David had made.

- Therefore as per Scripture, we can refer to Jesus Christ by the following names, "the God of Abraham, Isaac, and Jacob," "the God of Israel," "the Rock," "the LORD of hosts," "Shiloh," "the King of Israel," and by the name of "the King of glory."

Where did Isaiah See the King of Israel Sitting?

King David reigned over the children of Israel for forty years (seven years in Hebron and thirty-three years. in Jerusalem); he died in 971 BC. After his death, his Son Solomon began to reign on his throne for forty years also. Solomon died in 931 BC.

Although the record states that the borders of Israel kept expanding during the reign of King David and King Solomon because they and the children of Israel did the will of Christ the LORD of hosts, the expansion did not last because Solomon, in his twilight years, chose to reject Christ the King of glory and began to worship the pagan gods of his multiple wives. And because he fell into apostasy, Christ the King of Israel said to him that his kingdom will be divided in to two (the house of Israel—10 tribes and the house of Judah—2 tribes).

And so it was, the house of Israel and the house of Judah were like roller coasters. At one point, they would repent, but most of the time, they remained in apostasy. And, in their apostate state, they gradually lost the majority of the Promised Land, dwindled in numbers, and they both lost their kingdoms.

The house of Israel lost its kingdom in 722 BC during the reign of King Hoshea because they were entrenched in pagan worship.

And during that period of time (722 BC), the attack by the Assyrians, upon the house of Israel, left the house of Judah vulnerable because during that period of time the house of Judah and their king (Ahaz) were also worshipping idols.

But, as always, Christ the King of Israel sent His prophets to speak to them and waited compassionately for them to repent and return to Him. One of those prophets, who was sent to them, was Isaiah.

Isaiah, the prophet of Christ the LORD of hosts, was the son of Amon and of the royal line. His ministry spanned

David Crowned a King

through the reign of four kings—Uzziah, Jotham, Ahaz, and Hezekiah. He was called to the prophetic office towards the close of the reign of Uzziah (Azariah 790-737), as Isaiah's presentation indicates. This would place the call of Isaiah between the years 750-739 B.C.

Therefore the following vision took place as it is recorded during the year Uzziah the king died. Isaiah starts by saying, "1 In the year that king Uzziah died I saw also the LORD sitting upon a throne, high and lifted up, and His train filled the temple. 2 Above it stood the seraphims; each one had six wings; with twain he covered his face, and with twain he covered his feet, and with twain he did fly. 3 And one cried unto another, and said, Holy, holy, holy, is the LORD of hosts: the whole earth is full of His glory. 4 And the posts of the door moved at the voice of him that cried, and the house was filled with smoke. 5 Then said I, Woe is me! for I am undone; because I am a man of unclean lips, and I dwell in the midst of a people of unclean lips: for mine eyes have seen the King,   the LORD of hosts." Isaiah 6:1-5

In the above verses, Isaiah "saw the LORD sitting upon a throne" (v.1), and a number of activities taking place around His throne. And one of the seraphims saying, "Holy, holy, holy, is the LORD of hosts" "the whole earth is full of His glory" (v.3). And then Isaiah adds, "mine eyes have seen the King, the LORD of hosts" (v.5).

There is no confusion in the above verses. Isaiah plainly states that the LORD who was sitting on His throne, in heaven, is the "King" of Israel; and further identifies Him by the name of "the LORD of hosts."

So, who is "the King of Israel" and by what other name does He identify Himself? ____When Christ started his ministry, He focused His Gospel message to the house of Judah (Jews) because He had promised through His prophets that He

Moses Wrote About Me By: *Philip Mitanidis* _____ 157

Where did Isaiah See the King of Israel Sitting?

would come to them in the flesh, save them from their sins, and work with them to save the rest of the sinners of the world by offering Himself a sacrifice. Therefore when Christ went into their synagogues, He revealed to the priest, scribes, and leaders of Israel that He was "the King of Israel" and the "Messiah" (Christ) of whom the prophets wrote about. But as it turned out, many of the powerful leaders of the house of Judah did not want to acknowledge or accept, what looked like, a helpless human being claiming to be their God. Therefore they rejected Christ, the Messianic prophecies, Isaiah chapter fifty-three, and branded Him an impostor and a pest who was trying to wipeout the Jewish system.

But, although the majority of the Jewish leaders rejected Christ as their LORD God of their fathers, the Gentiles did not reject Christ, His miracles, and His Gospel message of hope. And whenever it was appropriate, Christ would reveal Himself to those who were sincere in their belief that Christ was the Messiah.

Here is an example:

"25 And the woman said unto Him [Christ], I know that Messias [Messiah] cometh, which is called Christ: when He is come, He will tell us all things. 26 Jesus saith unto her, I that speak unto thee [you] am He." John 4:25, 26

Like the woman above, the masses that came from all over the land did acknowledge Christ to be the Messiah and followed Him wherever He went.

According to the above verses Christ the LORD of hosts did come in the flesh as He had promised the prophets of old. And when He started His ministry, He did proclaim to everyone that He was the Messiah (Christ); but, more predominantly to the Jewish authorities. Christ not only

Where did Isaiah See the King of Israel Sitting?

revealed Himself to the house of Judah that He was the Christ but He also revealed to them that He was the King of Israel.

Christ the LORD of hosts said, "5 Tell ye [all of you] the daughter of Sion [Zion], Behold, thy [Your] King cometh unto thee [you], meek, and sitting upon an ass, and a colt the foal of an ass." Matthew 21:5 (See Genesis 49:10, 11.)

The blind, the lame, the lepers, those that were dead, the crippled, the sorrowful, the diseased who were healed, curious, and those who received hope from the Gospel message lined up on either side of the road, which led to the city of Jerusalem shouting hosanna's and proclaiming Christ the King of Israel.

And when Christ entered Jerusalem He proclaimed to the Jewish authorities, as a witness that He is "the King of Israel," and that proclamation was not welcomed by the leaders of the house of Judah. They said to Him make the people stop shouting hosannas; make them stop proclaiming You the King of Israel.

But Christ rebuked them by saying to them, "If they did not proclaim Me, the stones would do it." And that statement made the Jewish authorities mad and started to plot His death. And when they succeeded to crucify Christ their King, they said that He was an imposter and therefore they refuted the inscription on the cross, which read, "THE KING OF THE JEWS".

In their anger because they did not want to associate or acknowledge Christ as the King of the Jews, they went to Pilate and told him to rewrite the inscription to read, "He said I am King of the Jews."

Here is the reference: "21 Then said the chief priests of the Jews to Pilate, Write not, The King of the Jews; but

Where did Isaiah See the King of Israel Sitting?

that He said, I am King of the Jews." John 19:21

But because Pilate was annoyed with them for killing an innocent man and because of his wife's dream about Christ, he was furious with the Jewish leaders and told them to leave his presence promptly.

Therefore Christ's verbal and written claims to the common people and to the Jewish authorities that He was the "Messiah" (Christ) and "the King of Israel" stood their ground as a witness to the masses but more so to the house of Judah.

Although the above verses clearly identify Christ by the names of "the King of Israel," and "the LORD of hosts," I want to reveal to you, another character name of Christ, which further testifies that Christ is the King of Israel and the LORD of host.

Here is the reference: "6 Thus saith the LORD the King of Israel, and his Redeemer the LORD of hosts; I am the first, and I am the last; and beside Me there is no God" (Isaiah 44:6).

So, who is the King of Israel that identifies Himself by the character name "the first and the last" in the above verse? _____
The above verse is self-explanatory; Christ the King of Israel identifies Himself by the names of: "the King of Israel," "Redeemer," "the LORD of hosts," and "the first and the last." And since Christ the King of Israel identifies Himself by the character name of "the first and the last," let Apostle John identify and confirm the fact that Christ is the One who claims in the above verse that He is "the first and the last" in the following verses;

"17 And when I saw Him [Christ], I fell at His feet as

Where did Isaiah See the King of Israel Sitting?

dead. And He laid His right hand upon me, saying unto me, Fear not; I am the first and the last; 18 I am He that liveth, and was dead; and, behold, I am alive for evermore" (Revelation 1:17, 18).

Therefore, as per the above verses, since Christ the LORD God of Israel in Isaiah 44:6 personally claims to be "the King of Israel" and "the first and the last," and since Christ (Messiah) personally claims to be "the King of Israel" (Matthew 21:5; John 1:49) and "the first and the last" of Revelation 1:17, 18, it follows, according to Apostle John, Christ is the King of Israel.

Consequently, as per the above verses and like verses throughout the Bible, Christ the LORD God of Abraham" is identified by the name of "the King of Israel," and "the King of Israel" is identified by the name of "the LORD of hosts," and "the LORD of hosts is identified by the character name of "the first and the last," and the "first and the last" is identified by the name of "Messiah" (Christ), and visa versa.

Therefore the LORD of the Old Testament (Isaiah 44:6) is the same LORD of the New Testament (Revelation 1:17, 18; John 1:49).

In addition, we can further conclude, as Apostle John has concluded, by testifying in the following verses that Isaiah saw Christ sitting on His throne in heaven, by saying, "37 But though He [Christ] had done so many miracles before them, yet they believed not on Him: 38 That the saying of Esaias [Isaiah] the prophet might be fulfilled, which he spake, LORD, who hath believed our report? and to whom hath the arm of the LORD been revealed? 39 Therefore they could not believe, because that Esaias said again, 40 He hath blinded their eyes, and hardened their heart; that they should not see with their eyes, nor understand with their heart, and be converted, and I should heal them."

In reference to the above verses, Apostle John says,

"41 These things said Esaias [Isaiah], when he saw His [Christ's] glory, and spake of Him [Christ]." John 12:37-41

Therefore, as per the above Scripture references, we, like Apostle John, can accept Christ's personal claims and conclude that Isaiah saw Christ "the King of Israel" (v.41), who is also identified by the character name of "the first and the last," setting upon His throne in heaven during the year King Uzziah died.

But, the bottom line is the fact, since Christ personally claims a number of times that He is "the King of Israel," should not that personal claim suffice for us and acknowledge Him as such?

* Therefore as per Scripture, we can refer to Jesus Christ by the following names, "the God of Abraham, Isaac, and Jacob," "the God of Israel," "the Rock," "the LORD of hosts," "Shiloh," "the King of Israel," "the King of glory," "Zion," "Redeemer," and by the name of "the first and the last."

Why were the Sanctuaries in Shiloh and in Jerusalem Destroyed?

A falling away from Christ the King of Israel or in total apostasy, if you like, most of the time, creeps in very slowly. Satan and his evil angels rarely make a person fall into apostasy abruptly. If people fall abruptly, they would more alert about their transgressions and harder to continue in them. And in the case, of Eli and Samuel, it was not different than the previous apostasies; all it took to send the children of Israel into apostate spiral was the gradual

Why were the Sanctuaries in Shiloh & in Jerusalem Destroyed?

influence of the leaders and priests of Israel, which encouraged them by their actions to go and worship the pagan idols instead of Christ the God of Israel. The majority of the elders, priests, and leaders of Israel polluted the Sanctuary of Christ the LORD of hosts in Shiloh with abominable diverse acts of lust, having sex with the worshippers, payment for favors, idol worship, drinking, vomit, flies, maggots, and creepy crawlies in the Sanctuary.

And, if that was not bad enough, they worshiped the sun from within the Sanctuary, gave incense to variety of idols, which they bowed down, and worshipped their man made gods. They had reached a point where these priests and elders of Israel had revealed no remorse for their abominable evil acts.

Christ the LORD of hosts warned the priests, elders of Israel, and the children of Israel to refrain from their debase evil acts, stop polluting His Sanctuary, and return to a righteous living; if they did not, the Philistines would come in vengeance, sweep across the country, demolish the town of Shiloh, and the Sanctuary of Shiloh to the ground.

Unfortunately, as you have read before, the children of Israel did not repent from their evil acts, therefore Christ the LORD of hosts removed His divine protection from the children of Israel and from the Sanctuary, which was in Shiloh. Then Christ the LORD of hosts removed the fear that was instilled in the Philistines. Once the fear of the children of Israel was removed from the Philistines, the Philistines rallied themselves and declared war upon the children of Israel. They took the Ark of the Covenant; and later, in another fight, they killed King Saul.

After king Saul died, David became the king of Judah in 1011 BC and reigned from Hebron for seven years. After the seven years David was asked by the tribes of Israel to be their king also. As soon as he was made king of Israel, David

Why were the Sanctuaries in Shiloh & in Jerusalem Destroyed?

captured Jerusalem from the Jebusites and made it the capital of the nation. And when he moved to Jerusalem, after he put his enemies down, he started to think of building a permanent Sanctuary for Christ the LORD of hosts. But because David had too much blood on his hands, Christ the LORD of hosts told him that he was not going to build the Sanctuary; his son was going to do it for him.

And so it was, King David with his son planned and collected funds and prepared for the building of the Sanctuary. After serving Israel for forty years, King David died in 971 BC. Although King Solomon reigned jointly for few years with his father before David died, Solomon did not start to build the Sanctuary for Christ the LORD of hosts until the fourth year of his reign. It took him seven years to build it; and on the eleventh year of his reign, the building of the Sanctuary in Jerusalem was completed; and then the task was to place the furniture in the Sanctuary. And once the furniture was in, Solomon dedicated the Sanctuary to Christ the LORD of hosts.

The reign of Solomon lasted forty years (971-931 BC); and during those forty years Christ the LORD of hosts gave the condition for the blessings and warnings of which the following was given to him after his dedication prayer for the newly built Sanctuary in Jerusalem.

The admonition: "3 And the LORD said unto him[Solomon], I have heard thy [your] prayer and thy supplication, that thou [you] hast made before Me: I have hallowed this house, which thou hast built, to put My name there for ever; and Mine eyes and Mine heart shall be there perpetually. 4 And if thou [you] wilt walk before Me, as David thy [your] father walked, in integrity of heart, and in uprightness, to do according to all that I have commanded thee [you], and wilt keep My statutes and My judgments: 5 Then I will establish the throne of thy [your] kingdom upon Israel for ever, as I promised to David thy [your] father, saying, There shalt not fail thee a man upon the throne of Israel.

The warning: "6 But if ye [all of you] shall at all turn from following Me, ye or your children, and will not keep My commandments and My statutes which I have set before you, but go and serve other gods, and worship them: 7 Then will I cut off Israel out of the land which I have given them; and this house, which I have hallowed for My name, will I cast out of My sight; and Israel shall be a proverb and a byword among all people:

"8 And at this house, which is high, every one that passeth by it shall be astonished, and shall hiss; and they shall say, Why hath the LORD done thus unto this land, and to this house? 9 And they shall answer, Because they [the children of Israel] forsook the LORD their God, who brought forth their fathers out of the land of Egypt, and have taken hold upon other gods, and have worshipped them, and served them: therefore hath the LORD brought upon them all this evil." 1 Kings 9:3-9

Nonetheless, the reason I have brought you this far historically in the lives of the children of Israel is to not only reveal to you that Christ the LORD of hosts was the Individual who was worshipped for over 400 years in Shiloh, but to also reveal to you that later, from the time King David began to reign form Jerusalem and up until the third siege of Jerusalem, Christ the LORD was worshipped in His Sanctuary in Jerusalem, and why the Sanctuary in Jerusalem was allowed to be destroyed by King Nebuchadnezzar's forces. I want you to peek, by the pen of the prophet, at the

Why were the Sanctuaries in Shiloh & in Jerusalem Destroyed?

evil abominable acts the priests, scribes, elders, and the leaders of Israel practiced in secret in the Sanctuary in Jerusalem as they did in the Sanctuary in Shiloh.

Here are the events: As per 1 Kings 9:3-9, most of King Solomon's life was a blessing. But, when king Solomon fell into apostasy in his twilight years, his kingdom was divided into two kingdoms. There was "the house of Israel (ten tribes of Israel) and there was "the house of Judah" (which consisted of the two tribes —Benjamin and Judah).

Appallingly, to Christ's disapproval, these two kingdoms, the house of Israel and the house of Judah, not only fought between themselves for supremacy, but the house of Israel encouraged by its king (Jeroboam), from the very beginning chose to serve idols, which he built, on the altars of Dan and Bethel.

And, ** "When the protection by a merciful God was removed from the house of Israel because they chose to serve Satan and his satanic agencies, the Assyrians attacked the house of Israel, took many of them into bondage, and in 722 BC the house of Israel disintegrated.

This attack, upon the house of Israel, left the house of Judah very vulnerable because during this period of time (722 BC) Ahaz, who started his rule in 735 BC, was ruling the house of Judah; and he, like many of his predecessors, practiced idol worship and sought help from the pagan nations instead of the LORD God of Abraham.

One of the reasons why King Ahaz worshipped satanic agencies was due to a psychological assessment, which he had of the Assyrians. He noticed that the Assyrian gods were helping them to win the war against the house of Israel. He thought, if he was to worship their gods, they would help him also.

That is why "24 Ahaz gathered together the vessels of the

house of God [the Sanctuary in Jerusalem], and cut in pieces the vessels of the house of God, and shut up the doors of the house of the LORD, and he made him altars in every corner of Jerusalem. 25 And in every several city of Judah he made high places to burn incense unto other gods, and provoked to anger the LORD God of his fathers" (2 Chronicles 28:24, 25).

On the other hand, if Ahaz looked at the history of his forefathers and observed how many of his predecessors were successful under the guidance of the LORD God of his fathers, he and the house of Judah should have worshipped the LORD of hosts because He always blessed and protected His people.

But since Ahaz chose to worship the gods of Assyria, he failed miserably in his endeavors to bring salvation to himself and to his subjects.

Because of his pagan worship, Ahaz reign was cut short. He reigned for only sixteen years in Jerusalem and died at the age of forty-one.

After the death of Ahaz, his son Hezekiah became the king of the house of Judah in 729 BC.

Because Ahaz practiced paganism and served the Assyrian king, the Assyrians did not bother Hezekiah to a large degree because they thought, like Ahaz his father, he would continue to serve the Assyrians and to promote paganism throughout his kingdom." ** 2

As a reminder to the house of Judah because of its apostasy, Christ the LORD of hosts gave a decree that the house of Judah would never again place a king upon the throne of King David. And so it is today, Judah (Jews) does

_____
** 2 Mitanidis, Philip *Christians Headed Into the Time of Trouble* pgs 26, 27 BeeHive Publishing House Inc. 2007

not have a king reigning on King David's throne!

But before "the house of Judah" lost her king and kingdom in 586 BC, Christ the LORD of hosts raised Jeremiah in 627 BC to help Judah's king, elders, and priests to repent from their evil acts of fornication and submit to King Nebuchadnezzar in order to avert the destruction of the Sanctuary, Jerusalem, and its citizens.

Unfortunately, the elders and priests were so far gone in their apostasy, like the elders and priests of the Sanctuary in Shiloh, they did not believe that Christ the LORD of hosts existed in the Sanctuary or in Jerusalem. They said, "the LORD seeth us not; the LORD hath forsaken the earth." Therefore they continued with their idol worship, sun worship, giving incense and alms to their idols, etc., etc. And when Jeremiah exposed them; they turned against him and were eager to kill him.

Jeremiah was not the only prophet that revealed Judah's abominable sinful acts. Christ the LORD of hosts raised Ezekiel, who was taken into Babylon in captivity in 597 BC during the second siege of Jerusalem because King Jehoiachin rebelled.

Christ the LORD of hosts said to Ezekiel, "5 Son of man, lift up thine [your] eyes now the way toward the north, So I lifted up mine eyes the way toward the north, and behold northward at the gate of the altar this image of jealousy in the entry, 6 He said furthermore unto me, Son of man, seest thou [you] what they do? even the great abominations that the house of Israel committeth here, that I should go far off from My sanctuary? but turn thee [you] yet again, and thou [you] shalt see greater abominations. 7 And He brought me to the door of the court; and when I looked, behold a hole in the wall. 8 Then said He unto Me, son of man, dig now in the wall: and when I had digged in the wall, behold a door. 9 And He said unto me, Go in, and

Why were the Sanctuaries in Shiloh & in Jerusalem Destroyed?

behold the wicked abominations that they do there. 10 So I went in and saw; and behold every form of creeping things, and abominable beasts, and all the idols of the house of Israel, portrayed upon the wall round about. 11 And there stood before them seventy men of the ancients of the house of Israel, and in the midst of them stood Jaazaniah the son of Shaphan, with every man his censer in his hand; and a thick cloud of incense went up.

"12 Then said He unto me, Son of man, hast thou [you] seen what the ancients of the house of Israel do in the dark, every man in the chambers of his imagery? for they say, The LORD seeth us not; the LORD hath forsaken the earth.

"13 He said also unto me, Turn thee [you] yet again, and thou [you] shalt see greater abominations that they do. 14 Then he brought me to the door of the gate of the LORD'S house which was toward the north; and, behold, there sat women weeping for Tammuz [a pagan cult god that was worshipped in Egypt and all around the Middle East.].

"15 Then said He unto me, Hast thou [you] seen this, O son of man? turn thee yet again, and thou shalt see greater abominations than these. 16 And He brought me into the inner court of the LORD'S house [Sanctuary], and, behold, at the door of the temple of the LORD, between the porch and the altar, were about five and twenty men, with their backs towards the temple of the LORD, and their faces toward the east; and they worshipped the sun toward the east.

"17 Then He said unto me, Hast thou [you] seen this, O son of man? Is it a light thing to the house of Judah that they commit the abominations which they commit here? for they have filled the land with violence, and have returned to provoke Me to anger; and lo, they put the branch to their nose." Ezekiel 8:5-17

Why were the Sanctuaries in Shiloh & in Jerusalem Destroyed?

Unfortunately, the elders of the house of Judah, the kings of the house of Judah, and the priests who polluted the Sanctuary, they would not listen to the words of Christ the LORD of hosts as they were given by Ezekiel and Daniel the prophets. And neither did they listen to the words of Jeremiah the prophet who lived amongst them.

These personal fresh warnings were not the first warnings that were given to the house of Judah; they were given many times before and in the form of prophecy, which revealed what would happen if the children of Israel would not repent from their evil acts. They were told; the Sanctuary and Jerusalem would become like "Shiloh," and they would be taken into captivity for 70 years, if they did not reform and become subservient to the Babylonian king.

Christ the LORD of hosts said by the mouth of Jeremiah,

"12 go ye now unto My place which was in Shiloh, where I set My name at the first, and see what I did to it for the wickedness of My people Israel. 13 And now, because ye [all of you] have done all these works, saith the LORD, and I spake unto you, rising up early and speaking, but ye heard not; and I called you, but ye answered not; 14 Therefore will I do unto this house [Sanctuary in Jerusalem], which is called by My name, wherein ye trust, and unto the place which I gave to you and to your fathers, as I have done to Shiloh. 15 And I will cast you out of My sight, as I have cast out all your brethren, even the whole seed of Ephraim." Jeremiah 7:12-15

But because the children of Israel, their priests, and their leaders would not repent from their abominable evil works, Christ the LORD of hosts said to Jeremiah,

"16 Therefore pray not thou [you] for this people,

neither lift up cry nor prayer for them, neither make intercession to Me; for I will not hear thee [you]." Jeremiah 7:16

That is a very, very, strong rebuke volleyed to the house of Judah and to her king.

The warnings and admonitions that were given by Daniel, Obadiah, Ezekiel, and Jeremiah were not heeded; and neither were the calls for reform heeded when the previous prophets of Christ the LORD of hosts expressed to the house of Judah

The overthrow of the city of Jerusalem and the Sanctuary occurred in 586 B.C. during the third siege, which lasted for over a year. The destruction of the Sanctuary in Jerusalem by the Chaldeans, like the destruction of the Sanctuary in Shiloh by the Philistines, was demolished to the ground, all because the priests, scribes, elders, and the king of Judah wanted to live in their abominable evil lust. That is why they refused to listen to Christ the LORD of hosts when He said to them,

"13 I spake unto you, rising up early and speaking, but ye heard not; and I called you, but ye [all of you] answered not;" Jeremiah 7:13

By reading the above events, it is quite clear that Christ the LORD of hosts was the One who occupied His Sanctuary in "Shiloh" and His Sanctuary in Jerusalem. And, Christ has revealed to us why the Sanctuary in Jerusalem and the Sanctuary in Shiloh were demolished to the ground and why He abandoned both of them. In fact, He even utterly abandoned the tribe of Ephraim because of their debase whoredom, which they committed with the pagan gods of the surrounding nations.

In addition, since Christ the LORD of hosts was worshipped by the children of Israel in Shiloh, they automatically thought about Christ the LORD of hosts when they thought about the Sanctuary in Shiloh. (See Genesis 49:10, 11.) The name "Shiloh" was synonymous with the name of Christ the LORD of hosts when it was used by the children of Israel up until such time King David started the campaign to build a new Sanctuary in Jerusalem. And when Christ the LORD of hosts moved into the Sanctuary in Jerusalem, the children of Israel referred to the Temple area by the name of "Zion" because that is where Christ the LORD of hosts dwelt above "the mercy seat" and in between the two cherubims of the Ark of the Covenant (Isaiah 2:3; 8:18).

THE ARK OF THE COVENANT

* Therefore as per Scripture, we can refer to Jesus Christ by the following names, "the God of Abraham, Isaac, and Jacob," "the God of Israel," "the Rock," "the LORD of hosts," "Shiloh," "the King of Israel," "the King of glory," "Redeemer," "the first and the last," and by the name of "Zion."

Jehovah the Most High God

Approximately twenty-three years after Josiah's reign, as we have read because of the rebellion of the house of Judah, Jerusalem and its Sanctuary were utterly destroyed to the ground.

*** "the destruction of the house of Judah, the Sanctuary, and the destruction of Jerusalem, began during the first siege of Jerusalem (about 606 BC), which was during the third year of Jehoiakim's reign (Daniel 1:1-3).

The record states, "5 Jehoiakim was twenty and five years [25 years] old when he began to reign, and he reigned eleven years in Jerusalem: and he did that which was evil in the

the sight of the LORD his God."

Eight years later, on the eleventh year of Jehoiakim's reign, "6 Against him came up Nebuchadnezzar king of Babylon, and bound him in fetters, to carry him to Babylon. 7 Nebuchadnezzar also carried of the vessels of the house of the LORD to Babylon, and put them in his temple at Babylon."

When Jehoiakim was removed from his throne, by King Nebuchadnezzar, Nebuchadnezzar left Jehoiakim's young son Jehoiachin to reign. "9 Jehoiachin was eight years old when he began to reign, and he reigned three months and ten days in Jerusalem: and he did that which was evil in the sight of the LORD. 10 And when the year was expired, king Nebuchadnezzar sent, and brought him to Babylon, with the goodly vessels of the house of the LORD, and made Zedekiah his brother king over Judah and Jerusalem.

"11 Zedekiah was one and twenty years [21 years] old when he began to reign, and reigned eleven years in Jerusalem. 12 And he did that which was evil in the sight of the LORD his God, and humbled not himself before Jeremiah the prophet speaking from the mouth of the LORD. 13 And he also rebelled against king Nebuchadnezzar, who had made him swear by God: but he stiffened his neck, and hardened his heart from turning unto the LORD God of Israel" (2 Chronicles 36:5-7, 9-13).

After Zedekiah swore allegiance, in the name of God, to Nebuchadnezzar, Zedekiah sought support from the Egyptians in order to overthrow the kingdom of Nebuchadnezzar. Zedekiah thought that the combined forces of the house of Judah and of Egypt were enough to depose the kingdom of Babylon. But the king of Babylon could not be overthrown because the word of the LORD had stated over and over again by Isaiah, Micah, Ezekiel, and Jeremiah that if the house of Judah or any other nation did not submit to the Babylonian king, they would be destroyed.

So, what was Zedekiah and his advisors thinking to go against the word of the LORD of hosts?

Needless to say at this point, when King Nebuchadnezzar learned of Zedekiah's plans, he was so mad that he surrounded and attacked Jerusalem for over a year and a half, which caused the inhabitants of Jerusalem to suffer severe hardships, horror, famine, pain, and traumatized deaths.

The third siege of Jerusalem ended in 586 BC. The combined forces of the house of Judah and Egypt were defeated. Zedekiah and his family, while trying to escape, were captured. His family was killed. Zedekiah's eyes were poked out of their sockets with a knife and he was taken to Babylon. There he died a miserable death; fulfilling the prophecy which stated "13 My net also will I spread upon him, and he shall be taken in My snare: and I will bring him to Babylon to the land of the Chaldeans; yet shall he not see it, though he shall die there" (Ezekiel 12:13).

In spite of the warning and of the prophetic evidence that was taking place before the house of Judah and their king, the leaders did not want to listen to the LORD'S admonition by the mouth of Jeremiah. Instead, they rebelled, suffered affliction, oppression, and death. They lost Jerusalem, lost their autonomy, lost the Promised Land in 586 BC, and during that year, the rest of the house of Judah was carried into fifty years of captivity by the hand of the Babylonian army; all because they chose to reject the LORD of hosts, the God of their forefathers. Instead, they chose to listen to the false prophets who caused the destruction upon the house of Judah and upon the house of Israel. (See Jeremiah 27:14-18.)

At this point in time, 586 BC, the house of Judah and the house of Israel were left without a country, homeless, in

Jehovah the Most High God

captivity, and without a human ally to turn to for
help." *** 3

And, while the house of Judah was held into captivity by
the Babylonian king for seventy years, Daniel the prophet of
the LORD of hosts sought through books (the books of his
contemporary prophets and through the former prophets) as
to why the house of Judah was held into captivity. And when
he searched through their pages, he found out a stunning
revelation as to why they were held into captivity.

Daniel said; "3 I set my face unto the LORD God, to
seek by prayer and supplications, with fasting, and sackcloth,
and ashes: 4 And I prayed unto the LORD my God, and
made my confession, and said, O LORD, the great and
dreadful God, keeping the covenant and mercy to them that
love Him, and to them that keep His commandments; 5 We
have sinned, and have committed iniquity, and have done
wickedly, and have rebelled, even by departing from Thy
[Your] precepts and from Thy judgments: 6 Neither have we
hearkened unto Thy servants the prophets, which spake in
Thy name to our kings, our princes, and our fathers, and to
all the people of the land. 7 O LORD, righteousness
belongeth unto Thee [You], but unto us confusion of faces,
as at this day; to the men of Judah, and to the inhabitants of
Jerusalem, and unto all Israel, that are near, and that are far
off, through all the countries whither Thou [You] hast
driven them, because of their trespass that they have
trespassed against Thee." Daniel 9:3-7

Read up to verse nineteen if you want to know what
Daniel said in conclusion.

In addition, Daniel in chapter seven (see verse 25 for an

*** 3   Mitanidis, Philip *Christians Headed Into the Time of
Trouble* pgs 53-56 BeeHive Publishing House Inc. 2007

Jehovah the Most High God

example) refers to Christ the LORD of hosts a number of times by the name of "the Most High."

Although Daniel, the patriarchs, and prophets of old, and the children of Israel identified and acknowledged Christ the LORD of hosts by the names of "LORD," "God," "the King of Israel," "Shiloh," "Rock," "the Most High God," and "Jehovah," you would be surprised to know that today, rarely, if few, refer to Christ the King of Israel by the names of " the Most High" and "Jehovah"!

In North America and probably elsewhere, people like myself have been confronted with the Arian doctrine in one point of time or another. My experience has been when Arian representatives come knocking on my door, normally they try not to disclose who they are because they fear they would be turned away before they give their little canvass. But irrespective of the outcome, they try to leave their magazines for me to read; that way, they feel that I will receive their doctrinal Arian message, which predominantly states throughout their writings that God the Father is Jehovah.

Ironically, although they claim that God the Father is Jehovah, if you were to confront them to show you one single verse from the entire Bible where it states that God the Father is Jehovah, they are not able to produce a single verse to support their Arian belief!

Are you surprised!

No, I am not making this up! If I was, I would be lying to you; and that I would not knowingly do because if I did lie to you, I would re-crucify my LORD God and Savior Jesus Christ and put Him into open shame. (See Hebrew 6:6)

Nonetheless, The Arians insist that God the Father is Jehovah? And to prove their point, their first response is to claim that they can show you over 6,000 verses where God the Father is identified by the name of Jehovah. The reason

Jehovah the Most High God

reason they make that claim is due to the fact that they have
been taught to believe that the word LORD (יהוה) means
is Jehovah, which is one hundred percent in error. As I have
stated before, the word LORD (יהוה) does not translate
into English or any other language—and that includes the
Hebrew language—to read Jehovah. Let me say again; the
Hebrew word יהוה translates into all languages to read
LORD. But, regarding the Hebrew word Jehovah, you will
find the word appearing only seven times. And then again,
some will tell you that the word Jehovah appears eight times
in the entire Bible; but that is another study.

Here are some of the references out of the seven:
Jehovah-jireh (Genesis 22:14); it means, Jehovah will
provide.   Jehovah-nissi (Exodus 17:15, 16); it means,
Jehovah is my banner. Jehovah-shalom (Judges 6:23, 24); it
means Jehovah is peace. See also Exodus 6:3; Isaiah 12:2,
and the rest, I will let you search for them.

Therefore, since there are only seven references with the
word Jehovah, they cannot claim that the word Jehovah
appears over 6,000 times in their Bible or any other Bible
that has translated the Hebrew word יהוה to read
incorrectly, Jehovah.

But, if you were to dispute their claim that the Hebrew
word יהוה does not translate to read Jehovah, they will
quickly go to one of their favorite verses (Psalms 83:18) and
point out to you that the verse contains the Hebrew word
Jehovah and it refers to God the Father.

Well, if you do go to your Bible and look at the verse,
you will definitely find the Hebrew word Jehovah there,
which is one of the seven references, and not the word
יהוה (LORD); but does the verse and the word Jehovah
refer to God the Father?

They claim that it does, but can they show you the words
God the Father in that verse? Or prove that the verse refers

Jehovah the Most High God

to God the Father?

Obviously not because the words God the Father have been added to the verse; these words do not exist in that verse. Therefore all they have done is to reveal to you that One of the Individual from the Godhead is identified by the name of "Jehovah."

So! Who is identified in Psalms 83:18 by the name of "Jehovah"?
To answer according to the inspired Scriptures, Jehovah is none other than Christ the Creator of Genesis 1:1.

How do we know?

Consider the following; the verse reads as follows,

"18 That men may know that Thou [You], whose name alone is JEHOVAH, art the Most High over all the earth" (Psalms 83:18).

So, who is "the Most High"? And "whose name alone is Jehovah"?

As you have read in the above verse, the answer is given; Jehovah is "the Most High."

"The Most High" is one of Christ's character names; and in the New Testament, "the Highest" is God the Father's character name.

Nonetheless, to confirm the fact that the character name "the Most High" refers to Jesus Christ the LORD, as we know Him now in the New Testament, here are the references, which reveal that the children of Israel tempting Christ "the Most High God" during His travel with them towards the Promised Land and in the Promised Land.

"56 Yet they tempted and provoked the Most High God, and kept not His testimonies; 57 But turned back, and dealt unfaithfully like their fathers: they were turned aside like a

Jehovah the Most High God

deceitful bow. 58 For they provoked Him to anger with their high places, and moved Him to jealousy with their graven images.

"59 When God heard this, He was wroth, and greatly abhorred Israel; 60 So that He forsook the tabernacle of Shiloh, the tent which He placed among men; 61 And delivered His strength into captivity, and His glory into the enemy's hand.

"62 He gave His people over also unto the sword; and was wroth with His inheritance. 63 The fire consumed their young men; and their maidens were not given to marriage. 64 Their priests fell by the sword; and their widows made no lamentation.

"65 Then the LORD awakened as one out of sleep, and like a mighty man that shouteth by reason of wine. 66 And He smote His enemies in the hinder parts: He put them to a perpetual   reproach.

"67 Moreover He refused the tabernacle of Joseph, and chose not the tribe of Ephraim: 68 But chose the tribe of Judah, the mount Zion which He loved. 69 And He built His sanctuary like high places, like the earth which He hath established for ever" (Psalms 78:56-69).

Briefly, as you have read in the above verses "the Most High God" was tempted by the children of Israel (v.56). The Most High God abandoned His dwelling place in the Sanctuary, which was pitched in "Shiloh" by Joshua (v.60). In other words, the Most High God refused the tabernacle of Joseph, and chose not the tribe of Ephraim (v.67). The Most High God "chose the tribe of Judah, the mount Zion which He loved" (v.68).   Who chose to dwell in the Sanctuary in Jerusalem? Why it was none other than Jesus Christ the LORD of hosts— remember? We have studied this point earlier. And then, the psalmist acknowledges that

Jehovah the Most High God

the Most High God is the Creator by saying: "And He built His sanctuary like high places, like the earth which He hath established for ever" (v.69).

To further confirm the fact that Christ the LORD of hosts is the Most High God, read the chapters on the "Three Overviews" (Psalms 78; Nehemiah 9; 1 Corinthians 10) to refresh your memory that Jesus Christ the Creator is the God of Israel, is the King of Israel, is the One who took the children of Israel out of Egypt and led them into the Promised Land, is the One who gave the children of Israel water to drink from rocks, is the One who fed them, is the One who protected them, is the One who dwelt in His Sanctuary in Shiloh and in Jerusalem, is the Creator, is the Most High God etc., etc.

And when you finish reading the "Three Overviews," you would have noticed according the Psalmist, Nehemiah, and Apostle Paul, the Individual who was temped was Christ the LORD of hosts. Christ is identified by the psalmist in verse fifty-six by the name of "the Most High God" and Creator of the "earth" (v.69). And since Christ is the One who was tempted by the children of Israel and is the sole Creator, the words "the Most High God" can only refer to Christ the LORD of hosts.

But, simplistically, Christ identifies Himself as the "first and the last," in Revelation 1:17, 18, to Apostle John. And in Isaiah 44:6 Christ also identifies Himself as the "first and the last," as "the LORD of hosts," and as "the King of Israel." Therefore Christ the LORD of hosts who is the King of Israel identifies Himself by the character name of "the Most High" in Psalms 47:2. The verse reads as follows:

"2 For the LORD Most High is terrible; He is a great King of all the earth." Psalms 47:2 (See also Matt. 21:5; Mark 15:9; Luke 23:38; John 1:49 where Christ is

Jehovah the Most High God

revealed as the King of Israel.)

Consequently, since Christ is the King of Israel, it follows that the words "the most high" refer only to Christ the LORD of hosts. The verse reads:

> "18 That men may know that Thou whose name alone is JEHOVAH, art the Most High over all the earth" (Psalms 83:18).

But more simplistically, compare Psalms 78:56 with Psalms 78:35 and notice how Christ the "Rock" and "Redeemer" is identified by the names of "the most high God" and "the high God." See also where Christ is identified by the name of "Rock" 1 Corinthians 10:4; 2 Samuel 22:32.) And notice how Christ the "Rock" of v.15 is identified as the Creator in v.5 and by the name of "the Most High" in vs. 1, and 8 of Psalms 92; and notice how Christ "the Most High" is further identified by the Psalmist by the name "Jehovah" in Psalms 83:18.

Therefore, for anyone to use Psalms 83:18 to prove that God the Father's name is Jehovah is futile because, as we have seen, according to Scripture, especially in the other six references, which contain the name of Jehovah, they all refer to Christ the LORD of hosts "whose name alone is Jehovah" (v.18).

By the way, did you know that the Arians, today, contrary to their belief, identify Christ (Χριστος) by the name of "Jehovah" over 6,000 times in their Bible—the "New World Translation of the Holy Scriptures" (NWT) 1961 Edition and onward—and yet, they refuse to call Christ by His name Jehovah!

Go figure?

As an example, see Numbers 21:4-6 and 1 Corinthians 10:9 in their Bible where Christ is identified by the name of

Jehovah." And for the Greek text, see pgs 128 - 133 in this book.

*   Therefore as per Scripture, we can refer to Jesus Christ by the following names, "the God of Abraham, Isaac, and Jacob," "the God of Israel," "the Rock," "the LORD of hosts," "Shiloh," "the King of Israel," "the King of glory," "Zion," "Redeemer," "the first and the last," "Jehovah," and by the name of "the Most High God."

<u>The Messiah</u>

After Cyrus the Persian king overthrew King Nebuchadnezzar's kingdom in 538 BC, he permitted, as it was prophesied that he would allow the house of Judah to return to their homeland after the seventy years of captivity in Babylon. Unfortunately, to their detriment, many chose not to return.

And when a minority of the house of Judah returned to Jerusalem after their 70 years of captivity, they became tardy and indifferent to the building of the Sanctuary; and when Nehemiah, the king's cup bearer, heard that the progress of the Sanctuary in particular was a secondary consideration, he asked the king of Persia for a leave of absence so that he could go and help to speed up the building of Jerusalem and the Sanctuary. The king granted him his request; and Nehemiah went to Jerusalem to organize the people and to finish building the city and its Sanctuary and implement its services.

But shortly after the restoration of the city and its Sanctuary, the house of Judah began again to erode into apostasy. They failed to take heed to Daniel the prophet when he said that they were to prepare the way for the coming of the King of Israel in the flesh, for His appearing, and for the transition from the Old Covenant to the New Covenant. Daniel gave the house of Judah a complete timetable, which they were admonished to follow.

The Messiah

The timetable reads as follows:

"24 Seventy weeks are determined upon thy people and upon thy holy city, to finish the transgression, and to make an end of sins, and to make reconciliation for iniquity, and to bring in everlasting righteousness, and to seal up the vision and prophecy; and to anoint the most Holy [Christ the LORD]. 25 Know therefore and understand that from the going forth of the commandment to restore and to build Jerusalem unto the Messiah the Prince shall be seven weeks, and threescore and two weeks: the street shall be built again, and the wall, even in troublous times. 26 And after threescore and two weeks shall Messiah be cut off, but not for Himself: and the people of the prince that shall come shall destroy the city [Jerusalem] and the sanctuary; and the end thereof shall be with a flood, and unto the end of the war desolation are determined. 27 And He shall confirm the covenant with many for one week: and in the midst of the week He shall cause the sacrifice and the oblation to cease, and for the overspreading of abominations He shall make it desolate, even until the consummation, and that determined shall be poured upon the desolate." Daniel 9:24-27

Since a day in prophecy equals to a year (Ezekiel 4:6), the following diagram is calculated in years to depict Daniel's time table of the coming of the Messiah and His death on Calvary's cross.

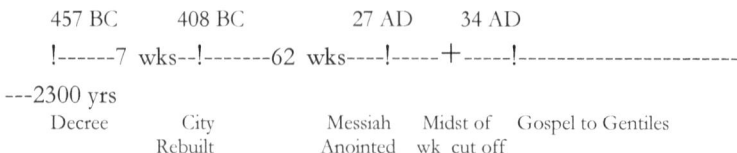

```
457 BC      408 BC            27 AD    34 AD
!------7 wks--!-------62 wks----!-----+-----!-----------------------
---2300 yrs
    Decree      City           Messiah   Midst of  Gospel to Gentiles
                Rebuilt        Anointed  wk  cut off
```

The Messiah

Although the house of Judah was admonished to prepare for the coming of their King in the flesh, they rejected Daniel's timetable, the Messianic prophecies, the messages of the Minor Prophets, and stuck to a form of worship that was steeped in tradition and man made cumbersome laws. And because of their apostasy, the house of Judah was rapidly abandoning Christ the King of Israel. Therefore Christ continued to send the Minor Prophets, to not only reveal their condition, but to also admonish them to prepare for His soon coming in the flesh.

Unfortunately, as I stated before, the leaders of the house of Judah chose to reject the messages of the prophets, to prepare for the coming of Christ the LORD of hosts in the flesh, and to accept Him as their LORD, God, and Savior as their forefathers had done. And because the house of Judah rejected the messages of the Minor Prophets, and failed to prepare the way for the Messiah (Christ), John the Baptist was sent to prepare the people for the coming of Christ the King of Israel in the flesh. And when Christ appeared in the flesh, the house of Judah (Jews) rejected Christ the LORD of hosts who claimed all along that He is the God of Abraham, the King of Israel, and Christ (the Messiah). (See John 1:41; 4:25, 26.)

Likewise, today a handful of Christian denominations, Jews, Muslims, and non-Bible believers have chosen to reject and refuse to acknowledge Jesus Christ the LORD of hosts by the names of "LORD," "Jehovah," "Most High God," "the God of Abraham," "Christ" (Messiah), and by His other character names.

But, regardless of peoples' attitude, the Old Testament and the New Testament prophets, as we have seen thus far, complement each other's writings, accept Moses' writings, and acknowledge that Moses' writings are predominantly about Christ the LORD of hosts. And that being a fact, you

The Messiah

will further witness that the New Testament prophets, like the Old Testament prophets, confirm that Christ the God of Abraham is "the Creator," "the Word," "God," "the God of Israel," "the Lamb," "the King of Israel," and "the Messiah (Christ)."

In confirmation to the above paragraph, although the house of Israel failed to proclaim the arrival of the "Messiah" to their own people and to the Gentiles, the prophets of Christ the LORD of hosts did. As an example, Apostle John identifies the "Messiah" by the following names.

*The Creator*_____ When you read verse one of John chapter one, you will notice, after you compare this verse with Genesis 1:1, the prophet of Christ the Creator goes beyond Genesis 1:1. Apostle John gives us a glimpse of what was like before the creation of the Universe took place.

He writes: "1 In the beginning was the Word, and the Word was with God, and the Word was God." John 1:1

The phrase "in the beginning" reads, "In beginning" in the Greek text. The definite article "the" is omitted in the Greek text, which leaves the impression that there was no beginning of time during the existence of Christ the "Word" (Gr. ΛΟΓΟΣ: Logos) and "God" the Father (Christ's Associate).

In addition, the verse does not reveal a time frame between the time "the Word was with God" and the creation of "All things" (John 1:3). But, since the words "All things" are used, these words imply that there was not a single thing created during the fellowship between Christ the "Word" and "God" (Christ's Associate); verse three testifies to that fact. The universe as we know it now with its teeming creation did not exist during the fellowship between Christ the "Word" and "God" (Christ's Associate). And neither did the angels, who were created over nine and a half billion years before man was created.

The portion of non-existent time between the fellowship of Christ the "Word" and "God" (Christ's Associate), prior to the creation of the universe, appears to be silent in the Scriptures. Therefore we can only minutely relate to a pre-existing relationship between Christ the "Word" and "God" (Christ's Associate) before Christ the "Word" created the universe and everything that is in it.

But, Apostle John does not stop there with his information regarding Christ the "Word"; he goes one step further and says that the "Word" of verse one is the sole Individual who created "All thing" and that includes the "world."

Apostle John, like Moses, and Isaiah says,

"3 All things were made by Him [Christ the Word of v.1]; and without Him [Christ] was not anything made that was made. 10 He [Christ] was in the world, and the world was made by Him [Christ]." John 1:3, 10

"1 In the beginning God created the heaven and the earth." Genesis 1:1

"24 Thus saith the LORD, thy [your] redeemer, and He that formed thee [you] from the womb, I am the LORD that maketh all thing; that stretcheth forth the heavens alone; that spreadeth abroad the earth by Myself;" Isaiah 44:24

Like Isaiah 44:24, in a complementary tone to John's presentation of Christ the Creator (the Word) that He

The Messiah

created "All thing" "alone" and "by Himself," Apostle Paul also says that Christ (the Word) created all things" by Himself ("by Him") and for Himself ("for Him")

The verse reads as follows: "16 For by Him [Christ] were all things created, that are in heaven, and that are in earth, visible and invisible, whether they be thrones, or dominions, or principalities, or powers: all things were created by Him [Christ], and for Him [Christ]." Colossians 1:16

And then, Apostle Paul adds, "17 and by Him [Christ] all things consist." Colossians 1:17

The Psalmist agrees with Apostle Paul by saying, "3 For the LORD is a great God, and a great King above all gods

.

"4 In His hand are the deep places of the earth: the strength of the hills is His also. 5 The sea is His, and He made it: and His hands formed the dry land. 6 O come, let us worship and bow down; let us kneel before the LORD our maker, 7 For He is our God." Psalms 95:3-7

Did you hear?

The Psalmist says, "He [the King] made it [earth]" (vs. 3, 5).

Apostle Paul, like Isaiah and the Psalmist says, "by Him [Christ] were all things created." And again Paul insists, "all things were created by Him [Christ], and "for Him [Christ]." And then the apostle goes one step further and adds, "by Him [Christ] all things consist." Colossians 1:17

Did you notice?

By Christ the King of Israel "all things consist" and not by somebody else. Therefore, the universe and everything that is in it was created by Christ (the Word); and it is sustained by the word of Christ the LORD of hosts.

The "Word"? _____ The reason Christ the Creator is

identified by the character name of "Word" is due to the fact that He created the heavens, the earth, and the earth's ecosystem by simply speaking them into existence. Christ the Creator said, "Let there be light" and there was light. And Christ said; "Let there be a firmament in the midst of the waters" and there was a firmament. Christ the Creator said; "Let there be grass..." etc.

If you have read chapter one of Genesis you would have noticed that the "Word" (Christ) spoke the creation into existence. He said and it was done. (See Isaiah 48:13.)

King David, like Apostle John, confirms the fact that Christ the Creator of Genesis chapter one brought the creation into existence by speaking it into existence. He said, "6 By the word of the LORD were the heavens made; and all the host of them by the breath of His mouth."

"9 For He spake, and it was done; He commanded, and it stood fast." Psalms 33:6, 9

Consequently because Christ the Creator of Genesis chapter one spoke the creation into existence, Apostle John identifies Christ the LORD of hosts in John 1:1, by the character name of "Word" (ΛΟΓΟΣ).

*God*_____ Furthermore, as you have noticed in John 1:1, the prophet of Christ the Creator, to avoid confusion, stated that the "Word was with God." He did not say God was with God as Moses has stated in Genesis 1:26, 27, and then, identifying One of the Individuals as the Creator.

First the prophet of Christ the LORD of hosts stated that the "Word was with God" and then he identifies the "Word" by the same name as the Word's Associate and that name is "God." The prophet added, "and the Word was

The Messiah

God." And if you were to read the Greek text, you would notice that the Greek text emphasizes the fact that the "Word" is God by saying, "and God is the Word." it reads:

"ΚΑΙ   ΘΕΟΣ   ΗΝ   Ο   ΛΟΓΟΣ
"and   God   is   the   Word."
ΙΩΑΝΝΗΝ 1:1. (Βιβλικη Εταιρεια)
John 1:1 (Translation is mine.)

"1 IN the beginning was the Word, and the Word was with God, *and the Word was God."* John 1:1 (OKJV) *Italics mine*

As per the above verse, four things are quite apparent; one, Christ the "Word" pre-existed with "God" His Associate. Two, Christ the "Word" created "all things" (v.3). Three, Christ the "Word" is also identified in the predicate (of v.1) by the name of "God." The Greek text emphasizes in the predicate that Christ the "Word" is "God." The Greek text says, "and God is the Word." Four, Apostle John identifies two Individuals by the name of God (God the Christ and God the Father) because that is their name. (See Matthew 28:19.)

*The God of Israel*_____ After revealing that the "Word" was the sole Creator of "All things" (John 1:3) and pre-existed with His Associate before the creation of "All things," Apostle John makes the statement that Christ the "Word" is the God of Israel by saying,

"11 He came unto His own, and His own received Him not." John 1:11

To clarify the above verse, it will read, "11 He [Christ the

The Messiah

Word of v.1] came unto His own [the children of Israel], and His own received Him not." John 1:11

Christ the LORD of hosts came to His own people who are called by His name; but His own people rejected Him because Christ said to them that He was their King; and that He pre-existed before Abraham and Abraham saw His day and was glad.

Christ said to the Jewish authorities,

"56 Your father Abraham rejoiced to see My day: and he saw it, and was glad. 57 Then said the Jews unto Him, Thou [you] art not yet fifty years old, and hast thou seen Abraham? 58 Jesus said unto them, Verily, verily, I say unto you, Before Abraham was, I am. 59 Then took they up stones to cast at Him: but Jesus hid Himself, and went out of the temple, going through the midst of them, and so passed by." John 8:56-59

And when Jesus confessed before Caiaphas, the high priest, that Christ was the Son of God, Caiaphas condemned Him to death (Mark 14:60-64). "11 He came unto His own, and His own received Him not" (John 1:11). Then the leaders of Judah brought Him before Pilate the governor so that he would pass judgment and have Him crucified.

*King of Israel*_____ As you have read before Christ acknowledged publicly as well as personally many times to the Jewish authorities and to the common people that He is the King of the Jews.

Publicly Christ the "Word" said,

"5 Tell ye [all of you] the daughter of Sion [Zion], Behold, thy [Your] King cometh unto thee [you], meek, and sitting upon an ass, and a colt the foal of an ass."

The Messiah

Matthew 21:5
And personally, Christ said that He is the King of the Jews; but they rejected His claim when Christ said, "I am the King of the Jews."

> "21 Then said the chief priests of the Jews to Pilate, Write not, The King of the Jews; but that He said, I am King of the Jews." John 19:21

And to Nathanael, Jesus personally acknowledged that He is the King of Israel.

> "49 Nathanael answered and saith unto Him [Christ], Rabbi, thou [You] art the Son of God; thou [You] art the King of Israel." John 1:49

And when Jesus heard Nathanael, He acknowledged his words by saying to him, "50 Because I said unto thee [you], I saw thee under the fig tree, believest thou [you]?" John 1:50

Yes, Nathanael, like many others, did believe that Christ was "the King of Israel" and went on to become one of Christ's disciples. The throng that followed Jesus did believe that He was the King of the Jews; and Pilate proclaimed it as such. He said, to the crowd, what do you want me to do "unto Him whom ye call the King of the Jews?" Mark 15:12 (See also Mark 15:2, 9, 31, 32.)

*The Word became flesh*_____ The other astonishing fact the prophet of Christ the God of Israel reveals to us is by saying, "the Word" of verse one, who is identified by the name of "God," became "flesh."

> "14 And the Word [of v.1] was made flesh, and dwelt among us," John 1:14

Abraham's Seed

Apostle John says that they the disciples and all those individuals who saw Christ "(beheld His glory, the glory as of the only begotten of the Father,) full of grace and truth.

"15 John [the Baptist] bare witness of him, and cried, saying, This was He of whom I spake, He that cometh after me is preferred before me: for He was before me." John 1:14-15

But the Sadducees and Pharisees did temp John the Baptist in order to discredit him. But John stood his ground and continued to say to them that he was not the Christ. But John testified that Christ

"31 should be made manifest to Israel," and "32 bare record, saying, I saw the Spirit descending from heaven like a dove, and it abode upon Him." John 1:31, 32

And during Christ's ministry, Christ revealed Himself to the people throughout the land that He came in the "flesh" by claiming to be the "Messiah."

When the "Word" became "flesh," by what name was He identified? _____ According to the prophets of Christ the King of Israel, Christ the King of Israel is identified by the name of "Messiah"; and when the name "Messiah" is interpreted it means "Christ," and visa versa.

Here is the reference: "41 He [Andrew] first findeth his own brother Simon, and saith unto him, We have found the Messias [Eng. Messiah], which is, being interpreted, the Christ." John 1:41

Thus as per the above verse, the "Word," who was with "God" (Christ's Associate), became "flesh" (a human being); and that "flesh" is identified by the name of "Christ," which means "Messiah" (John 1:41).

In conclusion, although I stated earlier that Apostle John condensed the Torah in seven verses in his first chapter in order to reveal the Messiah; you would be surprised to know that Isaiah almost condenses the Torah in one single verse by revealing Christ's character names.

The verse reads as follows:

"16 O LORD of hosts, God of Israel, that dwellest between the cherubims, thou [you] art the God, even thou [you] alone, of all the kingdoms of the earth: thou [you] hast made heaven and earth." Isaiah 37:16

*   Therefore as per Scripture, we can refer to Jesus Christ by the following names, "the God of Abraham, Isaac, and Jacob," "the God of Israel," "the Rock," "the LORD of hosts," "Shiloh," "the King of Israel," "the King of glory," "Zion," "Redeemer," "the first and the last," "Jehovah," "the Most High God," "the LORD God of Abraham," "King of the Jews," "Creator," "God," "Messiah" (Christ), and by the character name of "the Word."

Abraham's Seed

According to the scientific community—if their calculations are correct—Adam, Eve, and their children lived a sinless life for about three billion years. And then, war erupted in heaven between Lucifer (Satan) and Christ the LORD of hosts. Satan's angels fought with Christ's angels. And eventually, Christ and His angels prevailed and cast Lucifer and his evil angels to planet earth because they had nowhere else to go.

The reason they were cast upon the earth was due to the fact that Eve and Adam sinned about six thousand years ago and threw their allegiance with Satan and his angels. They

Abraham's Seed

threw their allegiance with Satan because Satan promised them that they would become gods. Therefore Satan claimed dominion, which was Adam's and Eve's, over the earth and everything that was in it; and that included Adam's and Eve's sinless children.

> Here are the references,   "7 And there was war in heaven: Michael and his angels fought against the dragon; and the dragon fought and his angels, 8 And prevailed not; neither was their place found any more in heaven. 9 And the great dragon was cast out, that old serpent, called the Devil, and Satan, which deceiveth the whole world: he was cast out into the earth, and his angels were cast out with him." Revelation 12:7-9

It should be noted; Satan and his evil angels were cast down to planet earth after Adam sinned. Up until then, even though Eve had sinned first, Adam still had dominion over the earth and everything that was in it. But, as soon as Adam sinned, the earth became Satan's dominion.

Shortly after Adam chose to sin, Christ the LORD of hosts came down to the Garden of Eden and spoke to Adam and Eve regarding their sins. And when they heard Christ's voice, they recognized Him right away and hid from Him because they thought it was retribution time for their transgressions.

When Christ the LORD of hosts asked Adam and Eve what they did, in their defense, they began the blame game; Eve said that the serpent (dragon) deceived her and blamed it for her transgression; and Adam, in his defense, said to Christ the LORD of hosts that it was Eve's fault.

But, when they heard that Christ the LORD of hosts did not come down to punish them, they were relieved. And when they showed remorse for their transgressions, Christ

Abraham's Seed

the LORD offered them the Plan of Salvation. And when they heard that Christ the LORD was willing to die for them in order to pay for their sins, they were stunned and overwhelmed that their Creator the LORD God of the universe was willing to sacrifice Himself on their behalf in order to save them from their eternal demise.

Adam and Eve accepted the Plan of Salvation; and when they did, Christ the LORD of hosts partially unveiled the Plan of Salvation to them and to Satan (Lucifer) who was there listening to them. Christ the LORD of hosts assured them that when the fullness of time came, He would come out of the seed of a women through the lineage of Adam and save them.

And then, Christ the LORD of hosts said to the serpent (dragon),

> "14 Because thou [you] hast done this, thou art cursed above all cattle, and above every beast of the field; upon thy [your] belly shalt thou go, and dust shalt thou eat all thy days of thy [your] life:" Genesis 3:14

Today, according to Christ's curse, the dragon (serpent) has lost its legs and wings and it is slithering on the ground breathing dust as it travels from place to place.

And when Christ the LORD of hosts arrives in the flesh through a woman, Christ would "put enmity between thee [Satan] and the woman, and between thy [Satan's] seed and her seed."

> Christ said,   "15 And I [Christ the LORD of hosts] will put enmity between thee [you] and the woman, and between thy [your] seed and her seed; it shall bruise thy [your] head, and thou [you] shalt bruise His heel." Genesis 3:15

Abraham's Seed

As you have read in the above verse, the "Seed" that was going to come out of a woman to save Adam and Eve and their offspring is the personal pronoun "I." As a result, since Christ the LORD of hosts was speaking to Adam, Eve, snake (dragon), and Satan, it follows that the "I" of v.15 refers to Christ the LORD of hosts. Therefore Christ the LORD of hosts is the "Seed" that Adam, Eve, and their offspring were to look forward to His coming from a woman, in the flesh, and die for their sins. And to that end, the prophets of the Old Testament were looking to the coming of the "Seed" in the flesh.

The prophet of Christ the LORD agrees and says, "9 Receiving the end of your faith, even the salvation of your souls.

"10 Of which salvation the prophets have inquired and searched diligently, who prophesied of the grace that should come unto you: 11 Searching what, or what manner of time the Spirit of Christ which was in them did signify, when it testified beforehand the sufferings of Christ, and the glory that should follow.

"12 Unto whom it was revealed, that not unto themselves, but unto us they did minister the things, which are now reported unto you by them that have preached the gospel unto you with the Holy Ghost sent down form heaven; which things the angels desire to look into." 1 Peter 1:9-12

Therefore, for the Old Testament prophets, their message was that Christ the "Seed" was to come. And so it was, before the flood, the message was understood. The "Seed" (Christ) that was going to come out of a woman was to be procreated through the lineage of Adam, Seth, Enos, Cainan, Enoch, Methusalah, Lamech, and Noah. After the flood, the "Seed" (Christ) that was going to come out of a

Abraham's Seed

woman was to be procreated through the lineage of Noah, Shem, Abraham, Isaac, Jacob, and through Judah, the son of Jacob.

The reason Christ the LORD of hosts had chosen these individuals was due to their character. They loved Christ the LORD of hosts and because they loved Christ the LORD of hosts they did His will. And because they loved Christ the LORD, and wanted others to be saved, the Plan of Salvation was spread throughout the world by them. Through these holy men, Christ the "Seed" was to come out of a woman from the tribe of Judah.

So, how was Christ the LORD of hosts going to transfer Himself from an awesome Spirit Being, whose creation could not contain Him (1 Kings 8:27), into a woman and become the "Seed" (Baby) that was promised to Adam, Noah, Abraham, and to the rest of the prophets of Christ the LORD of hosts that followed?

If you recall, the coming of Christ the God of Israel in the flesh was explained by the pen of Isaiah. Christ the LORD of hosts was going to make the transfer from a spirit being and into a human being by His own desire, will, and "zeal."

Here is the prediction: "6 For unto us a child is born, unto us a son is given: and the government shall be upon His shoulder: and His name shall be called Wonderful, Counsellor, The mighty God, The everlasting Father, The Prince of Peace. 7 Of the increase of His government and peace there shall be no end, upon the throne of David, and upon His kingdom, to order it, and to establish it with judgment and with justice from henceforth even for ever."

Then the prophet of the LORD of hosts adds, "The zeal of the LORD of hosts will perform this." Isaiah 9:6, 7

Abraham's Seed

Did you notice who was going to perform the transfer? That's right! Christ the LORD of hosts was going to perform the transfer by His "zeal."

As you have read in the above verse, we are told that the transfer of Christ the LORD of hosts was going to take place by His own "zeal." Christ the LORD of hosts was going to make the transfer happen from an awesome powerful Spirit Being, whose creation could not contain Him (1 Kings 8:27), into a human being. If Christ the LORD did not want the transfer to take place, it would not have taken place. Therefore Christ had to take the initiative and accomplish the transfer from a Spirit being into a single cell in a woman who had to be from the tribe of Judah. And in order for that transfer to take place, Christ the LORD of hosts had to strip Himself from all of His awesome powers.

Here are the references: "5 Let this mind be in you, which was also in Christ Jesus: 6 Who, being in the form of God, thought it not robbery to be equal with God [Associate]: 7 But made Himself of no reputation, and took upon Him the form of a servant, and was made in the likeness of men: 8 And being found in fashion as a man, He humbled Himself, and became obedient unto death, even the death of the cross." Philippians 2:5-8

And once Christ the LORD of hosts removed His awesome powers from Himself, Christ the LORD of hosts, God the Holy Spirit, and Christ's Associate (God the Father) came to Mary and Christ turned Himself into a single cell and was implanted by God the Holy Spirit into Mary's ovary so that Christ the LORD of hosts would take on the form of human flesh.

Here are the references   "34 Then said   Mary unto the

Abraham's Seed

angel, How shall this be, seeing I know not [had no intercourse] a man? 35 And the angel answered and said unto her, The Holy Ghost shall come upon thee [you], and the power of the Highest [Christ's Associate] shall overshadow thee [you]: therefore also that holy thing which shall be born of thee [you] shall be called the Son of God." Luke 1:34, 35

Once the single cell of Christ the LORD of hosts was transferred by His "zeal" (Isaiah 9:7) into Mary by God the Holy Spirit, the cell began to take on the human nature of Mary. And after nine months, the "seed" (Christ the LORD of hosts) emerged from Mary in the form of a sinful "flesh."

Now before you start jumping up and down and tie your shirt into knots, please, I did not say Christ is a sinner! I am merely stating a fact that Christ was born out of a sinful woman.

> Apostle Paul agrees and says,   "4 when the fullness of time was come, God sent forth his Son, made of a woman, made under the law." Galatians 4:4

As per the above verses, Mary who gave birth to Jesus Christ the LORD of hosts was "under the law," therefore she (Mary) was a sinner (Romans 6:23); and therefore, she was in need to be saved from the law (the Ten Commandments as they are given in Exodus 20). And as a sinner, she gave Jesus Christ a body of a sinful flesh, just like your own body. You were born from a sinful flesh that is why your body degenerates and becomes old and eventually dies—Just as Christ's body did.

Apostle Paul confirms that fact. He says, "3 For what the law could not do, in that it was weak through the flesh, God [Christ's Associate] sending his own Son in the likeness of sinful flesh, and for sin, condemned sin in the flesh:"

Abraham's Seed

Romans 8:3

Therefore the "Seed" that was promised to Adam, Noah, Abraham, and Judah was not of seeds of many but of one "Seed" and that "Seed" that was promised in the beginning was Christ the LORD of hosts better known in the Old Testament by the name of the LORD God of Abraham.

Here is the reference: "16 Now to Abraham and his seed were the promises made. He saith not, And to seeds, as of many; but as of one, And to thy [your] seed, which is Christ" (Galatians 3:16).

And so it was, as per the prophetic clock of Daniel, and as per the fullness of time, Christ came into this world of ours in the form of a sinful flesh so that He could destroy sin as He promised.

And regards to Christ's birth, it was proclaimed by the angels throughout the land and by those individuals who saw the baby Jesus. Shepherds came to see Jesus, dignitaries came to see Jesus, even those individuals who waited for Christ's birth to take place saw baby Jesus. In fact even unbelievers saw baby Jesus all the way down to Egypt. And as a testimony and a witness to the house of Judah (Jews), as per the prophecies that their King had arrived, God (Christ's Associate) sent the wise men from the east to witness before the house of Judah and Herod the pagan king.

Following the prophetic events, the wise men from the east assembled a caravan and followed the star (angels) who led them to Jerusalem. When they arrived in Jerusalem, they began to ask the people saying, "Where is He that is born King of the Jews?" People were stunned; they said, "Herod was their king! They did not know of another king?"

"But we have seen His star!" they said.

Abraham's Seed

Through the commotion, the people did not know what to make of their query?

"Do we have another king?" they asked each other.

"What happened to King Herod?" others asked.

And as the wise men moved within the city stirring up the emotions of the people, and asking questions, they created quite a commotion. And when King Herod heard about the wise men and what they were seeking, they were quickly whisked before the king and found themselves explaining to the king how they came to believe that the King of the Jews had arrived?

The mere mention that King Herod had a rival ignited the fury of the king and anxiously wanted an explanation and answers. He wanted to know where was the King of the Jews?

The wise men stated the prophecies of the coming King and how they came here to look for Him.

"3 When Herod the king had heard these things, he was troubled, and all Jerusalem with him. 4 And when he had gathered all the chief priests and scribes of the people together, he demanded of them where Christ [Messiah] should be born.

"5 And they said unto him, In Bethlehem of Judaea: for thus it is written by the prophet [Micah 5:2], "6 And thou you] Bethlehem, in the land of Juda, art not the least among the princes of Juda: for out of thee [you] shall come a Governor, that shall rule my people Israel.

"7 Then Herod, when he had privily called the wise men, inquired of them diligently what time the star [angels] appeared. 8 And he sent them to Bethlehem, and said, Go and search diligently for the young child; and when ye [all of you] have found Him, bring me word again, that I may come

Abraham's Seed

and worship Him also. 9 When they had heard the king, they departed; and, lo, the star, which they saw in the east, went before them, till it came and stood over where the young child was. 10 When they saw the star, they rejoiced with exceeding great joy." Matthew 2:3-10

The wise men went into the manger and worshipped Jesus Christ the LORD of hosts and gave Him gifts. And when they finished worshipping Christ the King of Israel, they prepared for their journey; but, in a dream the wise men were warned not to go to Jerusalem and tell King Herod where baby Jesus was staying. Therefore the wise man with their caravan took another route to go home.

Likewise Joseph was told to take Mary and Jesus and flee to Egypt because Herod the king wants to do Jesus harm.

And when the king did not receive word from the wise men, "16 he saw that he was mocked of the wise men, was exceeding wroth, and sent forth, and slew all the children that were in Bethlehem, and in all the coasts thereof, from two years old and under, according to the time which he had diligently inquired of the wise men. 17 Then was fulfilled that which was spoken by Jeremy the prophet, saying, 18 In Rama was there a voice heard, lamentation, and weeping, and great mourning, Rachel weeping for her children, and would not be comforted, because they are not." Matthew 2:16-18

Isn't it strange, a pagan king believed the wise men and the prophecies that were quoted to him by the wise men, scribes, and by the priest of Judah; and yet, the scribes, priests, and the leaders of the Sanhedrin failed to document the incident, failed to investigate the event, and failed to see if Christ the King of Israel did arrive in the flesh as the prophecy of Micah the prophet had stated! (See Micah 5:2.)

Why did they not bother to investigate?

Why did they not go with the wise men to Bethlehem and confirm Christ's birth?

Abraham's Seed

Don't you find it odd, abnormal, weird, peculiar, unusual—should I go on—that the scribes did not go with the wise men to document the birth of Christ (Messiah)?

By the way, wasn't that the job of the scribes?

This was the first rejection of Jesus Christ the LORD of hosts by the house of Judah; but more particularly by the leaders of the house of Judah and not by the common men and women of Judah because many of them believed in the birth of Christ.

Nonetheless, although the motives of King Herod were self-serving, he at least believed the prophecies and implemented the plan to eradicate the baby Jesus. And so were Satan's motives. He encouraged Herod to go and destroy Jesus. And like before in heaven, Satan failed again to destroy Christ the LORD of hosts. But the battle had just begun on earth between Satan and Christ the LORD and between Satan's seed (followers) and Christ's seed (followers). But the battle between Christ and Satan would not come into fruition until such time Jesus Christ became of age where He would be able to distinguish between right and wrong.

Meanwhile, Joseph and his family remained in Egypt safe and sound and were sustained by selling the expensive gifts that were given to Jesus by the wise men. And when Herod the king died, the angel of the LORD of hosts was sent to Egypt to tell Joseph that it was safe to return to his home.

But when Joseph returned, he chose not to stay in the province of Judah; he chose the province of Galilee to live in; and he also chose a corrupt little town called Nazareth. There, Joseph set up his carpenter's shop and worked to sustain his family. As time went on, Joseph and Mary had a number of children who had diverse interest. But, in regards to Jesus, He chose to work in Joseph's carpenter shop. And as far as Christ's education was concerned, He received it

Abraham's Seed

from Mary by the power of God the Holy Spirit.

As Jesus was growing spiritually, so was His cousin John (the Baptist) growing spiritually in the wilderness of Judah. When John reached a mature spiritual growth by the help of God the Holy Spirit, he set out to preach that the Kingdom of God was at hand and baptized those who repented and accepted that the Kingdom of Christ the LORD of hosts was at hand.

By preaching that the kingdom of God the Christ was at hand, John was telling people that Christ (Messiah) was to appear very soon and they were to go to Him for the forgiveness of their sins and for their salvation.

But, the Pharisees and Sadducees tempted John and tried to discourage him from preaching the message of repentance and baptism; and when he saw them coming, "7 he said unto them, O generation of vipers, who hath warned you to flee from the wrath to come? 8 Bring forth therefore fruits meet for repentance: 9 And think not to say within yourselves, We have Abraham to our father: for I say unto you, that God is able of these stones to raise up children unto Abraham."

And then, a stern warning was given to them. John went to the core of the problem, which was the leadership of the house of Judah. John said, "10 And now also the axe is laid unto the root of the trees therefore every tree which bringeth not forth good fruit is hewn down, and cast into the fire." Matthew 3:7-10

The leaders of the house of Judah had fallen into apostasy; they were not there to hear the Plan of Salvation; they were there to discredit John the Baptist in order not to lose their church members to John the Baptist and amass followers to his cause. But, John could not be stopped; neither could the Sadducees, Pharisees, priests, elders, and the leaders of the Sanhedrin stop the message of repentance and of the coming of the Messiah (Christ).

Abraham's Seed

John said to his followers, "11 I indeed baptize you with water unto repentance: but He that cometh after me is mightier than I, whose shoes I am not worthy to bear: He shall baptize you with the Holy Ghost, and with fire: 12 Whose fan is in His hand, and He will throughly purge His floor, and gather His wheat into the garner; but He will burn up the chaff with unquenchable fire." Matthew 3:11, 12

John was the forerunner for Christ the LORD of hosts; John explained that he was not the Christ (Messiah). He was preparing the people for Christ's appearance. John was not there to build and accumulate followers to his own cause. He was to direct the people to Christ the LORD of hosts.

And when Jesus finally left His home in Nazareth at the age of about thirty, He set out to meet His cousin and be baptized of him before He started His ministry and proclaim to the house of Judah that He is the Messiah (Christ), the God of their fathers, the King of the Jews, and of the One Moses wrote about.

One day, as John was preaching the message of repentance and of the appearing of Christ, his spirit was agitated. And, as Jesus approached the crowd that was gathered and listening to John message, John realized that Christ was amongst them. And when Jesus came through the crowed and approached John, John said,

> "29 Behold the Lamb of God, which taketh away the sin of the world." John 1:29

Then Jesus asked John to baptize Him, "14 John forbad Him, saying, I have need to be baptized of thee [You], and comest thou [You] to me? 15 And Jesus answering said unto him, Suffer it to be so now: for thus it becometh us to fulfill all righteousness, Then he suffered Him." Matthew 3:14, 15

Although John understood that Jesus Christ the LORD

Abraham's Seed

of hosts was sinless and therefore He did not need to repent or to be baptized, John understood when Jesus said to him that He was leaving an example for others to follow, after they repent. Thus John acknowledged Christ's request and did perform the baptism.

> "16 And Jesus, when He was baptized, went up straightway out of the water: and, lo, the heavens were opened unto Him, and He saw the Spirit of God descending like a dove, and lighting upon Him: 17 And lo a voice from heaven, saying, This is my beloved Son, in whom I am well pleased." Matthew 3:16, 17

After Jesus was baptized, a person would think that Jesus would celebrate some sort of festivities for the fact that God (Christ's Associate) and God the Holy Spirit acknowledged and confirmed by their presence that Christ is the Messiah; instead, God the Holy Spirit took Christ the LORD of hosts to the wilderness to be tempted by Satan!

We are told, "12 And immediately the spirit driveth Him into the wilderness." Mark 1:12

"2 And when He had fasted forty days and forty nights, He was afterward an hungred. 3 And when the tempter [Satan] came to Him, he said, If thou [You] be the Son of God, command that these stones be made bread. 4 But He answered and said, It is written, Man shall not live by bread alone, but by every word that proceedeth out of the mouth of God. 5 Then the devil taketh Him up into the holy city, and setteth Him on a pinnacle of the temple, 6 And saith unto Him, If thou [You] be the Son of God, cast Thyself down: for it is written, He shall give His angels charge concerning thee [you]: and in their hands they shall bear thee [You] up, lest at any time thou [You] dash thy [Your] foot against a stone.

Abraham's Seed

"7 Jesus said unto him, It is written again, Thou [you] shalt not tempt the LORD thy [your] God. 8 Again, the devil taketh Him up into an exceeding high mountain, and sheweth Him all the kingdoms of the world, and the glory of them; 9 And saith unto Him, All these things will I give thee [You], if thou [You] wilt fall down and worship me. 10 Then saith Jesus unto him, Get thee hence, Satan: for it is written, Thou [you] shalt worship the LORD thy [your] God, and Him only shalt thou [you] serve.

"11 Then the devil leaveth Him, and, behold, angels came and ministered unto Him." Matthew 4:2-11

Satan was defeated again; he was defeated while Christ was in a lower form, a human being. This was the third time he was defeated. Satan was so mad at himself that he had to take a break for a little season before he went to pester Christ the LORD again with evil deceptive mind games.

But the question is; why did God the Holy Spirit take Jesus Christ the LORD of hosts to the wilderness to be tempted by the devil (Satan)?

He did in order to not only strengthen Christ for His mission at hand, which would eventually lead Him to be nailed on the cross, but also to meet His adversary so that Christ would know with whom He had to do mental and physical battle with.

After Christ's temptation and victory over Satan's temptations, hearing that John the Baptist was put in prison, Jesus went to His home in Galilee for a while. We are told, "14 And Jesus returned in the power of the Spirit into Galilee: and there went out a fame of Him through all the region round about. 15 And He taught in their synagogues, being glorified of all. 16 And he came to Nazareth, where He had been brought up: and, as His custom was, He went into the synagogue on the Sabbath day [Saturday], and stood up for to read. 17 And there was delivered unto Him the book

Abraham's Seed

of the prophet Esaias [Isaiah]. And when He had opened the book, He found the place where it was written,

> "18 The Spirit of the Lord is upon Me, because he hath anointed Me to preach the gospel to the poor; he hath sent Me to heal the brokenhearted, to preach deliverance to the captives, and recovering of sight to the blind, to set at liberty them that are bruised, 19 To preach the acceptable year of the Lord.

"20 And He closed the book, and He gave it again to the minister, and sat down. And the eyes of all them that were in the synagogue were fastened on Him. 21 And He began to say unto them, This day is this scripture fulfilled in your ears. 22 And all bare Him witness, and wondered at the gracious words which proceeded out of His mouth. And they said, Is not this Joseph's son? 23 And He said unto them, Ye [all of you] will surely say unto Me this proverb, Physician, heal thyself [Yourself]: whatsoever we have heard done in Capernaum, do also here in thy [your] country. 24 And He said, Verily [truly] I say unto you, No prophet is accepted in his own country. 25 But I tell you of truth, many widows were in Israel in the days of Elias, when the heaven was shut up three years and six months, when great famine was throughout all the land; 26 But unto none of them was Elias sent, save unto Sarepta, a city of Sidon, unto a woman that was a widow. 27 And, many lepers were in Israel in the time of Eliseus the prophet; and none of them was cleansed, saving Naaman the Syrian. 28 And all they in the synagogue, when they heard these things, were filled with wrath, 29 And rose up, and thrust Him out of the city, and led Him unto the brow of the hill whereon their city was built, that they might cast Him down headlong. 30 But He passing through the midst of them went His way." Luke 4:14-30 (Christ

Abraham's Seed

rejected in Galilee.)

And then He departed to "13 Capernaum, which is upon the sea coast, in the borders of Zabulon and Nephthalim: 14 That it might be fulfilled which was spoken by Esaias [Isaiah] the prophet, saying, 15 The land of Zabulon, and the land of Nephthalim, by the way of the sea, beyond Jordan, Galilee of the Gentiles; 16 The people which sat in darkness saw great light; and to them which sat in the region and shadow of death light is sprung up.

"17 From that time Jesus began to preach, and to say, Repent: for the kingdom of heaven is at hand." Matthew 4:13-17

"37 And the two disciples heard Him speak, and they followed Jesus.

"38 Then Jesus turned, and saw them following, and saith unto them, What seek ye? They said unto Him, Rabbi, (which is to say, being interpreted, Master,) where dwellest thou? 39 He saith unto them, Come and see. They came and saw where He dwelt, and abode with Him that day for it was about the tenth hour. 40 One of the two which heard John speak, and followed Him, was Andrew, Simon Peter's brother.

> "41 He first findeth his own brother Simon, and saith unto him, We have found the Messias [Messiah], which is, being interpreted, the Christ.

"42 And he brought him to Jesus. And when Jesus beheld him, He said, Thou art Simon the son of Jona: thou [you] shalt be called Cephas, which is by interpretation, A stone.

"43 The day following Jesus would go forth into Galilee, and findeth Philip, and saith unto him, Follow Me. 44 Now Philip was of Bethsaida, the city of Andrew and Peter.

Abraham's Seed

"45 Philip findeth Nathanael, and saith unto him, We have found Him, of whom Moses in the law, and the prophets, did write, Jesus of Nazareth, the son of Joseph.

"46 And Nathanael said unto him, Can there any good thing come out of Nazareth? Philip saith unto him, Come and see.

"47 Jesus saw Nathanael coming to Him, and saith of him, Behold an Israelite indeed, in whom is no guile! 48 Nathanael saith unto Him, Whence knowest thou me? Jesus answered and said unto him, Before that Philip called thee [you], when thou was under the fig tree, I saw thee.

"49 Nathanael answered and saith unto Him, Rabbi, thou [You] art the Son of God; thou [You] art the King of Israel. 50 Jesus answered and said unto him, Because I said unto thee [you], I saw thee under the fig tree, believest thou? thou shalt see greater things than these. 51 And He saith unto him, Verily, verily, I say unto you, Hereafter ye [all of you] shall see heaven open, and the angels of God ascending and descending upon the Son of man." John 1:37-51

From the above you can readily see that it was Jesus Christ the LORD of hosts who picked the eleven disciples; but the twelfth disciple was welcomed by the disciples.

Although Jesus did not choose Judas by saying to him follow Me," as He did with the other disciples, instead Christ revealed His poor homeless condition by saying to him,

"20 The foxes have holes, and the birds of the air have nests; but the Son of man hath not

210 _____ Moses Wrote About Me By: *Philip Mitanidis*
Abraham's Seed

where to lay His head." Matthew 8:20

But, since Judas wanted to follow Christ, Christ gave Judas the opportunity to repent from his selfish motives and to become part of the twelve disciples. Jesus would not turn anyone away without giving a person the opportunity to be saved from his or her eternal demise. Jesus came to save everyone who wants to be saved; none are excluded. Jesus loves the human race so much that He gave his life on the cruel cross to save it.

Nonetheless, Jesus ordained the twelve disciples; and then, "1 He gave them power against unclean spirits, to cast them out, and to heal all manner of sickness and all manner of disease." Matthew 10:1

And then Jesus gave the warning before He sent them to preach the Gospel to the entire world. Christ the LORD of hosts said to them, "16 Behold, I send you forth as sheep in the midst of wolves: be ye [all of you] therefore wise as serpents, and harmless as doves. 17 But beware of men: for they will deliver you up to the councils, and they will scourge you in their synagogues; 18 And ye shall be brought before governors and kings for My sake, for a testimony against them and the Gentiles. 19 But when they deliver you up, take no thought how or what ye shall speak: for it shall be given you in that same hour what ye shall speak. 20 For it is not ye [all of you] that speak, but the Spirit of your Father which speaketh in you." "22 And ye shall be hated of all men for My name's sake: but he that endureth to the end shall be saved. 23 But when they persecute you in this city, flee ye into another: for verily I say unto you, Ye shall not have gone over the cities of Israel, till the Son of man be come." Matthew 10:16-20, 21-23

Although Christ the LORD of hosts was giving the disciples the warning that same warning applied to Jesus

Abraham's Seed

Christ. He was constantly hounded by the leaders of the house of Judah, tempted, and looked for entrapment. But as hard as they would try, they could not win an argument with Him. Instead Christ the LORD of hosts revealed their state of apostasy and they did not like that. They grew callous hearts and tried very hard not to lose their members from their synagogues because Christ continued to draw the people to Himself.

The leaders of the house of Judah were worried of losing their members; and if they lost their members they would lose their status, the homage of the people, their elite club, the preferred upper rooms in the meeting places, their rule of law, tradition, etc.

Nonetheless, Christ and His disciples "21 went into Capernaum; and straightway on the Sabbath day [Saturday] He entered into the synagogue, and taught. 22 And they were astonished at His doctrine: for He taught them as one that had authority, and not as the scribes. 23 And there was in their synagogue a man with an unclean spirit; and he cried out, 24 Saying, Let us alone; what have we to do with thee [You], thou [You] Jesus of Nazareth? Art thou [You] come to destroy us? I know thee [You] who thou art, the Holy One of God. 25 And Jesus rebuked him, saying, Hold thy [your] peace, and come out of him. 26 And when the unclean spirit had torn him, and cried with a loud voice, he came out of him. 27 And they were all amazed, insomuch that they questioned among themselves, saying, What thing is this? what new doctrine is this? for with authority commandeth He even the unclean spirits, and they do obey Him. 28 And immediately His fame spread abroad throughout all the region round about Galilee.

"29 And forthwith, when they were come out of the synagogue, they entered into the house of Simon and Andrew, with James and John. 30 But Simon's wife's mother

212 _____ Moses Wrote About Me By: *Philip Mitanidis*

Abraham's Seed

lay sick of a fever, and anon they tell Him of her, 31 And He came and took her by the hand, and lifted her up; and immediately the fever left her, and she ministered unto them.

"32 And at even, when the sun did set, they brought unto Him all that were diseased, and them that were possessed with devils. 33 And all the city was gathered together at the door. 34 And He healed many that were sick of divers diseases, and cast out many devils; and suffered not the devils to speak, because they knew Him. 35 And in the morning, rising up a great while before day, He went out, and departed into a solitary place, and there prayed. 36 And Simon and they that were with Him followed after Him. 37 And when they had found Him, they said unto Him, All men seek for thee [you]. 38 And He said unto them, Let us go into the next towns, that I may preach there also: for therefore came I forth. 39 And He preached in their synagogues throughout all Galilee, and cast out devils,

"40 And there came a leper to Him, beseeching Him, and kneeling down to Him, and saying unto Him, If thou [You] wilt, thou [You] canst make me clean. 41 And Jesus, moved with compassion, put forth His hand, and touched him, and saith unto him, I will; be thou [you] clean. 42 And as soon as He had spoken, immediately the leprosy departed from him, and he was cleansed. 43 And He straitly charged him, and forthwith sent him away; 44 And saith unto him, See thou [you] say nothing to any man: but go thy [your] way, shew thyself [yourself] to the priest, and offer for thy [your] cleansing those things which Moses commanded, for a testimony unto them [leaders of the house of Judah].

"45 But he went out, and began to publish it much, and to blaze abroad the matter, insomuch that Jesus could no more openly enter into the city, but was without in desert places: and they came to Him from

Abraham's Seed

every quarter." Mark 1:21-45

"1 And again He entered into Capernaum after some days; and it was noised that He was in the house. 2 And straightway many were gathered together, in somuch that there was no room to receive them, no, not so much as about the door: and He preached the word unto them. 3 And they came unto Him, bringing one sick of the palsy, which was borne of four. 4 And when they could not come nigh unto Him for the press, they uncovered the roof where he was: and when they had broken it up, they let down the bed wherein the sick of the palsy lay. 5 When Jesus saw their faith, He said unto the sick of the palsy, Son, thy [your] sins be forgiven thee [you].

"6 But there were certain of the scribes sitting there, and reasoning in their hearts, 7 Why doth this man thus speak blasphemies? who can forgive sins but God only? 8 And immediately when Jesus perceived in His spirit that they so reasoned within themselves, He said unto them, Why reason ye these things in your hearts. 9 Whether is it easier to say to the sick of the palsy, Thy sins be forgiven thee [you]; or to say, Arise, and take up thy [your] bed, and walk? 10 But that ye [all of you] may know that the Son of man hath power on earth to forgive sins (He saith to the sick of the palsy,) 11 I say unto thee [you], Arise, and take up thy [your] bed, and go thy way into thine house, 12 And immediately he arose, took up the bed, and went forth before them all; insomuch that they were all amazed, and glorified God, saying, We never saw it on this fashion." Mark 2:1-12

"1 And He entered again into the synagogue; and there was a man there which had a withered hand. 2 And they watched Him, whether He would heal him on the sabbath day [Saturday]; that they might accuse Him. 3 And He saith unto the man which had the withered hand, Stand forth. 4 And He saith unto them, Is it lawful to do good on the

Abraham's Seed

Sabbath days, or to do evil? to save life, or to kill? But they held their peace. 5 And when He had looked round about on them with anger, being grieved for the hardness of their hearts, He saith unto the man, Stretch forth thine hand. And he stretched it out: and his hand was restored whole as the other. 6 And the Pharisees went forth, and straightway took counsel with the Herodians against Him, how they might destroy Him." Mark 3:1-6

"7 But Jesus withdrew Himself with His disciples to the sea: and a great multitude from Galilee followed Him, and from Judaea, 8 And from Jerusalem, and from Idumaea, and from beyond Jordan; and they about Tyre and Sidon, a great multitude, when they had heard what great things He did, came unto Him.

"9 And He spake to His disciples, that a small ship should wait on Him because of the multitude, lest they should throng Him. 10 For He had healed many; insomuch that they pressed upon Him for to touch Him, as many as had plagues. 11 And unclean spirits, when they saw Him, fell down before Him, and cried, saying, Thou [You] art the Son of God." Mark 3:7-11

"1 And they came over unto the other side of the sea, into the country of the Gadarenes. 2 And when He was come out of the ship, immediately there met Him out of the tombs a man with an unclean spirit, 3 Who had his dwelling among the tombs; and no man could bind him, no, not with chains: 4 Because that he had been often bound with fetters and chains, and the chains had been plucked asunder by him, and the fetters broken in pieces: neither could any man tame him. 5 And always, night and day, he was in the mountains, and in the tombs, crying, and cutting himself with stones.

"6 But when he saw Jesus afar off, he ran and

Abraham's Seed

worshipped Him. 7 And cried with a loud voice, and said, What have I to do with thee [You], Jesus, thou [You] Son of the most high God? [Grk. Son of God the highest] I adjure thee [You] by God, that thou [You] torment me not. 8 For He said unto him, Come out of the man, thou unclean spirit. 9 And He asked him, What is thy [your] name? And he answered, saying, My name is Legion; for we are many. 10 And he besought Him much that He would not send them away out of the country.

"11 Now there was there nigh unto the mountains a great heard of swine feeding. 12 And all the devils besought Him, saying, Send us into the swine, that we may enter into them. 13 And forthwith Jesus gave them leave. And the unclean spirits went out, and entered into the swine: and the herd ran violently down a steep place into the sea. (they were about two thousand;) and were choked in the sea." Mark 5:1-13

"1 And He went out from thence, and came into His own country; and His disciples follow Him. 2 And when the Sabbath day was come, He began to teach in the synagogue: and many hearing Him were astonished, saying, From whence hath this man these things? and what wisdom is this which is given unto Him, that even such mighty works are wrought by His hands? 3 Is not this the carpenter, the son of Mary, the brother of James, and Joses, and of Juda, and Simon? and are not His sisters here with us? And they were offended at Him. 4 But Jesus said unto them, A prophet is not without honour, but in his own country, and among his own kin, and in his own house. 5 And He could there do no mighty work, save that He laid His hands upon a few sick folk, and healed them. 6 And He marveled because of their unbelief. And He went round about the villages, teaching." Mark 6:1-6   (rejection at Nazareth)

Abraham's Seed

"53 And when they had passed over, they came into the land of Gennesaret, and drew to the shore. 54 And when they were come out of the ship, straightway they knew Him, 55 And ran through that whole region round about, and began to carry about in beds those that were sick, where they heard He was. 56 And whithersoever He entered, into villages, or cities, or country, they laid the sick in the streets, and besought Him that they might touch if it were but the border of His garment: and as many as touched Him were made whole." Mark 6:53-56

"1 Then came together unto Him the Pharisees, and certain of the scribes, which came from Jerusalem. 2 And when they saw some of His disciples eat bread with defiled, that is to say, with unwashen, hands, they found fault. 3 For the Pharisees, and all the Jews, except they wash their hands oft, eat not, holding the tradition of the elders. 4 And when they come from the market, except they wash, they eat not. And many other things there be, which they have received to hold, as the washing of cups, and pots, brazen vessels, and of tables.

"5 Then the Pharisees and scribes asked Him, Why walk not thy [your] disciples according to the tradition of the elders, but eat bread with unwashen hands?

"6 He [Christ] answered and said unto them, Well hath Esaias [Isaiah] prophesied of you hypocrites, as it is written, This people honoureth Me with their lips, but their heart is far from Me. 7 Howbeit in vain do they worship Me, teaching for doctrines the commandments of men. 8 For laying aside the commandment of God, ye [all of you] hold the tradition of men, as the washing of pots and cups: and many other such like things ye [all of you] do. 9 And He said unto them, Full well ye [all of you] reject the commandment of God, that ye may keep your own tradition.

"10 For Moses said, Honour thy [your] father and thy

Abraham's Seed

[your] mother; and, Whoso curseth father or mother, let him die the death: 11 But ye say, If a man shall say to his father or mother, It is Corban, that is to say, a gift, by whatsoever thou [you] mightest be profited by Me; he shall be free. 12 And ye suffer him no more to do ought for his father or his mother; 12 Making the word of God of none effect through your tradition, which ye have delivered: and may such like things do ye." Mark 7:1-13

"10 And straightway He entered into a ship; with His disciples, and came into the parts of Dalmanutha. 11 And the Pharisees came forth, and began to question with Him, seeking of Him a sign from heaven, tempting Him. 12 And He sighed deeply in His spirit, and saith, Why doth this generation seek after a sign? verily I say unto you, There shall no sign be given unto this generation. 13 And He left them, and entering into the ship again departed to the other side." Mark 8:10-13

"34 And when He had called the people unto Him with His disciples also, He said unto them, Whosoever will come after Me, let him deny himself, and take up his cross, and follow Me. 35 For whosoever will save his life shall lose it; but whosoever shall lose his life for My sake and the Gospel's, the same shall save it. 36 For what shall it profit a man, if he shall gain the whole world, and lose his own soul? 37 Or what shall a man give in exchange for his soul? 38 Whosoever therefore shall be ashamed of Me and of My words in this adulterous and sinful generation; of him also shall the Son of man be ashamed, when He cometh in the glory of His Father with the holy angels." Mark 8:34-38

"14 And when He came to His disciples, He saw a great multitude about them, and the scribes questioning with

Abraham's Seed

them. 15 And straightway all the people, when they beheld Him, were greatly amazed, and running to Him saluted Him. 16 And He asked the scribes, What question ye with them?

"17 And one of the multitude answered and said, Master, I have brought unto Thee [You] my son, which hath a dumb spirit: 18 And wheresoever he taketh him, he teareth him: and he foameth, and gnasheth with his teeth, and pineth away: and I spake to thy [Your] disciples that they should cast him out; and they could not.

"19 He answereth him, and saith, O faithless generation, how long shall I be with you? how long shall I suffer you? bring him unto Me. 20 And they brought him unto Him [Jesus]: and when He saw him, straightway the spirit tare him; and he fell on the ground, and wallowed foaming. 21 And He [Christ] asked his father, How long is it ago since this came unto him? And he said, Of a child. 22 And ofttimes it hath cast him into the fire, and into the waters, to destroy him: but if thou canst do any thing, have compassion on us, and help us. 23 Jesus said unto him, If thou [you] canst believe, all things are possible to him that believeth.

"24 And straightway the father of the child cried out, and said with tears, LORD, I believe; help thou mine unbelief.

"25 When Jesus saw that the people came running together, He rebuked the foul spirit, saying unto him, Thou [you] dumb and deaf spirit, I charge thee [you], come out of him, and enter no more into him. 26 And the spirit cried, and rent him sore, and came out of him and he was as one dead; insomuch that said, He is dead. 27 But Jesus took him by the hand, and lifted him up; and he arose." Mark 9:14-27

"30 And they departed thence, and passed through Galilee; and He would not that any man should know it. 31 For He taught His disciples, and said unto them, the Son of man is delivered into the hands of men, and they shall kill Him; and after that He is killed, He shall rise the third day. 32

Abraham's Seed

But they understood not that saying, and were afraid to ask Him." Mark 9:30-32

"46 And they came to Jericho: and as He went out of Jericho with His disciples and a great number of people, blind Bartimaeus, the son of Timaeus, sat by the highway side begging. 47 And when he heard that it was Jesus of Nazareth, he began to cry out, and say, Jesus, thou [You] son of David, have mercy on me. 48 And many charged him that he should hold his peace: but he cried the more a great deal, Thou Son of David, have mercy on me.

"49 And Jesus stood still, and commanded him to be called. And they call the blind man, saying unto him, Be of good comfort, rise; He calleth thee [you]. 50 And he casting away his garment, rose, and came to Jesus. 51 And Jesus answered and said unto him, What wilt thou [you] that I should do unto thee? The blind man said unto Him, LORD, that I might receive my sight.

"52 And Jesus said unto him, Go thy [your] way; thy [your] faith hath made thee [you] whole. And immediately he received his sight, and followed Jesus in the way." Mark 10:46-52

Heading towards the fourth Passover and His final days of ministry, Jesus decided to appear and claim publicly as a witness to the priests, scribes, elders, and to the leaders of the house of Judah that He is the King of the Jews and to also fulfill the prophecies of old, which Jacob foretold Christ riding an ass and ass's colt.

Here is the prophecy: "10 The sceptre shall not depart from Judah, nor a lawgiver from between his feet, until Shiloh come; and unto Him shall the gathering of the people be.

"11 Binding His foal unto the vine [the house of

Abraham's Seed

Israel], and His ass's colt unto the choice of vine [the house of Judah]" (Genesis 49:10, 11).

And here is the actual fulfillment: "1 And when they [Christ and the disciples] drew nigh unto Jerusalem, and were come to Bethphage, unto the mount of Olives, then sent Jesus two disciples, 2 Saying unto them, Go into the village over against you, and straightway ye shall find an ass tied, and a colt with her: loose them, and bring them unto Me. 3 And if any man say ought unto you, ye [all of you] shall say, The LORD hath need of them, and straightway he will send them. "4 All this was done, that it might be fulfilled which was spoken by the prophet, saying,

"5 Tell ye [all of you] the daughter of Sion [Zion], Behold, thy [Your] King cometh unto thee [you], meek, and sitting upon an ass, and a colt the foal of an ass." Matthew 21:1-5

And, the multitude that was standing on each side of the road did tell Zion that "thy [Your] King cometh unto thee [you]," by their actions and by the shouting of hosanna's.

Here is the account: "6 And the disciples went, and did as Jesus commanded them. 7 And brought the ass, and the colt, and put on them their clothes, and they set Him thereon. 8 And a very great multitude spread their garments in the way; others cut down branches from the trees, and strawed them in the way. 9 And the multitudes that were before, and that followed, cried, saying, Hosanna to the Son of David: Blessed is he that cometh in the name of the LORD; Hosanna in the highest.

"10 And when He was come into Jerusalem, all the city was moved, saying, Who is this? 11 And the multitude said, This is Jesus the prophet of Nazareth of Galilee.

Abraham's Seed

"12 And Jesus went into the temple of God, and cast out all them that sold and bought in the temple, and overthrew the tables of the moneychangers, and the seats of them that sold doves,

> "13 And said unto them, It is written My house shall be called the house of prayer; but ye have made it a den of thieves.

"14 And the blind and the lame came to Him in the temple; and He healed them. 15 And when the chief priests and scribes saw the wonderful things that He did, and the children crying in the temple, and saying, Hosanna to the son of David; they were sore displeased, 16 And said unto Him, Hearest thou [You] what these say? And Jesus saith unto them; Yea; have ye never read, Out of the mouth of babes and sucklings thou hast perfected praise? 17 And He left them, and went out of the city into Bethany; and He lodged there" with the twelve disciples. Matthew 21:6-17

As per the above, Christ (Messiah) claims, as He had claimed all along that He was the King of Israel. He not only testified that He was the King of Israel verbally but also by riding "His ass's colt" to the city of Jerusalem, just as Jacob had predicted. Christ said,

> "5 Tell ye [all of you] the daughter of Sion [Zion], Behold, thy [Your] King cometh unto thee [you] meek, and sitting upon an ass, and a colt the foal of an ass" (Matthew 21:5).

The next day, Jesus and His disciples came to "15 Jerusalem: and Jesus went into the temple, and began to cast out them that sold and bought in the temple, and overthrew the tables of the moneychangers, and the seats of them that

Abraham's Seed

sold doves; 16 And would not suffer that any man should carry any vessel through the temple. 17 And He taught, saying unto them, Is it not written, My house shall be called of all nations the house of prayer? but ye [all of you] have made it a den of thieves. 18 And the scribes and the chief priests heard it, and sought how they might destroy Him: for they feared Him, because all the people was astonished at His doctrine. 19 And when even was come, He went out of the city." Mark 11:15-19

The following day, "27 they come again to Jerusalem: and as He was walking in the temple, there come to Him the chief priests, and the scribes, and the elders, 28 And say unto Him, by what authority doest thou [You] these things? and who gave thee [You] this authority to do these things? 29 And Jesus answered and said unto them, I will also ask of you one question, and answer Me, and I will tell you by what authority I do these things. 30 The baptism of John, was it from heaven, or of men? answer Me. 31 And they reasoned with themselves, saying, If we shall say, From heaven; he will say, Why then did ye not believe him? 32 But if we shall say, Of men; they feared the people: for all men counted John, that he was a prophet indeed. 33 And they answered and said unto Jesus, We cannot tell. And Jesus answering saith unto them, Neither do I tell you by what authority I do these things." Mark 11:27-33

"1 Then spake Jesus to the multitude, and to His disciples, 2 Saying, The scribes and the Pharisees sit in Moses' seat: 3 All therefore whatsoever they bid you observe, that observe and do; but do not ye [all of you] after their works: for they say, and do not. 4 For they bind heavy burdens and grievous to be borne, and lay them on men's shoulders; but they themselves will not move them with one of their fingers. 5 But all their works they do for to be seen of men: they make broad their phylacteries, and enlarge the

Abraham's Seed

borders of their garments, 6 And love the uppermost rooms at feasts, and the chief seats in the synagogues, 7 And greetings in the markets, and to be called of men, Rabbi, Rabbi. 8 But be not ye [all of you] called Rabbi: for one is your Master, even Christ and all ye are brethren. 9 And call no man your father upon the earth: for one is your Father, which is in heaven. 10 Neither be ye called masters: for one is your Master, even Christ. 11 But he that is greatest among you shall be your servant. 12 And whosoever shall exalt himself shall be abased; and he that shall humble himself shall be exalted.

"13 But woe unto you, scribes and Pharisees, hypocrites! for ye [all of you] shut up the kingdom of heaven against men: for ye neither go in yourselves, neither suffer ye them that are entering to go in. 14 Woe unto you, scribes and Pharisees, hypocrites! for ye [all of you] devour widows' houses, and for a pretence make long prayer: therefore ye shall receive the greater damnation. 15 Woe unto you, scribes and Pharisees, hypocrites! for ye compass sea and land to make one proselyte, and when he is made, ye make him twofold more the child of hell than yourselves.

"16 Woe unto you, ye blind guides, which say, Whosoever shall swear by the temple, it is nothing; but whosoever shall swear by the gold of the temple, he is a debtor! 17 Ye fools and blind: for whether is greater, the gold, or the temple that sanctifieth the gold? 18 And, Whosoever shall swear by the altar, it is nothing; but whosoever sweareth by the gift that is upon it, he is guilty. 19 Ye fools and blind: for whether is greater, the gift, or the altar that sanctifieth the gift? 20 Whoso therefore shall swear by the altar, sweareth by it, and by all things thereon. 21 And

Abraham's Seed

whoso shall swear by the temple, sweareth by it, and by Him that dwelleth there in. 22 And he that shall swear by heaven, sweareth by the throne of God, and by him that sitteth thereon. 23 Woe unto you, scribes and Pharisees, hypocrites! for ye pay tithe of mint and anise and cumin, and have omitted the weightier matters of the law, judgment, mercy, and faith: these ought ye to have done, and not to leave the other undone. 24 Ye blind guides, which strain at a gnat, and swallow a camel. 25 Woe unto you scribes and Pharisees, hypocrites! for ye make clean the outside of the cup and of the platter, but within they are full of extortion and excess. 26 Thou [you] blind Pharisees, cleanse first that which is within the cup and platter, that the outside of them may be clean also. 27 Woe unto you, scribes and Pharisees, hypocrites! for ye are like unto whited sepulchers, which indeed appear beautiful outward, but are within full of dead men's bones, and of all uncleanness. 28 Even so ye also outwardly appear righteous unto men, but within ye are full of hypocrisy and iniquity.

"29 Woe unto you, scribes and Pharisees, hypocrites! because ye build the tombs of the prophets, and garnish the sepulchers of the righteous, 30 And say, If we had been in the days of our fathers, we would not have been partakers with them in the blood of the prophets. 31 Wherefore ye be witnesses unto your selves, that ye are the children of them which killed the prophets. 32 Fill ye up then the measure of you fathers. 33 Ye serpents, ye generation of vipers, how can ye escape the damnation of hell?

"34 Wherefore, behold, I send unto you prophets, and wise men, and scribes: and some of them ye shall kill and crucify; and some of them shall ye scourge in your synagogues, and persecute them from city to city: 35 That upon you may come all the righteous blood shed upon the earth, from the blood of righteous Abel unto the blood of

Abraham's Seed

Zacharias son of Barachias, whom ye slew between the temple and the altar. 36 Verily I say unto you, All these things shall come upon this generation.

"37 O Jerusalem, Jerusalem, thou [you] that killest the prophets, and stonest them which are sent unto thee [you], how often would I have gathered thy [your] children together, even as a hen gathereth her chickens under her wings, and ye would not! 38 Behold, your house is left unto you desolate [Read 1 Kings 9:6-9 to see why the Sanctuary has been left desolate.]. 39 For I say unto you, Ye shall not see Me hence forth, till ye shall say, Blessed is he that cometh in the name of the LORD." Matthew 23:1-39

"1 After two days was the feast of the passover, and of unleavened bread: and the chief priests and the scribes sought how they might take Him [Christ] by craft, and put Him to death. 2 But they said, Not on the feast day, least there be an uproar of the people." Mark 14:1, 2

"12 And the first day of unleavened bread, when they killed the Passover, His disciples said unto him, Where wilt thou [You] that we go and prepare that thou [you] mayest eat the passover?

"13 And He sendeth forth two of His disciples, and saith unto them, Go ye [all of you] into the city, and there shall meet you a man bearing a pitcher of water: follow him. 14 And wheresoever he shall go in, say ye to the goodman of the house, The Master saith, Where is the guestchamber, where I shall eat the passover with My disciples? 15 And he will shew you a large upper room furnished and prepared: there make ready for us. 16 And His disciples went forth, and came into the city, and found as He had said unto them: and they made ready the passover.

Abraham's Seed

"17 And in the evening He cometh with the twelve. 18 And as they sat and did eat, Jesus said, Verily I say unto you, One of you which eateth with Me shall betray Me. 19 And they began to be sorrowful, and to say unto Him one by one, Is it I? and another said, Is it I? 20 And He answered and said unto them, It is one of the twelve, that dippeth with Me in the dish. 21 The Son of man indeed goeth, as it is written of Him: but woe to that man by whom the Son of man is betrayed! good were it for that man if he had never been born.

"22 And as they did eat, Jesus took bread, and blessed, and brake it, and gave to them, and said, Take, eat: this is My body. 23 And He took the cup, and when He had given thanks, He gave it to them: and they all drank of it. 24 And He said unto them, This is My blood of the new testament, which is shed for many. 25 Verily I say unto you, I will drink no more of the fruit of the vine, until that day that I drink it new in the kingdom of God. 26 And when they had sung an hymn, they went out into the mount of Olives.

"27 And Jesus saith unto them, All ye shall be offended because of Me this night: for it is written, I will smite the shepherd, and the sheep shall be scattered. 28 But after that I am risen, I will go before you into Galilee. 29 But Peter said unto Him, Although all shall be offended, yet will not I. 30 And Jesus saith unto him, Verily, I say unto thee [you], That this day, even in this night, before the cock crow twice, thou [you] shalt deny Me thrice. 31 But he spake the more vehemently, If I should die with thee [You], I will not deny thee [You] in any wise. Likewise also said they all.

"32 And they came to a place which was named Gethsemane: and He saith to His disciples, Sit ye [all of you] here, while I shall pray. 33 And He taketh with Him Peter

Abraham's Seed

and James and John, and began to be sore amazed, and to be very heavy; 34 And saith unto them, My soul is exceeding sorrowful unto death: tarry ye here, and watch. 35 And He went forward a little, and fell on the ground, and prayed that, if it were possible, the hour might pass from Him. 36 And He said, Abba, Father, all things are possible unto thee [you]; take away this cup from Me: nevertheless not what I will, but what thou [you] wilt. 37 And He cometh, and findeth them sleeping, and saith unto Peter, Simon, sleepest thou? couldest not thou [you] watch one hour? 38 Watch ye and pray, lest ye enter into temptation. The spirit truly is ready, but the flesh is weak. 39 And again He went away, and prayed, and spake the same words, 40 And when He returned, He found them asleep again, (for their eyes were heavy,) neither wist they what to answer Him. 41 And He cometh the third time, and saith unto them, Sleep on now, and take your rest: it is enough, the hour is come; behold, the Son of man is betrayed into the hands of sinners. 42 Rise up, let us go; lo, he that betrayeth Me is at hand.

"43 And immediately, while He yet spake, cometh Judas, one of the twelve, and with him a great multitude with swords and staves, from the chief priests and the scribes and the elders. 44 And he that betrayed Him had given them a token, saying, Whomsoever I shall kiss, the same is He; take Him, and lead Him away safely. 45 And as soon as he was come, he goeth straightway to Him, and saith, Master, master; and kissed Him."

> And Jesus said unto him, "Judas, betrayest thou [you] the Son of man with a kiss?"

"46 And they laid their hands on Him, and took Him. 47 And one of them that stood by drew a sword, and smote a servant of the High priest, and cut off his ear. 48 And Jesus

Abraham's Seed

answered and said unto them, Are ye come out, as, against a thief, with swords and with staves to take Me? 49 I was daily with you in the temple teaching, and ye took Me not: but the scriptures must be fulfilled. 50 And they all forsook Him, and fled. 51 And there followed Him a certain young man, having a linen cloth cast about His naked body; and the young men laid hold on Him: 52 And he left the linen cloth, and fled from them naked.

"53 And they led Jesus away to the high priest: and with him were assembled all the chief priests and the elders and the scribes 54 And Peter followed Him afar off, even into the palace of the high priest: and he sat with the servants, and warmed himself at the fire. 55 And the chief priests and all the council sought for witness against Jesus to put Him to death; and found none. 56 For many bare false witness against Him, but their witness agreed not together. 57 And there arose certain, and bare false witness against Him, saying, 58 We heard Him say, I will destroy this temple that is made with hands, and within three day I will build another made without hands [Jesus was referring to His human body]. 59 But neither so did their witness agree together. 60 And the high priest stood up in the midst, and asked Jesus, saying, Answerest thou [You] nothing? what is it which these witness against thee [You]?

"61 But He held His peace, and answered nothing. Again the high priest asked Him, and said unto Him, Art thou [You] the Christ, The Son of the Blessed?

"62 And Jesus said, I am: and ye [all of you] shall see the Son of man sitting on the right hand of power, and coming in the clouds of heaven.

"63 Then the high priest rent his clothes, and saith, What

Abraham's Seed

need we any further witnesses? 64 Ye have heard the blasphemy: what think ye? And they all condemned Him to be guilty of death.

"65 And some began to spit on Him, and to cover His face, and to buffet Him, and to say unto Him, Prophesy: and the servants did strike Him with the palms of their hands.

"66 And as Peter was beneath in the palace, there cometh one of the maids of the high priest: 67 And when she saw Peter warming himself, she looked upon him, and said, And thou [you] also wast with Jesus of Nazareth. 68 But he denied, saying, I know not, neither understand I what thou sayest. And he went out into the porch; and the cock crew. 69 And a maid saw him again, and began to say to them that stood by, This is one of them. 70 And he denied it again. And a little after, they that stood by said again to Peter, Surely thou [you] art one of them: for thou [you] art a Galilaean, and thy [your] speech agreeth thereto. 71 But he began to curse and to swear, saying, I know not this man of whom ye [all of you] speak. 72 And the second time the cock crew. And Peter called to mind the words that Jesus said unto him, Before the cock crow twice, thou [you] shalt deny Me thrice. And when he thought thereon, he wept." Mark 14:12-72

"1 And straightway in the morning the chief priests held a consultation with the elders and scribes and the whole council, and bound Jesus, and carried Him away, and delivered Him to Pilate.

"2 And Pilate asked Him [Christ], Art thou [You] the King of the Jews? And He answering said unto him, Thou sayest it.

"3 And the chief priests accused Him of many things: but He answered nothing.

Abraham's Seed

"4 And Pilate asked Him again, saying, Answerest thou [You] nothing? behold how many things they witness against thee [You]. 5 But Jesus yet answered nothing; so that Pilate marveled.

"6 Now at that feast he released unto them one prisoner, whomsoever they desired. 7 And there was one named Barabbas, which lay bound with them that had made insurrection with him, who had committed murder in the insurrection. 8 And the multitude crying aloud began to desire him to do as he had ever done unto them.

"9 But Pilate answered them, saying, Will ye [all of you] that I release unto you the King of the Jews? 10 For he knew that the chief priests had delivered Him for envy.

"11 But the chief priests moved the people, that he should rather release Barabbas unto them.

"12 And Pilate answered and said again unto them, What will ye then that I shall do unto Him whom ye call the King of the Jews?

"13 And they cried out again, Crucify Him.

"14 Then Pilate said unto them, Why, what evil hath He done? And they cried out the more exceedingly, Crucify Him.

"15 And so Pilate, willing to content the people, released Barabbas unto them, and delivered Jesus, when he had scourged Him, to be crucified. 16 And the soldiers led Him away into the hall, called Praetorium; and they call together the whole band.

"17 And they clothed Him with purple, and platted a crown of thorns, and put it about His head.

"18 And began to salute Him, Hail, King of the Jews!

"19 And they smote Him, on the head with a reed, and did spit upon Him, and bowing their knees worshipped Him.

"20 And when they had mocked Him, they took off the purple from Him, and put His own clothes on Him, and led

Abraham's Seed

Him out to crucify Him.

"21 And they compel one Simon a Cyrenian, who passed by, coming out of the country, the father of Alexander and Rufus, to bear His [Christ's] cross. 22 And they bring Him unto the place Golgotha, which is, being interpreted, The place of a skull. 23 And they gave Him to drink wine mingled with myrrh: but He received it not.

"24 And when they had crucified Him, they parted His garments, casting lots upon them, what every man should take. 25 And it was the third hour, and they crucified Him.

"26 And the Superscription of His accusation was written over, THE KING OF THE JEWS.

"27 And with Him they crucify two thieves; the one on His right hand, and the other on His left. 28 And the scriptures was fulfilled, which saith, And He was numbered with the transgressors.

"29 And they that passed by railed on Him, wagging their heads, and saying, Ah, thou [You] that destroyest the temple, and buildest it in three days,

"30 Save thyself [Yourself] and come down from the cross. 31 Likewise also the chief priests mocking said among themselves with the scribes, He saved others; Himself He cannot save.

"32 Let Christ the King of Israel descend now from the cross, that we may see and believe. And they that were crucified with Him reviled Him.

"33 And when the sixth hour was come. There was darkness over the whole land until the ninth hour. 34 And at

Abraham's Seed

the ninth hour Jesus cried with a loud voice, saying Eloi, Eloi, Lama sabachthani? which is, being interpreted, My God, my God, why hast thou [you] forsaken Me?

"35 And some of them that stood by, when they heard it, said, Behold, He calleth Elias. 36 And one ran and filled a sponge full of vinegar, and put it on reed, and gave Him to drink, saying, Let alone; let us see whether Elias will come to take Him down."

"40 There were also women looking on afar off: among whom was Mary Magdalene, and Mary the mother of James the less and of Joses, and Salome; 41 (Who also, when He was in Galilee, followed Him, and ministered unto Him;) and many other women which came up with Him unto Jerusalem." Mark 15:1-35, 40, 41

"50 Jesus, when He had cried again with a loud voice, yielded up the ghost. 51 And, behold, the veil of the temple was rent in twain from the top to the bottom; and the earth did quake, and the rocks rent; 52 And the graves were opened; and many bodies of the saints which slept [were dead] arose, 53 And came out of the graves after His resurrection, and went into the holy city, and appeared unto many.

"54 Now when the centurion, and they that were with him, watching Jesus, saw the earthquake, and those things that were done, they feared greatly, saying, Truly this wast the Son of God." Matthew 27:50-54

"62 the next day [Saturday], that followed the day of the preparation [Friday], the chief priests and Pharisees came together unto Pilate.

"63 Saying, Sir, we remember that that deceiver said, while He was yet alive, After three days I will rise again. 64 Command therefore that the sepulcher be made sure until the third day, lest His disciples come by night, and

Abraham's Seed

steal Him way, and say unto the people, He is risen from the dead: so the last error shall be worse than the first.

"65 Pilate said unto them, Ye have a watch: go your way, make it as sure as ye can. 66 So they went, and made the sepulcher sure, sealing the stone, and setting a watch." Matthew 27:62-66

"1 In the end of the Sabbath [Saturday], as it began to dawn toward the first day of the week [Sunday], came Mary Magdalene and the other Mary to see the sepulcher. 2 And, behold, there was a great earthquake: for the angels of the LORD descended from heaven, and came and rolled back the stone from the door, and sat upon it. 3 His countenance was like lightning, and his raiment white as snow: 4 And for fear of him the keepers did shake, and became as dead men. 5 And the angel answered and said unto the women, Fear not ye; for I know that ye seek Jesus, which was crucified. 6 He is not here: for He is risen, as He said, Come, see the place where the LORD lay." Matthew 28:1-6

"He is not here:"
"For He is risen."

The grave could not hold Christ the LORD of hosts in its deadly grip because He was sinless. The Plan of Salvation that was sought after by the prophets of the Old Testament and by Christ's people was accomplished; now their sins can be eliminated and be saved from their deathbeds.

The angel said, "The LORD is risen, come and see."
They came and saw; but He was not there!

Later, after Christ the LORD of hosts saw Mary, He went to heaven briefly; then He came back and interacted with His disciples. He told them many things that they needed to know and assured them that He would be with

Abraham's Seed

them. And He also assured them that He would send the comforter (God the Holy Spirit) to empower them, guide them, and direct them as they preached the Gospel message. And then, He departed; by giving them an example of how His second coming is going to take place.

> "9 And when He [Christ] had spoken these things, while they beheld, He was taken up; and a cloud received Him out of their sight. 10 And while they looked steadfastly toward heaven as He went up, behold, two men stood by them in white apparel; 11 Which also said, Ye men of Galilee, why stand ye gazing up into heaven? this same Jesus, which is taken up from you into heaven, shall so come in like manner as ye have seen Him go into heaven." Acts 1:9-11

Yes, Christ the LORD of hosts has risen from the dead, which gives every person the hope of a resurrection from the grave (John 11:25). And yes, He is gone to heaven to prepare a place for the believers (John 14:1-3). And now He is preparing to come back to planet earth to take His people to heaven so that they may be where He is as His sons and daughters living in a sinless universal kingdom in happiness and contentment.

If you want more detailed information on Christ's second coming, based on the books of Daniel and Revelation, please read my book "Christians Headed into the Time of Trouble *By: Philip Mitanidis.* Published by BeeHive Publishing House Inc." 2007

Nonetheless, as you have observed in this chapter, Christ "the Seed" of Abraham accomplished His mission as He promised Adam, Eve, the patriarchs, and the prophets, even though His people (Israel) who are called by His name (2 Chronicles 7:14) rejected (John 1:11) and crucified Him on

Abraham's Seed

Calvary's cross.

A person cannot help but wonder, how was it possible for the house of Judah while holding in their hands the testimonies of the prophets to reject "the Seed" of Abraham and even to go as far as to crucify Him on the Roman barbaric cross?

But even more mind-boggling, is the question, how was the house of Judah going to receive salvation from their sins without accepting Christ as their LORD, God, and Saviour.

Christ said to them,   "11 I…am the LORD; and beside Me there is no Saviour" (Isaiah 43:11).

What were they thinking?

Oh, how far in darkness had the leaders, priests, and scribes of the house of Judah sunk into? Had they not read in the Scriptures where it says that the whole purpose of the God of Abraham was to come in the "flesh" so that He would "destroy sin in the flesh" and save a perishing world from their eternal demise? Had they not read Isaiah fifty-three, which reveals what would happen to the God of Israel after He came in the "flesh"? Had they not read all of the prophetic events, which applied to the God of Israel? Had they not read the Messianic references? Was the house of Judah and a remnant of the six tribes of the house of Israel so blinded by their traditions that they were not able to discern the plain revelations of Scripture, which they were privileged to have, study, and teach?

How is it that the Magi from the east came to see the King of the Jews? How is it that a pagan king believed when the scribes and the priest read how the King of Israel was going to come and where He was going to be born (Micah 5:2)? How is it that thousands upon thousands in the provinces of Galilee, Judah, in the surrounding provinces,

Abraham's Seed

and beyond believed and came to see Christ the LORD of hosts? They came from all over the various countries seeking Christ so much as to touch His garment, so that they would be healed from their diverse diseases—and they were healed!

How could the house of Judah not believe, when all they had to do is to look at the Scriptures that were given to them and confirm the authenticity of Christ the LORD of hosts as others had done and believed? How could the leaders of the house of Judah lie, deny, and persecute Christ the God of their fathers and at the end even execute Him by the pagan Roman hand? All they had to do is to confirm that Christ was the "Seed" of Abraham, as others had done and are doing today and believe. There is no other seed to look forward to! There is only one "Seed" of Abraham! Scripture says,

> "16 Now to Abraham and his seed were the promises made. He saith not, And to seeds, as of many; but as of one, And to thy [your] seed, which is Christ" (Galatians 3:16).

That's it!
The "Seed" of Abraham has come and gone!
There is no other seed that can save a penitent sinner (Acts 4:12). So, why wait or look for another?

In closing, let me give you a little bit more info on Christ's character names. As you have seen, the character names, which we have studied thus far, overwhelmingly refer to Christ the LORD of hosts. And, you should also know that there are a handful of other character names that apply to Christ the LORD, which have not studied. But because now, you have been exposed to the majority of Christ's character names, I am confident that you will be able to spot these character names while you read your Bible.

Abraham's Seed

How do I know?

I know because you can cross-reference Christ's character names; and because Christ the LORD of hosts said,

> "39 Search the scriptures; for in them ye [all of you] think ye have eternal life; and they are they which testify of Me" (John 5:39).

In addition, since over ninety percent of the Scriptures (Bible) testify of Christ the LORD of hosts, why are people saying to us that the majority of the Scriptures testify of God the Father? Why do they say, "Moses mainly wrote about God the Father"? Is Christ, Abraham's "Seed," lying to us when He says, "Moses wrote about Me," or are Christ's personal claims conveniently rejected by the masses when Christ says,

> "46 had ye [all of you] believed Moses, ye would have believed Me: for he wrote of Me. 47 But if ye [all of you] believe not his writings, how shall ye [all of you] believe My words?" John 5:46, 47

What do you think; is Christ lying to us?

If He is not lying to us, would you then accept Christ the LORD of hosts as the "Seed" of Abraham, and as your LORD, God, and Saviour as the prophets of old already have done?

* * *

> "1 O come, let us sing unto the LORD: let us make a joyful noise to the Rock of our salvation. 2 Let us come before His presence with thanksgiving, and make a joyful noise unto Him with psalms.

> "3 For the LORD is a great God, and a great King and

above all gods. 4 In His hand are the deep places of the earth: the strength of the hills is His also.

"5 The sea is His, and He made it: and His hands formed the dry land. 6 O come, let us worship and bow down: let us kneel before the LORD our maker.

" 7 To day if ye will hear His voice, 8 Harden not your heart, as in the provocation, and as in the day of temptation in the wilderness:" (Psalms 95:1-8).

*   Therefore as per Scripture, we can refer to Jesus Christ by the following names, "the God of Abraham, Isaac, and Jacob," "the God of Israel," "the Rock," "the LORD of hosts," "Shiloh," "the King of Israel," "the King of glory," "Zion," "Redeemer," "the first and the last," "Jehovah," "the Most High God," "the LORD God of Abraham," "Creator," "God," "Messiah" (Christ), "King of the Jews," "the Word," who "dwelt in between the cherubims" above "the mercy seat" of the "Ark of the Covenant" in His Sanctuary in "Shiloh" and after in "Jerusalem." And of course by the name of "the seed of Abraham."

Supplements

The God of Abraham

To further confirm the fact that the God of Abraham of the Old Testament and Jesus Christ the LORD of hosts of the New Testament is the same person, we have the following confirmation: "6 Thou, even thou, art LORD alone; thou hast made heaven, the heaven of heavens, with all their host, the earth, and all things that are therein, the seas, and all that is therein, and thou preservest them all; and the host of heaven worshippeth Thee [You]. 7 Thou art the LORD the God, who didst choose Abram, and broughtest him forth out of Ur of the Chaldees, and gavest him the name of Abraham;" Nehemiah 9:6, 7

The God of Abraham

As per the above verses, the Creator of v.6 is the God of Abraham (v.7). And the Creator as per the following verses is identified by the name of the King of Israel. "1 Hear ye [all of You] the word which the LORD speaketh unto you, O house of Israel:"

"10 But the LORD is the true God, He is the living God, and an everlasting King: at His wrath the earth shall tremble, and the nations shall not be able to abide His indignation.

"11 Thus shall ye [all of you] say unto them, The gods that have not made the heavens and the earth, even they shall perish from the earth, and from under these heavens. 12 He hath made the earth by His power, He hath established the world by His wisdom, and hath stretched out the heavens by His discretion." Jeremiah 10:1, 10-12

As you have read in verse ten above the "living God" is "an everlasting King." And this everlasting King, is the Creator. Jeremiah says,

"12 He hath made the earth by His power, He hath established the world by His wisdom, and hath stretched out the heavens by His discretion." Jeremiah 10:12

Did you notice? Jeremiah said "He" created; Jeremiah did not say "They" created. That means that there was no other Individual involved in the creation of the heavens and the earth.

Jeremiah in the above verse, like Moses, Isaiah, Apostle Paul, and Apostle John says, "10 the LORD is the true God… and an everlasting King…He hath made the earth by His power."

Did you notice; Jeremiah said, "the earth was made by His power," period.

Therefore, as per the above verses, we can conclude, the God of Abraham who is identified as the King of Israel is

The God of Abraham

the sole Creator of the "heavens and the earth." And, according to Apostles John and Paul, the sole Creator of the OT is the same sole Creator of the NT; and that Creator is Christ. (See John 1:3, 10; Colossians 1:16, 17 in the OKJV.) As a result, since God the Creator of the OT and God the Creator of the NT is Christ, it follows that Christ and the God of Abraham is the same person.

Who identifies Himself as the King of Israel? _____ Again, as we have read above, it is the God of Abraham who identifies Himself in the Old Testament as the "King of Israel" and when the King of Israel came in the "flesh," in the New Testament, He identified Himself by the character name of "Christ." And, at the same time, He claimed that He is the "King of Israel."

Here are the references: "1 And when they [Christ and the disciples] drew nigh unto Jerusalem, and were come to Bethphage, unto the mount of Olives, then sent Jesus two disciples, 2 Saying unto them, Go into the village over against you, and straightway ye shall find an ass tied, and a colt with her: loose them, and bring them unto Me. 3 And if any man say ought unto you, ye [all of you] shall say, The LORD hath need of them, and straightway he will send them. "4 All this was done, that it might be fulfilled which was spoken by the prophet, saying,

> "5 Tell ye [all of you] the daughter of Sion [Zion], Behold, thy [Your] King cometh unto thee [you], meek, and sitting upon an ass, and a colt the foal of an ass [Genesis 49:10, 11]" (Matthew 21:1-5).

And, the multitude that was standing on each side of the road did tell Zion (Jerusalem) that "thy [Your] King cometh unto thee [you]," by their actions and by the shouting of

The God of Abraham

Hosanna's.

Here is the account: "6 And the disciples went, and did as Jesus commanded them. 7 And brought the ass, and the colt, and put on them their clothes, and they set Him [Christ] thereon. 8 And a very great multitude spread their garments in the way; others cut down branches from the trees, and strawed them in the way. 9 And the multitudes that were before, and that followed, cried, saying, Hosanna to the Son of David: Blessed is he that cometh in the name of the LORD; Hosanna: in the highest.

"10 And when He was come into Jerusalem, all the city was moved, saying, Who is this? 11 And the multitude said, This is Jesus the prophet of Nazareth of Galilee." Matthew 21:6-11

Therefore as per the above overwhelming evidence, we can conclude that Christ is the King of Israel.

Why?

Because Christ said so!

But not only Christ proclaimed that He was the King of the Jews, so did the people who were shouting "hosanna to the highest"; they acknowledged that Christ was the King of the Jews. They said to Zion (Jerusalem),

"thy [Your] King cometh unto thee [you]."

In fact, about thirty years earlier, the Magi who came with their caravan from the east also acknowledged that Christ is the King of the Jews—remember? When they arrived in Jerusalem, they started to ask, "Where is He that is born King of the Jews"? And "3 When Herod the king had heard these things, he was troubled, and all Jerusalem with him. 4 And when he had gathered all the chief priests and scribes of the people together, he demanded of them where Christ should be born. 5 And they said unto him, In

The God of Abraham

Bethlehem of Judaea: for thus it is written by the prophet, 6 And thou [you] Bethlehem, in the land of Juda, art not the least among the princes of Juda: for out of thee [you] shall come a Governor, that shall rule My people Israel.

"7 Then Herod, when he had privily called the wise men, inquired of them diligently what time the star [angels] appeared. 8 And he sent them to Bethlehem, and said, Go and search diligently for the young child; and when ye [all of you] have found Him, bring me word again, that I may come and worship Him also." Matthew 2:3-8

And when the wise men did not report to Herod where Christ was, he ordered the insane brutal attack and killed all of the children under two years old in order to eliminate his rival.

And when Christ the King of Israel started His ministry, He proclaimed to the public that He was the "Messiah" (Christ) and the King of "the house of Judah." Therefore, everybody in and around the province of Judah heard that Jesus Christ was the King of the house of Judah; but the house of Judah, or Jews if you like, rejected Christ as their King, Saviour, and as the God of Abraham, and as they had often referred to the God of Abraham, as "the God of their fathers."

Here is the Jewish rejection of Christ;

"11 He [Christ] came unto His own [the house of Judah], and His own received Him not." John 1:11

Although the house of Judah (Jews) rejected Christ their LORD God, Savior, and King, the pagan Roman authorities still recognized Christ to be the King of the Jews because that is what Christ claimed a number of times to the Jewish authorities, to Pilate, and to the common people. In fact Pilate acknowledged that fact by saying to the mixed crowd, what do you want me to do to Christ, "whom ye [all of you] call King of the Jews?" Mark 15:12 Therefore the Roman authorities put three inscriptions upon the cross when they crucified Christ. The inscription read:

"38 And a superscription also was written over Him in letters of Greek, and Latin, and Hebrew, THIS IS THE KING OF THE JEWS." Luke 23:38

And when the Jewish authorities saw the inscription to read "THIS IS THE KING OF THE JEWS," they were furious with the Romans. They even went to Pilate and asked him to remove the inscription from the cross and make it read, "He said, I am King of the Jews."

"21 Then said the chief priests of the Jews to Pilate, Write not, The King of the Jews; but that He said, I am King of the Jews." John 19:21

But, Pilate still troubled by the dream of his wife and allowing an innocent man to be put to death in such a horrific way, rebuked them and told them to go on their way. And as far as the inscription was concerned, it remained in tact as it was over Christ's head, as a witness that they crucified their King.

Therefore as per the above verses, the King and Creator of the Old Testament is the same King and Creator of the New Testament. And that sole Creator is Christ the King of Israel, better known by the children of Israel as "the LORD God of Abraham."

One Creator or More?

Although the previous chapters have revealed how they all link Christ the LORD by the names of "Creator," "Word," "King of Israel," "the LORD of hosts," "the first and the last," "the God of Abraham," etc., etc.; at this point, I want to bring to your attention the pros and cons in this

One Creator or More?

and in the following chapter why people object to the Scriptural fact that Christ is the sole Creator of His universe and everything that is in it and outside of it? At the same time, I also want to reveal to you how Scripture positively singles out Christ the LORD of hosts as the sole Creator of "all things" and not God the Father. God the Father did not create a single thing; please go and search the Scriptures, I fervently encourage you.

To support the fact that Christ the LORD of hosts is the only Creator, we have the following penned by Nehemiah:

> "6 Thou [You], even thou, art LORD alone; thou hast made heaven, the heaven of heavens, with all their host, the earth, and all things that are therein, the seas, and all that is therein, and thou preservest them all: and the host of heaven worshippeth thee [You]. 7 Thou art the LORD the God, who didst choose Abram, and broughtest him forth out of Ur of the Chaldees, and gavest him the name of Abraham;" Nehemiah 9:6, 7

The above verses clearly state that the God of Abraham is the Creator who is "worshipped" by the "host of heaven" (v.6).

That is an overwhelming revelation. The verses state that the Creator who is worshipped by the "host of heaven" is the God of Abraham. Therefore all of the creation verses will identify the God of Abraham as the sole Creator because the noun "you" is used in the above verses to reveal that there is only one Creator that is worshipped by the "host of heaven."

In fact, even the New Testament prophet of the LORD of hosts is telling us to:

> "7 worship Him that made heaven, and the earth

One Creator or More?

and the sea, and the fountains of waters."
Revelation 14:7

Did you notice? The prophet of the LORD of hosts tells us to "worship Him"; he did not say worship them. I think Nehemiah and John are quite clear in their statements; we are to worship the Creator. And that means the Individual who created the heavens and the earth.

Likewise Moses reveals one Creator by saying, "1 In the beginning God created the heaven and the earth." Genesis 1:1

And several hundred years later, Isaiah, in agreement with Moses and Nehemiah, also acknowledged that the God of Abraham is the sole Creator by saying, "26 Lift up your eyes on high, and behold who hath created these things, that bringeth out their host by number: He calleth them all by names by the greatness of His might, for that He is strong in power; not one faileth." "28 Hast thou [you] not known? hast thou not heard, that the everlasting God, the LORD, the Creator of the ends of the earth, fainteth not, neither is weary? There is no searching of His understanding." Isaiah 40:26, 28

As per the above verses, the everlasting LORD God of Israel is the Creator.

Did you notice? Isaiah said, "Creator;" he did not say Creators. Therefore according to Isaiah, the everlasting God of Israel created "all things" by Himself and as He says, "alone."

Here is the reference: "24 Thus saith the LORD, thy [your] redeemer, and He that formed thee [you] from the womb, I am the LORD that maketh all things; that stretcheth forth the heavens alone that spreadeth abroad the earth by Myself." Isaiah 44:24

One Creator or More?

*So! Who is this individual who created "alone" and "by Myself"?*_____ Like Isaiah, Apostle Paul says that Christ created all thing alone and by himself. Here is his statement:

> "16 For by Him [Christ] were all things created, that are in heaven, and that are in earth, visible and invisible, whether they be thrones, or dominions, or principalities, or powers: all things were created by Him [Christ], and for Him [Christ]." Colossians 1:16

As you have read in the above verse, Christ created "all things" "by Him [Christ], and for Him [Christ]." In other words, Christ created them "alone" and as Apostle Paul says, "by Him." Therefore there was no co-creator or co-creators involved with Christ the God of Abraham when He created the universe and everything that is in it and outside of it.

Unfortunately, there are individuals, who disagree with the above verses, and with Christ the LORD of hosts when He says by the mouth of Isaiah,

> "24 I am the LORD that maketh all things; that stretcheth forth the heavens alone that spreadeth abroad the earth by Myself' (Isaiah 44:24).

In fact, there are over ninety percent of Christian believers that believe and teach, as a Bible doctrine that there was a co-creator involved with Christ the God of Israel; and therefore they argue fervently that the statements in Isaiah 44:24 and Colossians 1:16 are not true and therefore they mean something else!

But, if the statements in the above verses are not true, then we can say that the prophet Isaiah is lying to us, Apostle Paul is lying to us, and even worse, we can also say that Christ the God of Israel is lying to us because Christ the LORD of hosts says, "I am the LORD that maketh all things."

So, do we call Christ the LORD God of Israel a liar?

Obviously not because nowhere in the sixty-six books of the Bible do we find a written statement, which says that there was a co-creator involved with Christ the God of Abraham. Please go and look; I ardently encourage you.

Unwarranted Objections

The Creator of the universe said to Jeremiah,

"4 command them [the delegates, who came to Jerusalem] to say unto their masters, thus saith the LORD of hosts, the God of Israel; Thus shall ye [all of you] say unto your masters;

"5 I have made the earth, the man and the beast that are upon the ground, by My great power and by My outstretched arm, and have given it unto whom it seemed meet unto Me." Jeremiah 27:4, 5

You know, a person would think given that Christ acknowledges that He is "the LORD of hosts" and "the God of Israel" (v.4), and says by the mouth of Jeremiah, "5 I have made the earth, the man and the beast that are upon the ground, by My great power and by My outstretched arm" (Jeremiah 27:5), it should suffice for a person to acknowledge that Christ is the sole Creator; but, some people still disagree with the above Scripture references and with the previous chapter and state contrary to Scripture that there was a co-creator involved with the creation of the universe.

So, why are people insisting that there was a co-creator involved in the creation of "all things" when the above verses and in the previous chapters, the verses state so aptly

Unwarranted Objections

that there is only one Creator who created "all things" "alone"?

Generally, they base their belief on three suppositions.

1). They believe that the Creator is God the Father.

2). On Genesis 1:26

3). On mistranslated Bible verses in the New Testament. I say in the New Testament because the Old Testament creation verses have been translated correctly. They do not contradict each other as the New Testament verses do in many Bible translations.

Nonetheless, let us consider their first objection.

1)_____ Although the objectors claim that it was God the Father who created the heavens and the earth; when asked to produce one single verse, which states that God the Father is the Creator, it cannot be done because there is no such verse or verses that can be produced from anywhere in the entire Bible.

All the objectors can do is to produce the creation verses, which refer to Christ the LORD of hosts, and then say that these verses refer to God the Father. Other than that, there is not a single reference to God the Father where it states that he is the Creator. The Scriptures are silent on that point.

The reason the objectors assume that the creation verses of the Old Testament refer to God the Father is due to the fact that they have been brought up to believe that way and not as a fact of Scripture; and therefore they claim and base their belief that God the Father is referred to, throughout the Old Testament, by the prophets of old. And that belief as per Scripture is one hundred percent in error.

Therefore, if I ask you to find one verse in the Old Testament where the prophets are referring to God the Father, as the God of Abraham and as the Creator, would

Unwarranted Objections

you be able to produce one single verse? If you are unable to find one single verse, which refers to God the Father, as the God of Abraham and Creator of the universe, why would you believe that the Old Testament writers are writing about God the Father?

You know Christ the LORD of hosts personally stated to the house of Judah, particularly to the leaders of the house of Judah that the Scriptures testify of Him and not of God the Father. Christ said to His tempters:

> "39 Search the scriptures; for in them ye [all of you] think ye have eternal life; and they are they which testify of Me." John 5:39

How much plainer can Christ's statement be?

He said that the Old Testament Scriptures "testify of Me" and not about someone else. Christ the LORD of hosts referred to the Old Testament Scriptures because the New Testament Scriptures were not yet written.

Furthermore, Christ the LORD of hosts stated that the Torah (five books of Moses) testify of Him and not about His Associate (God the Father.) (I have used the word "Associate" throughout this book to refer to God the Father because God the Father did not become, God the Father until after Christ the LORD of hosts was born in the "flesh." Nonetheless Christ said to His tempters: "45 Do not think that I will accuse you to the Father: there is one that accuseth you, even Moses, in whom ye [all of you] trust.

And then, Jesus emphasizes the writings of Moses;

> "46 For had ye [all of you] believed Moses, ye would have believed Me: for he wrote of Me. 47 But if ye believe not his writings, how shall ye believe My words?" John 5:45-47

Unwarranted Objections

Did you hear that?

Christ the Creator of "all things" said that Moses wrote about Me and not about God the Father. Therefore we can agree with Christ the LORD of hosts when He says Moses wrote about Me; or we can call Christ a liar and disagree with Him and say like the objectors, "Moses wrote about God the Father."

It's your choice to make.

2)_____ Their second objection is found in the book of Genesis; it reads as follows:

"26 And God said, Let us make man in our image, after our likeness." Genesis 1:26

First, it should be noted that in verse twenty-six there was only a dialogue regarding the "image" of man; If man should be formed to look like the Creator and His Associate.

That's it!

Secondly, verse twenty-six does not deal with the creation of the heavens and of the earth as they are presented in Genesis chapter one. Therefore this verse cannot be applied to everything God the Christ had already created up until verses twenty-six. The only thing that was not created on the sixth day was man; otherwise everything else was created by Christ the Creator. Therefore up until that time period, there is no dialogue found anywhere in the Scriptures to reveal that there was a co-creator involved with Christ the Creator.

And thirdly, verse twenty-seven of Genesis chapter one deals with the creation of man; therefore the God who said "Let us make man in our Image" was none other than Christ the Creator because it was He who spoke the ecosystem of the earth, its inhabitants, as the previous creation verses have already stated. And then Christ created man as he is revealed to us in Genesis chapters one and two.

Nonetheless, if you were to consider verse twenty-six carefully, you will find, all Christ the Creator was asking His Associate, if it was all right to create man in "our image"? That's it! Asking to create man in "our image" does not involve the actual creation of man. And furthermore that statement does not involve a co-creator; verse twenty-seven explains why there was no co-creator involved in verse twenty-six or in verse twenty-seven. The verse reads,

> "27 So God created man in His image, in the image of God created He him; male and female created He them." Genesis 1:27

Did you notice? The verse says, "God created man in His image." And, the verse also says that God created man "in the image of God [Christ's Associate]." And to further clarify that it was God the Christ who created man, Moses uses the pronoun "He" to tell us that there was no co-creator involved in the creation of man. Moses says, "male and female created He them."

Did you hear that? Moses says, "God created He him; male and female created He them."

There is no confusion in the above verse regarding the creation of Adam and Eve. Christ the God of Abraham created "He them." As you can see, there is no statement in the above verse where it states we created. Read verse twenty-seven again and observe; there is no we or us anywhere to be found in the creation of man. But there are in confirmation, the pronouns "His" and "He" mentioned couple of times to specify that there was only one Creator involved in the creation of man.

To further confirm the fact that there was no co-creator

252 _____ Moses Wrote About Me By: *Philip Mitanidis*
Unwarranted Objections

involved with Christ the LORD of hosts, we are told, "6 for in the image of God [Christ's Associate] made He man." Genesis 9:6

To clarify the verse, the verse will read as follows:

"6 for in the image of God [the Father] made He [Christ] man." Genesis 9:6

In addition we are also told that Christ the Creator created man by Himself by saying,

"6 And it repenteth the LORD that He had made man on the earth, and it grieved Him at His heart. 7 And the LORD said, I will destroy man whom I have created from the face of the earth;" Genesis 6:6, 7

Did you notice? Christ the Creator said, "I will destroy man whom I have created." That's right, Christ the LORD of hosts said, "whom I have created." Therefore as per that statement and as per the previous verses, there was no co-creator involved with Christ the Creator in the creation of "all things."

As a result, Christ is the sole Creator of His universe; He did not need any help in the creation of the universe and man. If you think that Christ the Creator needed help by having someone to help Him, then you are putting limitation upon Him.

Do you really want to do that!

If you do, then you are mocking the Creator because the prophet of Christ the Creator says, "Is there anything impossible for the LORD?"

3)_____ The other references that are given to support a co-creator are found in the New Testament verses

Unwarranted Objections

where the objectors choose certain Bibles, which have the creation verses of the Greek text translated incorrectly.

Therefore, if you were to review some of these Bibles in the market place, you would notice that they not only contradict each other, but they also contradict the Greek inspired Scriptures.

Here are few examples:

"1 IN THE beginning [before all time] was the Word (d Christ), and the Word was with God, and the Word was God Himself. [Isa. 9:6]" "3 All things were made and came into existence through Him; and without Him was not even one thing made that has come into being." "10 He came into the world, and though the world was made through Him, the world did not recognize Him [did not know Him]." John 1:1, 3, 10 (Amp)

"1 In the beginning the Word already existed; the Word was with God, and the Word was God." "3 Through him God made all things; not one thing in all creation was made without him." "10 The Word was in the world, and though God made the world through him, yet the world did not recognize him." John 1:1, 3, 10 (TEV)

"1 In the beginning was the one who is called the Word. The Word was with God and was truly God." "3 And with this Word, God created all things. Nothing was made without the Word." "10 The Word was in the world, but no one knew him, though God had made the world with his Word." John 1:1, 3, 10 (CEV)

If you look in verses three and ten, in the above three translations, you will observe that they all corroborate that somebody created "all things" and the "world" "through" the "Word" (Christ) as we know Him now in the New Testament by His character name.

But, if you read the Old King James Version of the Bible

Unwarranted Objections

(OKJV), which is the closest translation of the Hebrew and Greek Scriptures that I know off, you will notice that it like the Greek Scriptures disagree with the above three Bible translations. (Amp.) (TEV) (CEV).

The Old King James Version reads as follows:

"1 IN the beginning was the Word, and the Word was with God, and the Word was God.

"3 All things were made by Him [Christ the Word of v.1]; and without Him [Christ] was not anything made that was made.

"10 He [Christ] was in the world, and the world was made by Him [Christ]." John 1:1, 3, 10 (OKJV)

Now take a good look in the above three verses of the (OKJV), and observe if the word "through" is present; obviously it is not. Verse three states that "All things were made by Him [Christ]." Likewise verse ten says the same thing. We are told that "He [Christ] was in the world, and the world was made by Him [Christ]." As you have observed, none of the verses say that somebody created "all things" and the "world" through Christ.

To further confirm the fact that the mistranslated word "through" does not exist in the Greek inspired Scriptures, look at verses three and ten in the following Greek text and observe the presence of the word δι' [by].

"3 Παντα δι' [by] αυτου εγειναν και χωρις αυτου δεν εγειναν ουδε εν το οποιον εγεινεν."

"10 Ητο εν τω κοσμω, και ο κοσμος εγεινε δι' [by] αυτου." Ιωαννην 1:3, 10 (Βιβλικη Εταιρεια) John 1:3, 10

Unwarranted Objections

As you can see the Greek word δι' [by] is present in the above two verses.

And to further confirm the fact that many of the Bible translators have altered the meaning of the New Testament creation verses by using the uninspired word "through," apostle Paul says in the Greek text "11 For of Him [Christ]…are all things" (1 Corinthians 11:36). Therefore, according to the Greek text ["εξ αυτου, και δι αυτου, και εις αυτου"], the creation of "all things" was "of Him [Christ]," "by [δι'] Him [Christ]," "for Him Christ]," and not of God the Father or of God the Holy Spirit or of anyone else. The fact that the creation of "all things" was "of Him [Christ]," Apostle Paul further added, "16 all things were created by [δι'] Him [Christ of v.15], and for Him [Christ]" (Colossians 1:16). Therefore the mistranslated word "through" should not be used as some Bible translators have taken the liberty to add in the New Testament creation verses.

A person should not delete the word of God or add his or her own words. Therefore the Greek word δι' [by] should not be deleted from all of the creation verses that are found in the New Testament. There was a reason why God the Holy Spirit used the word δι' [by], and that reason, like the Old Testament prophets, the New Testament prophets believed that there is only one Creator; and as a result, they had to use the word δι' [by].

Therefore the translators should not have removed the word δι' [by], and used the uninspired word "through" in the creation verses.

I do not know if you know that there is a very strong condemnation in the Old and New Testaments to individuals who add, delete, or preach the Gospel of Jesus Christ willfully in error. The warning is as follows: "8 But though we, or an angel from heaven, preach any other gospel unto you than that which we have preached unto you,

Unwarranted Objections

let him be accursed." Galatians 1:8

Did you hear that?

Very strong language, don't you think?

Nonetheless, by using the mistranslated word "through" in the creation verses of the New Testament it postures the New Testament against the Old Testament because nowhere in the Old Testament you will find in the creation verses where they state that somebody created "through" Christ the LORD of hosts or Christ the LORD of hosts created through somebody.

As a result, since there is no co-creator mentioned in any of the creation verses in the entire 66 books of the Bible, we can agree with the prophet Malachi and say,

> "10 Have we not all one father? Hath not one God created us? why do we deal treacherously every man against his brother by profaning the covenant of our fathers?" Malachi 2:10

So! Do you agree with Malachi the prophet of Christ the LORD of hosts that there is only "one God" who "created us"? Or do you disagree with him? But, if you agree with Malachi; then we can conclude that there is only one Creator, and that Creator, as per Scripture, is Christ the LORD of hosts who says, "4 command them [the delegates, who came to Jerusalem] to say unto their masters, thus saith the LORD of hosts, the God of Israel; Thus shall ye [all of you] say unto your masters;

> "5 I have made the earth, the man and the beast that are upon the ground, by My great power and by My outstretched arm," Jeremiah 27:4, 5

* * *   If you desire more detailed information on the subject of the

Creator, creation, the pros and cons of the creation verses, translators, the Hebrew and Greek texts, and much, much more, please read my book "The Creator of Genesis 1:1 Who is He" by: *Philip Mitanidis*, BeeHive Publishing House Inc. 2003

~~~~~~~~~

He Shall be Called the Son of God

The reason Christ's Associate (God the Father) is referred to as "God the Father" in relationship to Christ the LORD of hosts is simply because God the Father said, "I will be to Him [Christ] a Father, and He shall be to me a Son." Hebrews 1:5

Did you notice in the above quotation, God the Father as we know him now in the New Testament, says that he "shall be to Him a Father." God the Father in that statement does not claim to be a literal Father; he claims to be a Father to Jesus Christ as an arrangement and not that he is.

The proclamation by God the Father is straightforward; he says, "I will be to Him [Christ] a Father, and He [Christ] shall be to me a Son."

Likewise, the following verse supports the above quotation. The angel of the LORD of hosts said to Mary that Jesus Christ shall be called the Son of God (God the Father); and not that He literally is. "35 And the angel answered and said unto her, The Holy Ghost shall come upon thee [you]. And the power of the Highest [God the Father] shall overshadow thee [you] therefore also that holy thing which shall be born of thee [you] shall be called the Son of God." Luke 1:35

The reason why God the Father and God the Son, as we know them now in the New Testament are addressed by their character names of Father and Son, as an arrangement, is due to the fact that neither God the Father or Christ the LORD of hosts have a beginning as we rationalize the beginning of something. Both Christ the LORD of hosts

He shall be Called the Son of God

and God the Father according to Scripture, do not have a beginning; they are "from everlasting to everlasting."

So! How are we going to explain their origin or existence?

As an example, just before Moses died he stated that Christ the Creator was "from everlasting to everlasting" Psalms 90:1, 2. And before Moses went to Egypt, Moses asked Christ the LORD of hosts to reveal Himself to him. In response, Christ the LORD of hosts said to Moses, "I AM THAT I AM."

How is man going to explain Christ's statement "I AM THAT I AM"?

To answer, in reference to Christ the LORD of hosts, Apostle Paul said: "33 O the depth of the riches both of the wisdom and knowledge of God! How unsearchable are His judgments, and His ways past finding out! 34 For who hath known the mind of the LORD? or who hath been His counsellor? 35 Or who hath first given to Him, and it shall be recompensed unto Him again?" Roman 11:33-35

And Christ the LORD of hosts adds, "5 To whom will ye [all of you] liken Me, that we may be like?" Isaiah 46:5

And Isaiah says, "28 there is no searching of His understanding." Isaiah 40:28

So, who knows the mind of God (Christ the LORD of hosts); and to whom will we liken Him?

Obviously to no one, and therefore we cannot claim that we know God the Christ. And that equally applies to God the Father and to God the Holy Spirit.

But this much we do know, and that is whatever the Scriptures (Bible) have revealed. And Scripture says that Christ shall be called the Son of God the Father, and not that He literally is the Son of God Father; and that statement is further corroborated to be a fact because Christ was conceived by the Holy Spirit from an awesome Spirit Being

He shall be Called the Son of God

into human flesh.

Here is one of the references" "20 the angel of the LORD appeared onto him in a dream, saying, Joseph, thou [you] son of David, fear not to take unto thee [you] Mary thy [your] wife: for that which is conceived in her is of the Holy Ghost." Matthew 1:20

As you can see in the above verse, God the Father is not the Individual who inseminated or as Scripture says "sent" or made the transfer of Christ into Mary. That is why the Scriptures have stated that God the Father can only claim, "I will be to Him [Christ] a Father, and He [Christ] shall be to me a Son." And that is why Christ can only be "called" the Son of God the Father.

Therefore the recognition of a Son and a Father did not exist prior to Christ's birth from Mary; that recognition became only as an arrangement because Christ the LORD of hosts like God the Father and like God the Holy Spirit never had a beginning. Christ's birth was only a transfer from an all-powerful Spirit Being, whose creation cannot contain Him (1 Kings 8:27), into a helpless little baby called Jesus Christ.

QUESTIONS

1). Who told Abraham to leave his homeland?
2). Where was Abraham living before he left his homeland?
3). Where was Abraham told to go?
4). How many years did Abraham live in the new land?
5). Through whose seed was the world going to be blessed?
6). How many years did it take to inherit the Promised Land?
7). Where was Christ's Sanctuary erected in the Promised Land
8). How often did Israel come to worship Christ there?
9). Why was Christ's Sanctuary in Shiloh destroyed?
10). Where was a new Sanctuary built for Christ?
11). Why was Christ's new Sanctuary destroyed in 586 BC?
12). Who destroyed the new Sanctuary?
13). After the Sanctuary was rebuilt, who destroyed it in 70 AD?
14). Who abandoned the Sanctuary in Jerusalem? Why?
15). Are the ceremonial laws practiced in the Sanctuary today?
16). Who is the God of Abraham?
17). Why is Christ called the Son of God?
18). Why is Christ identified as "the LORD of hosts"?
19). Why is Christ identified as "the King of Israel"?
20). Why is Christ identified as "the Word"?
21). Why is Christ identified by the name of "Shiloh"?
22). Why did Christ ride a donkey and followed by ass's colt?
23). Why did Christ claim to be "the King of the Jews"?
24). How old was Christ when he started His ministry?
25). How many years did Christ preach His Gospel?
26). What miraculous miracles did Christ perform?
27). Why was Christ crucified?
28). Who crucified Christ?
29). Did Christ die?
30). Was Christ resurrected?
31). Where is Christ now?
32). When are the penitent sinners going to be saved?
33). What is going to happen to Satan, evil angels, evil men, and evil women?
34). Where are the redeemed going to live with Christ the LORD?
35). Why does the Bible say, the redeemed will reign on Christ's throne?

BIBLIOGRAPHY

Mitanidis, Philip: *The Creator of Genesis 1:1—Who is He?*
pgs. 48-49. BeeHive Publishing House Inc. 2003.

Mitanidis, Philip: *Christians Headed Into the Time of Trouble*
Pgs 26, 27 BeeHive Publishing House Inc. 2007

Mitanidis, Philip: *Christians Headed Into the Time of Trouble*
Pgs 53-56 BeeHive Publishing House Inc. 2007

www.ingramcontent.com/pod-product-compliance
Lightning Source LLC
Chambersburg PA
CBHW060232050426
42448CB00009B/1404